THEN & NOW

THE SANTA CLARITA VALLEY

OPPOSITE: The tiny Castaic train station opened at Castaic Junction in 1887 after the Southern Pacific Railroad ran a branch line from Saugus to Santa Barbara. In this 1909 photograph, two ladies with tennis equipment wait patiently for the next train. The station was destroyed in the St. Francis Dam disaster in March 1928. (Courtesy of scvhistory.com.)

THEN & NOW

THE SANTA CLARITA VALLEY

Dr. Alan Pollack,
Kim Stephens, and E.J. Stephens

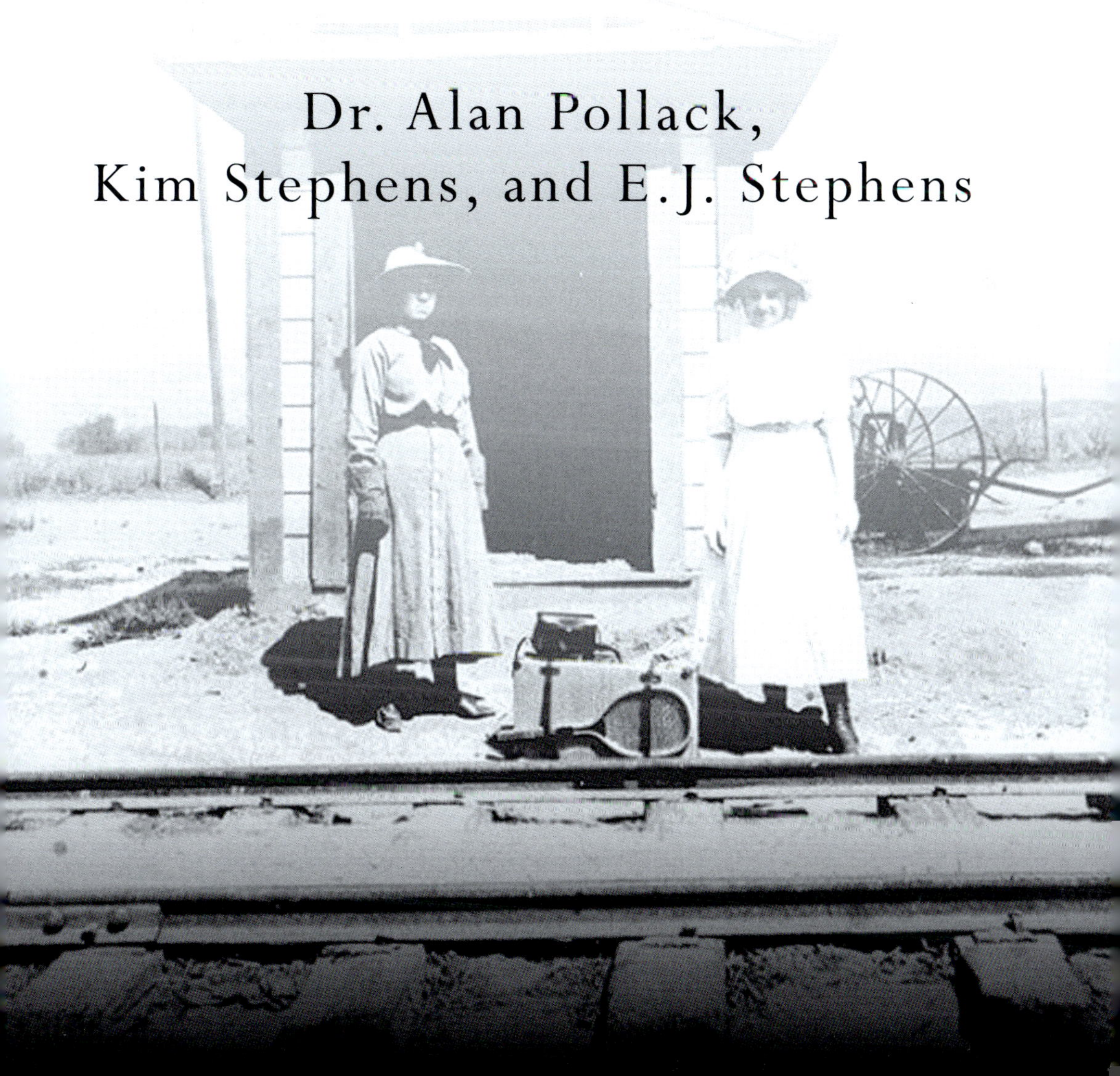

Alan would like to dedicate this book to his furball family: Bella, Montana, Bonnie, and Palmer. (Please adopt an animal today!) And many thanks go to my coauthors, Kim and E.J. They are dear friends and a joy to work with!

Kim and E.J. would like to dedicate this book to our children, Mariah and Dylan, who are beginning their individual paths of discovery. We could not be more proud of the two of you, and we look forward to reading your autobiographies (and to holding the grandchildren—but no rush on that!). We would also like to thank our great friend and creative partner Alan Pollack, whose love for Santa Clarita Valley history has made this book possible.

ISBN 978-1-4671-3153-7

Library of Congress Control Number: 2013950414

Published by Arcadia Publishing
Charleston, South Carolina

Printed in the United States of America

For all general information, please contact Arcadia Publishing:
Telephone 843-853-2070
Fax 843-853-0044
E-mail sales@arcadiapublishing.com
For customer service and orders:
Toll-Free 1-888-313-2665

Visit us on the Internet at www.arcadiapublishing.com

On the Front Cover: On the evening of November 10, 1929, former rodeo rider and cattle rustler "Buffalo Tom" Vernon loosened 60 feet of track next to Baker's Rodeo Arena, causing the derailment of the *West Coast Limited*. He then escaped, but not before robbing the passengers of about $300. Vernon was later captured in Pawnee, Oklahoma, and brought back to California to serve a life sentence in Folsom Prison. Today, the site of the train robbery is next to the Metrolink train station on Soledad Canyon Road. (Then image courtesy of scvhistory.com; now image courtesy of E.J. Stephens.)

On the Back Cover: Matinee Western superstar Tom Mix, atop Tony the Wonder Horse, appears to leap Newhall's Beale's Cut in this still from 1923's *Three Jumps Ahead*. It is uncertain whether the leap actually occurred, as the film is now lost. What is known is that Will Rogers spoofed the stunt that same year in *Uncensored Movies*, where he one-ups Mix by appearing to clear the cut on a horse that turns a complete loop, mid-leap! (Courtesy of scvhistory.com.)

CONTENTS

Acknowledgments

As in our previous publication, *Legendary Locals of the Santa Clarita Valley*, we were blessed with the assistance of a great many people who share our love for the Santa Clarita Valley during the creation of this book. At the top of the list is Leon Worden of SCVTV, who provided us with most of the historical images from his amazing website scvhistory.com.

We would also like to thank Mike Stephens for providing us with the camera equipment used in capturing most of the modern-day photographs.

Thanks also go to Jared Nelson of Arcadia Publishing, Laurene Weste, Bill West of *SCV in the Movies*, Megan Perez of SCVTV, Renaud and Sue Veluzat of the Melody Ranch Motion Picture Studio, Bobby Clark, Hugh Munro Neely, the Santa Clarita Valley Historical Society, and the Friends of Hart Park. Special thanks to our amazing Newhallywood Tours guests for helping us find many of the locations presented inside. And once again, thanks go to the wonderful folks at FreshWorks in Valencia for providing hours of free Wi-Fi and gallons of iced tea while we wrote this book. Unless otherwise noted, all historic images appear courtesy of scvhistory.com, and all modern image are by the authors.

INTRODUCTION

Welcome to the Santa Clarita Valley of yesterday and today.

Southern California's Santa Clarita Valley (SCV) is home to over a quarter-million residents who enjoy its mild Mediterranean climate, ample parks and green space, vibrant business environment, low crime rate, and close proximity to both the beach and the high desert. It is no wonder that the SCV consistently ranks among the best places to live in America.

The SCV stretches from north to south from the Angeles National Forest to the San Fernando Valley. The city of Palmdale lies at its eastern edge, and the Heritage Valley in Ventura County borders it on the west. Surrounded by the San Gabriel and Santa Susana Mountains, the SCV encircles the city of Santa Clarita—made up of the districts of Valencia, Newhall, Saugus, and Canyon Country—along with the communities of Castaic, Stevenson Ranch, Val Verde, Agua Dulce, and Acton.

While it is true that the Santa Clarita Valley is situated just minutes from the northern border of Los Angeles, please do not dismiss it as simply a bedroom community for the megalopolis to the south. The SCV has a rich history stretching back centuries.

A Native American tribe known as the Tataviam lived in the area for centuries before being subjugated by the Spanish, who arrived in 1769. During the Spanish Mission era that followed, the valley served as a cattle ranch for the friars. After Mexican independence, the area became the 48,000-acre Rancho San Francisco, owned by the Del Valle family.

Gold was discovered here in 1842, which predated the more famous strike at Northern California's Sutter's Mill by six years. Unlike its northern counterpart, the SCV's gold discovery created no noticeable "rush" and was largely overlooked by the press.

Americans took control of the valley after the land grab known as the Mexican-American War, which resulted in statehood for California in 1850. The valley's strategic location made it a vital transportation link between the cities and pueblos of Northern and Southern California.

During the Civil War, Edward F. Beale deepened a previously dug pathway between the SCV and the San Fernando Valley to 90 feet. It became known as Beale's Cut and was used for cattle drives and as a pathway for wagons and stagecoaches for decades.

Auctioneer and railroad speculator Henry Mayo Newhall later bought the remnants of the old Rancho San Francisco and, in 1876, established the town bearing his name as a stop on the Southern Pacific Railroad. During that same year, one of the world's longest railroad tunnels was dug nearby, and at the valley's Lang station, the Southern Pacific's rail lines between the two halves of California were first linked.

Oil had been discovered earlier in the valley, but the pivotal US centennial year of 1876 brought the state its first successful gusher in the valley's Pico Canyon. This well, known as CSO (California Star Oil) No. 4, pumped for the next 114 years. A pipeline was stretched from Pico Canyon to the first refinery in the state, Newhall's Pioneer Refinery.

For years, cattle rustling was a local pastime, and a decades-long "range war" raged between rival clans. Legendary bandit Tiburcio Vasquez visited during the 1870s and hid out for a time among the valley's otherworldly rocks, which now bear his name. Vasquez Rocks later became the backdrop for hundreds of Westerns.

While many cities claim to be the progeny of the Old West, few can profess to be where that colorful era's events occurred, as well as where those happenings were later recreated by Hollywood. The SCV can rightfully claim this two-tiered history as its own.

The first noted storyteller to arrive was Helen Hunt Jackson, who wrote a novel called *Ramona* about a young señorita who falls in love with a Native American man. The book sold millions of copies and created a travel boom of fans swarming to Southern California hoping to see the sites that modeled for locations in the story. One was reportedly Rancho Camulos at the valley's western end. The novel was later brought to film in 1910 by D.W. Griffith, who used Rancho Camulos as a backdrop.

Dozens of other filmmakers arrived in the area over the coming decades, mostly to make Westerns. The Santa Clarita Valley became such a popular filming site that Newhall earned the nickname "Newhallywood." Several stars, including William S. Hart, Hoot Gibson, and Harry Carey, chose to live in the area. In 1981, downtown Newhall began honoring this Western heritage with historic sidewalk plaques around Main Street, known as the Walk of Western Stars.

The next major import into the valley was water by way of the Los Angeles Aqueduct. This man-made channel brought the precious resource from the Owens Valley far to the north all the way to Los Angeles. The major shaker behind this project was Los Angeles "water czar" William Mulholland. Mulholland's motives and methods proved unpopular with the people of the Owens Valley, who sabotaged the waterway on multiple occasions. To keep the water flowing without interruption, Mulholland ordered the construction of the St. Francis Dam in the valley's San Francisquito Canyon. The dam was shoddily constructed in a geologically unstable location. It crashed down just before midnight on March 12, 1928, sending an 18-story torrent of water scouring through the canyon on a 53-mile path of destruction to the sea. At least 431 lives were lost that night.

Soon afterwards, one of the last Old West–style train robberies took place in Saugus when an ex-rodeo rider named "Buffalo Tom" Vernon derailed a train and gleaned $300 from the passengers at gunpoint.

In time, the Newhall Land and Farming Company, which owned most of the valley's property, shifted its priorities away from agriculture to land development. Seemingly overnight, square miles of empty land were transformed into residential areas, and the planned community of Valencia—complete with a major theme park that is today known as Six Flags Magic Mountain—sprouted on what had previously been bean and onion fields. Four towns, Newhall, Saugus, Valencia, and Canyon Country, joined forces in 1987, becoming the city of Santa Clarita. It was the first city in America created with an initial population greater than 100,000.

Over the past few decades, the economy of the valley has transitioned from agriculture to a broad spectrum of industries, including many in high-tech fields. Film and television production is still a major employer, with several studios and film ranches sprinkled throughout the valley.

But the Santa Clarita Valley still remembers its past. Nowhere is this more evident than at the city's annual Cowboy Festival, which takes place at Newhall's Melody Ranch Motion Picture Studio. It is here—on the same Western streets where *Gunsmoke*'s Marshal Matt Dillon used to stare down the bad guys—that the city gathers every April to honor its heritage.

CHAPTER 1

THE OLD WEST

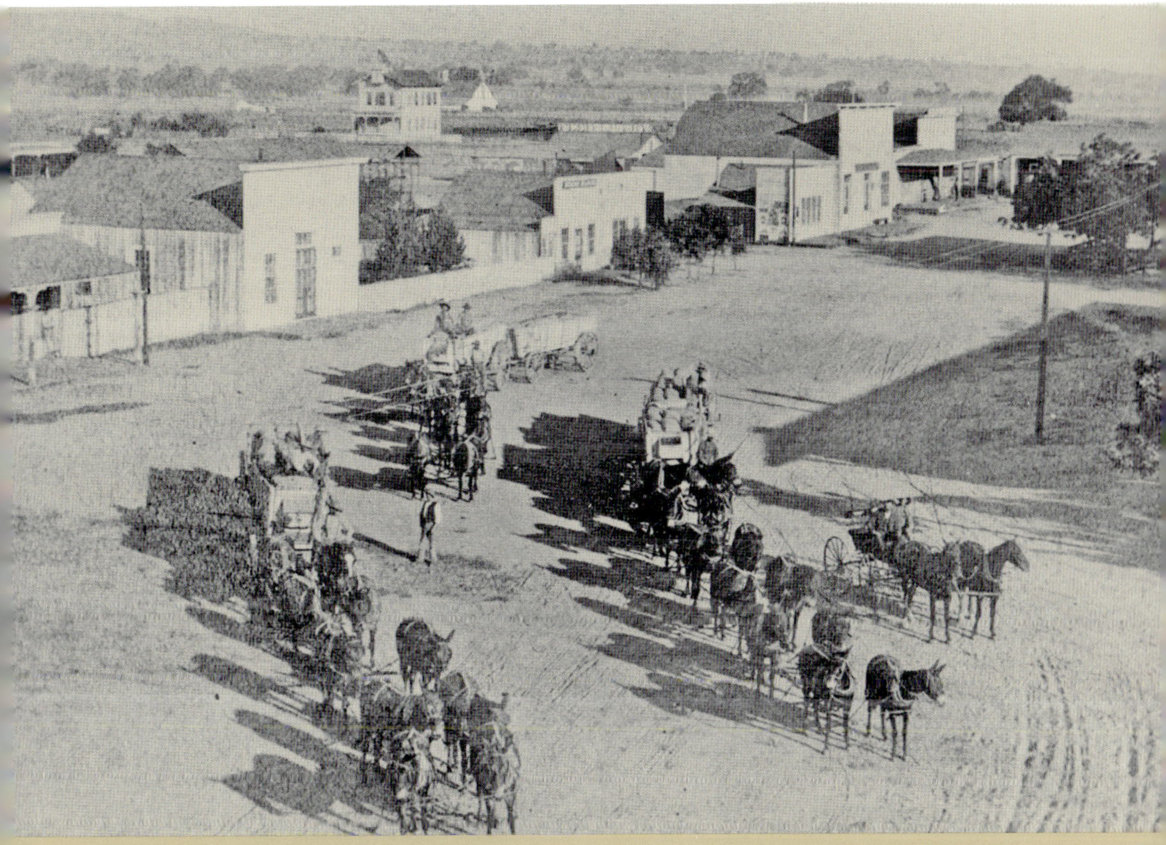

Mule teams, bringing feed and supplies into Newhall in 1887, round the corner from Railroad Avenue onto Market Street. Behind them is the main business district, including, from left to right, the home of Judge John Powell, the Rivera Saloon, Mike Powell's Palace Saloon, and George Campton's general store. The first Newhall school is in the background.

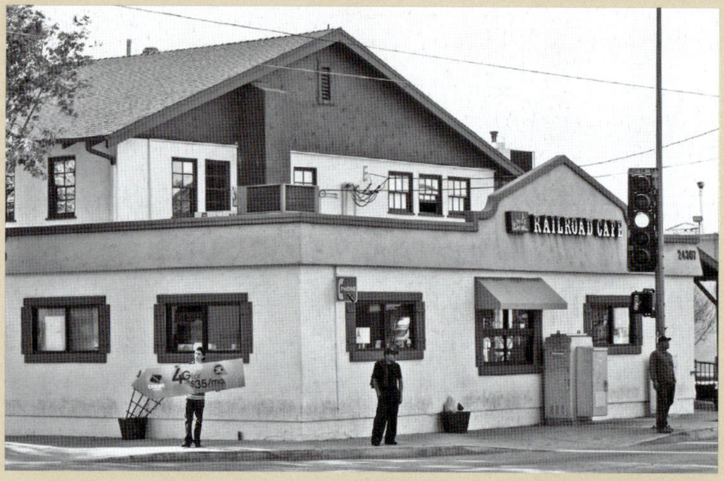

Four patrons, two horses, and one dog posed for this 1880s-era photograph outside of this general store on the northwest corner of Railroad Avenue and Market Street. The store was built by town founder Henry Mayo Newhall's brother (some sources say cousin) Joshua O. Newhall. The store later changed hands a few times before becoming the Hap-A-Lan dance hall. After the St. Francis Dam disaster in 1928, the building served as a morgue for many of the victims. It was torn down shortly thereafter, and this current structure was later built.

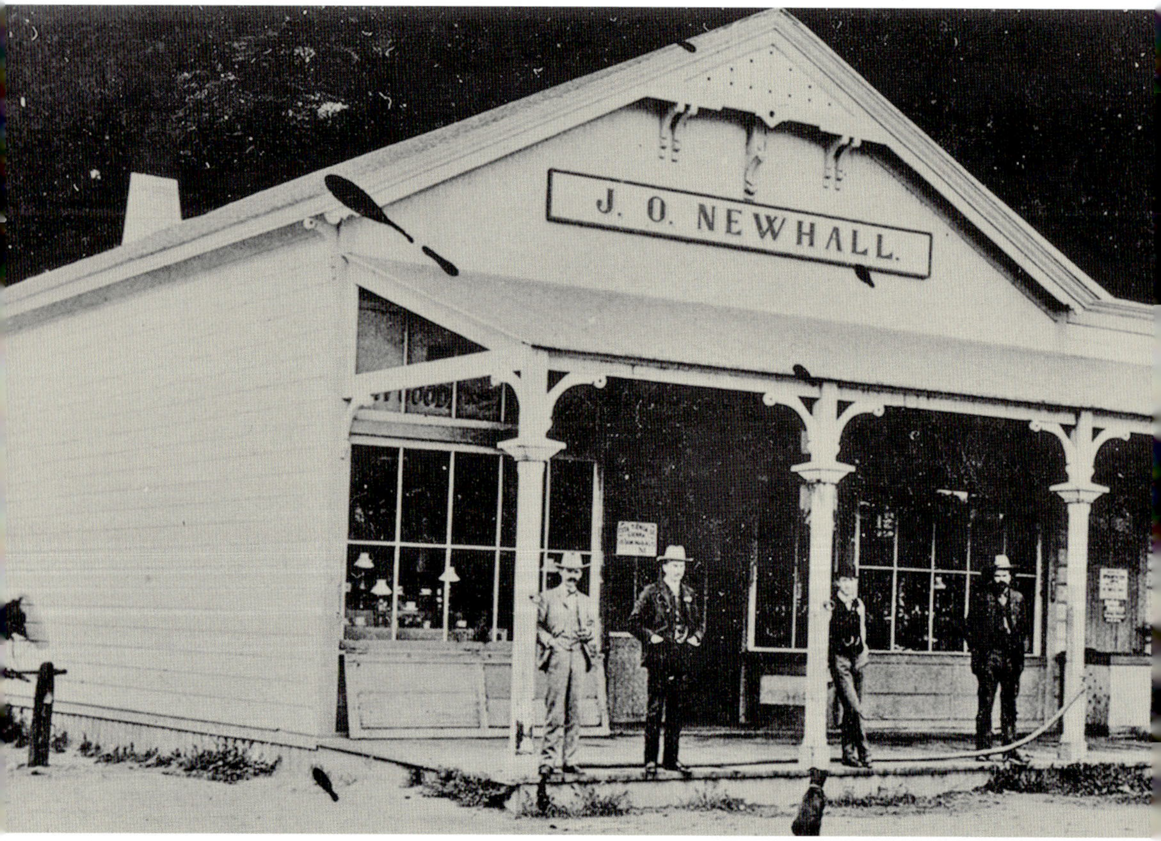

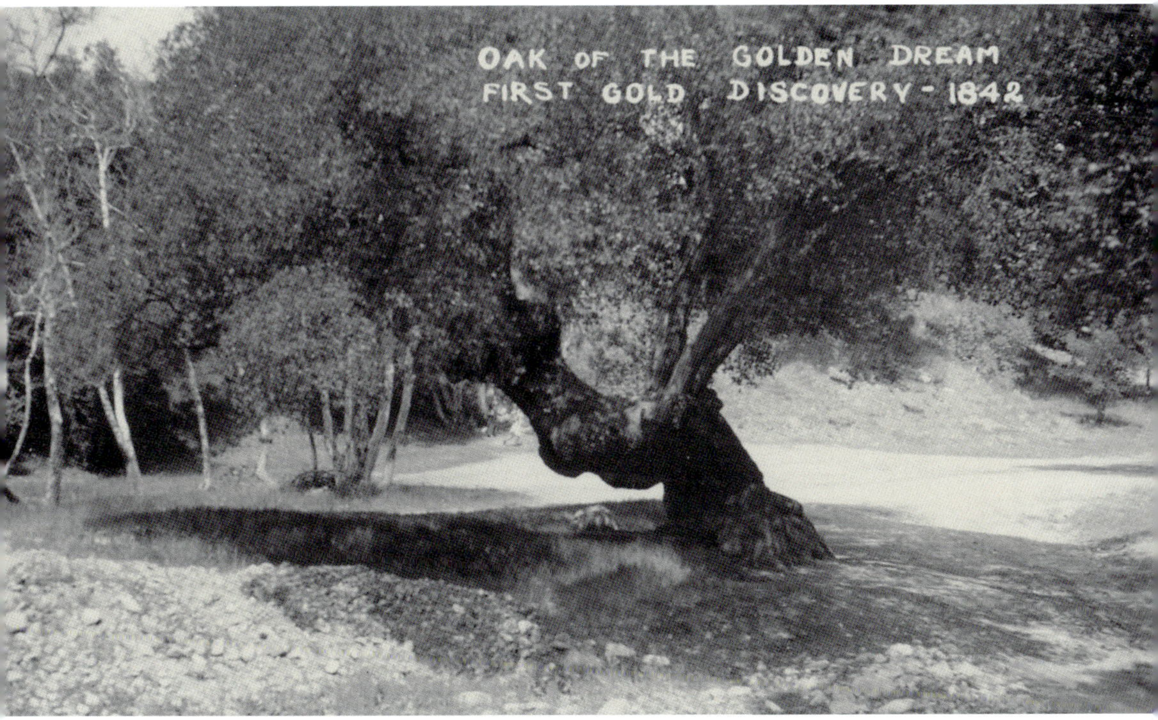

Everyone's heard about the gold strike at Sutter's Mill in 1848. But the first documented gold discovery in California actually occurred over six years earlier, near an oak tree in Placerita Canyon. The story (which is most likely dubious) is that Francisco Lopez fell asleep under the tree and dreamed of gold. After awakening, he dug up wild onions under some nearby sycamore trees and found gold clinging to the roots. Today, the Oak of the Golden Dream is a California historic landmark.

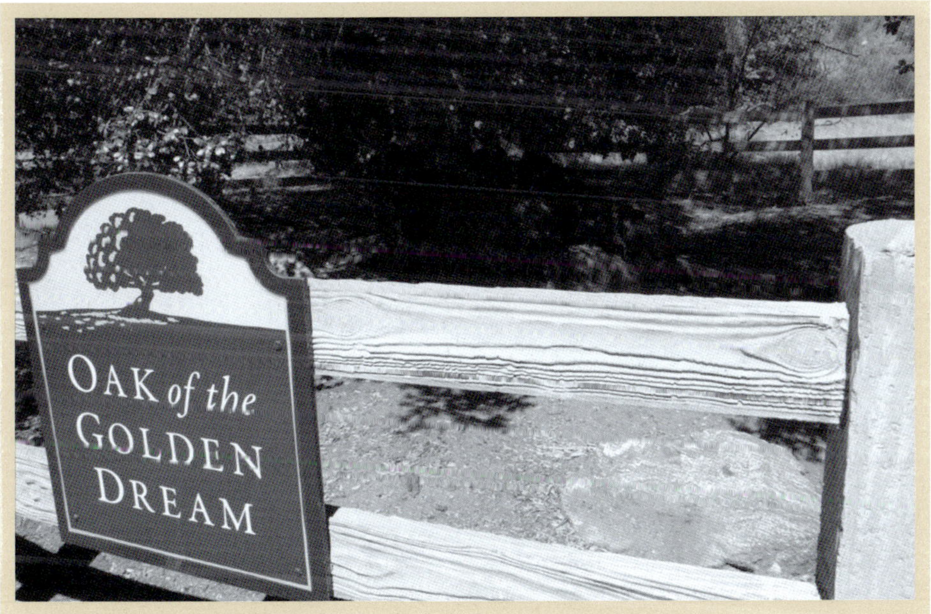

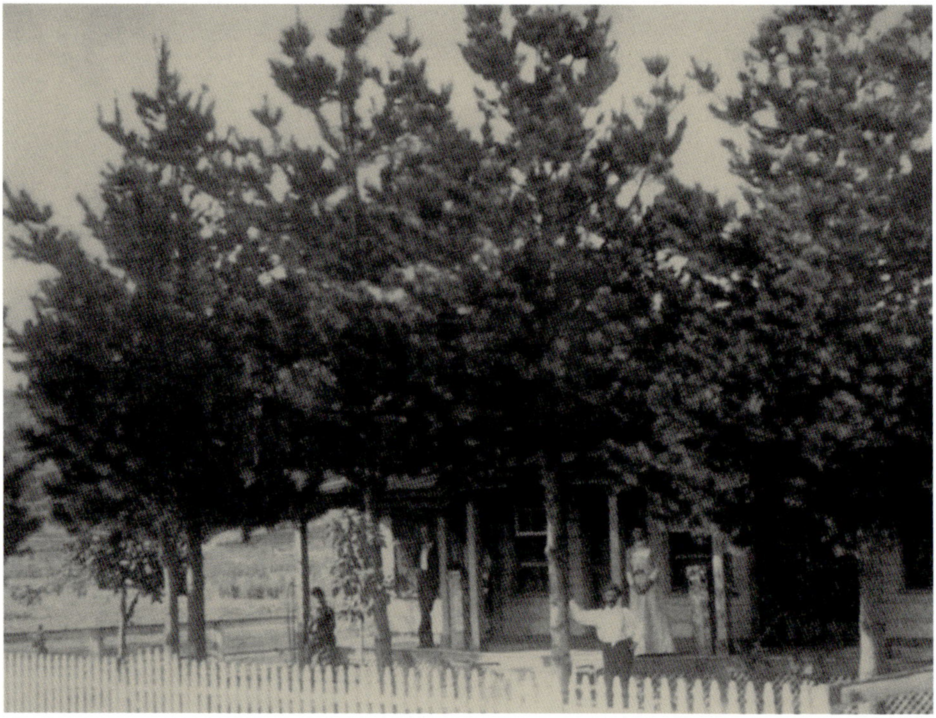

Around 1855, brothers Sanford and Cyrus Lyon purchased a stagecoach stop at the base of the Fremont Pass somewhere in the vicinity of present-day Eternal Valley Cemetery. The structure in the old photograph may have been built in the 1850s for the stationmaster. It was thought to have been located under today's Sierra Highway or just to the east, across from the cemetery. Some believe that the house was moved and still exists today on Thirteenth Street in Newhall.

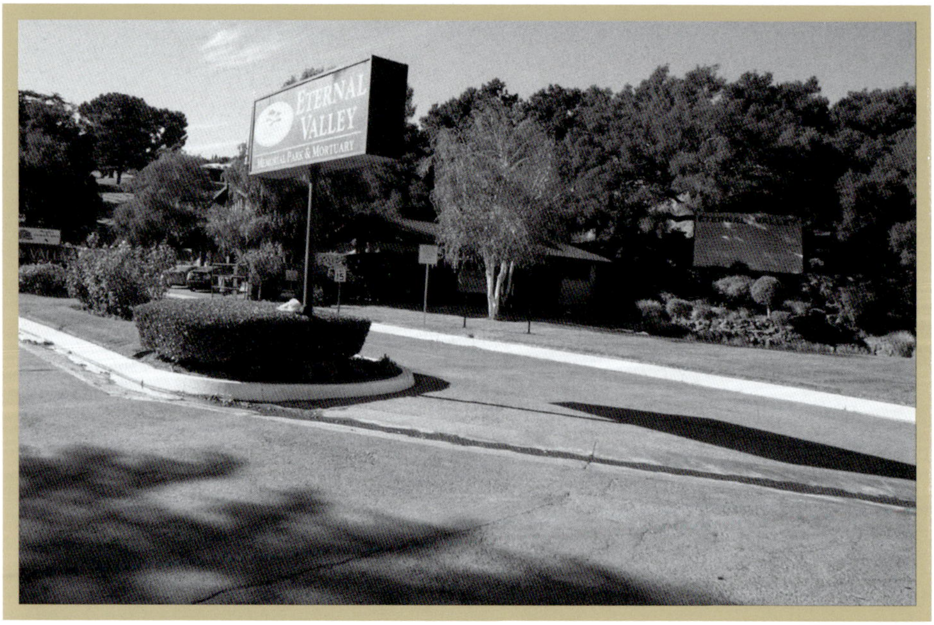

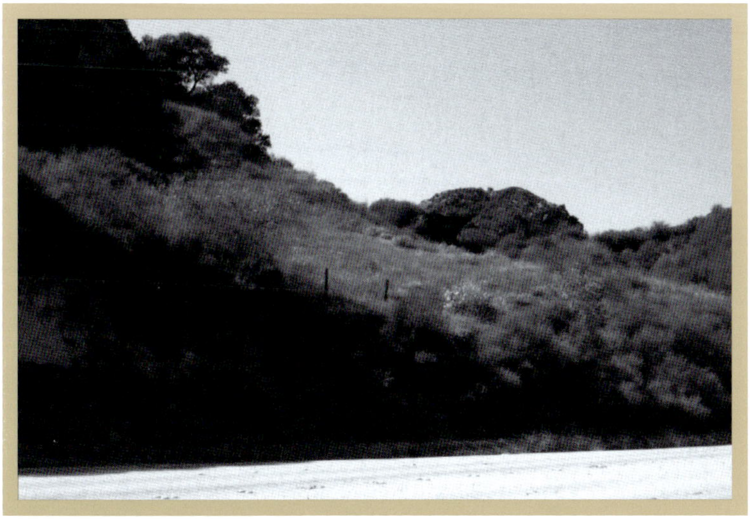

In exchange for deepening what was then known as Banning's Cut in 1863, Edward Beale was given a 20-year franchise to charge tolls on all passengers traveling through. A small five-room adobe tollhouse was built near the foot of the south grade of what was renamed Beale's Cut. Toll rates ranged from 10¢ per animal to $2.75 for a team of 12. Today, Sierra Highway runs through the site.

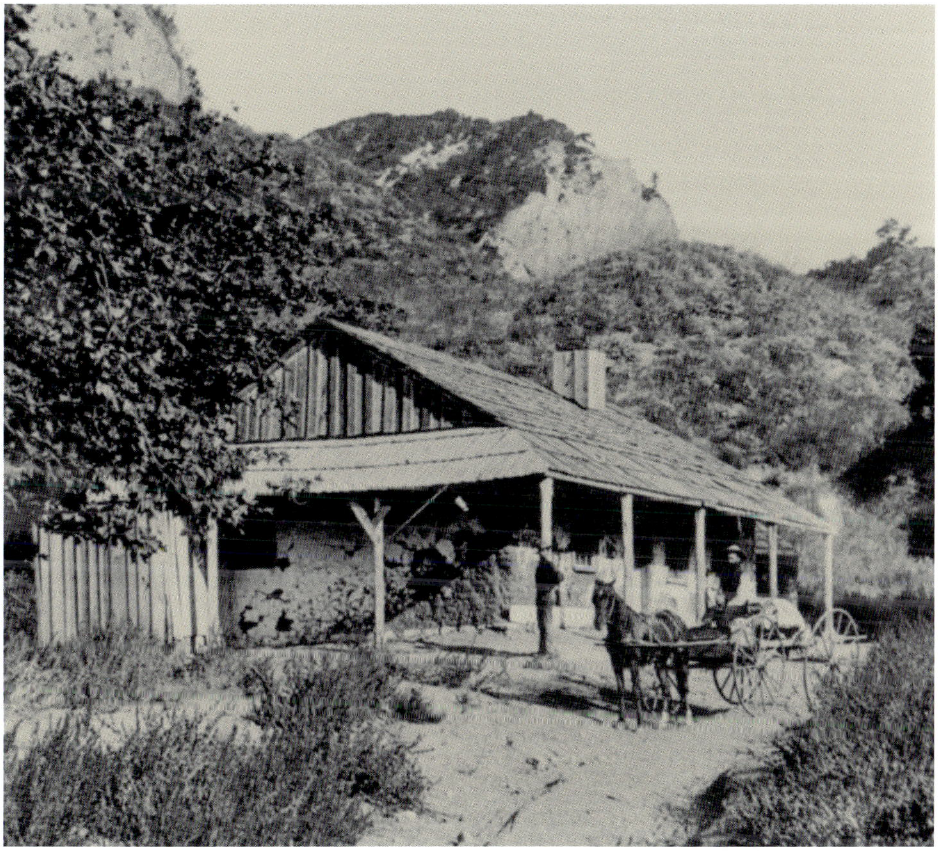

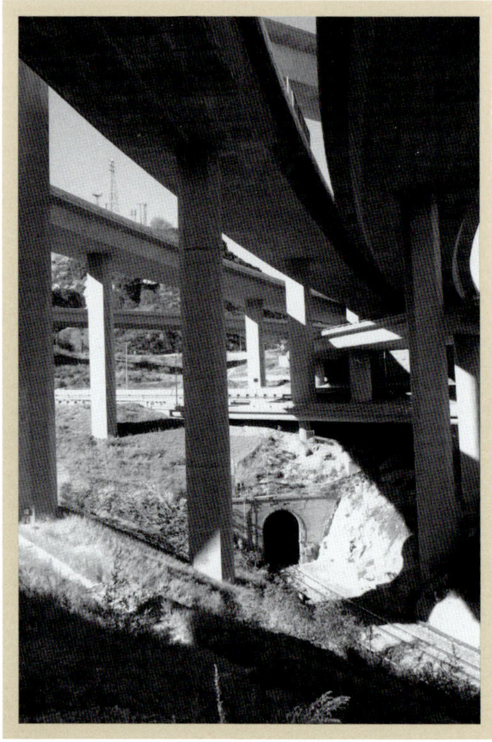

Unbeknownst to thousands of daily commuters passing overhead, far beneath the Interstate 5/Antelope Valley Interchange in the Newhall Pass lies one of California's great historic treasures. The completion of the 6,967-foot San Fernando Railroad Tunnel in 1876 made it possible to link both segments of the Southern Pacific Railroad. Some historians speculate that California may have split into separate states were it not for the tunnel, which was once the fourth-longest in the world. The postcard from 1908 shows the tunnel's southern entrance.

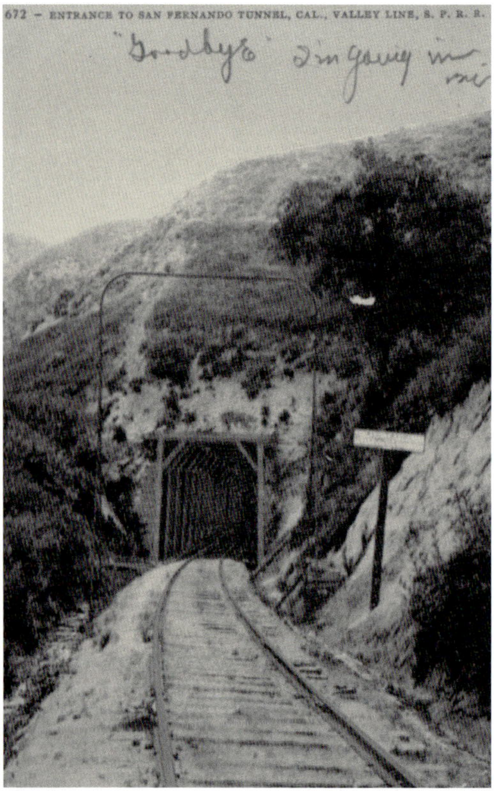

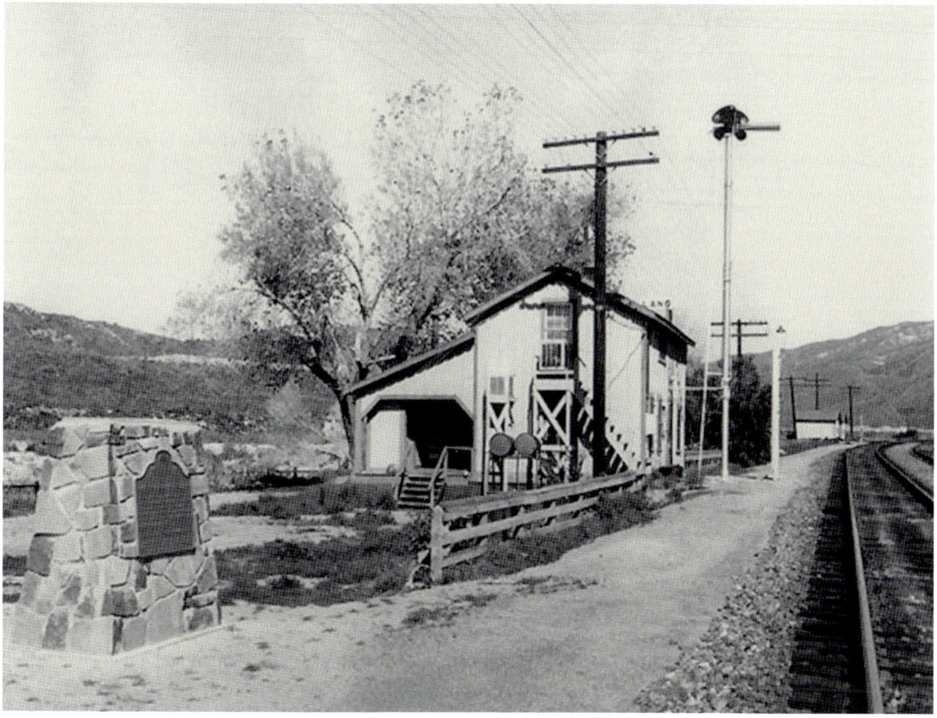

In 1870, New Yorker John Lang purchased 160 acres in Soledad Canyon for $300. Here, he built a train depot, express office, post office, and a hotel and spa. On September 5, 1876, a golden spike ceremony here marked the completion of the Southern Pacific Railroad connecting Los Angeles and San Francisco. Lang's original depot burned down in 1888 and was replaced by the depot pictured here. This depot was demolished in 1971.

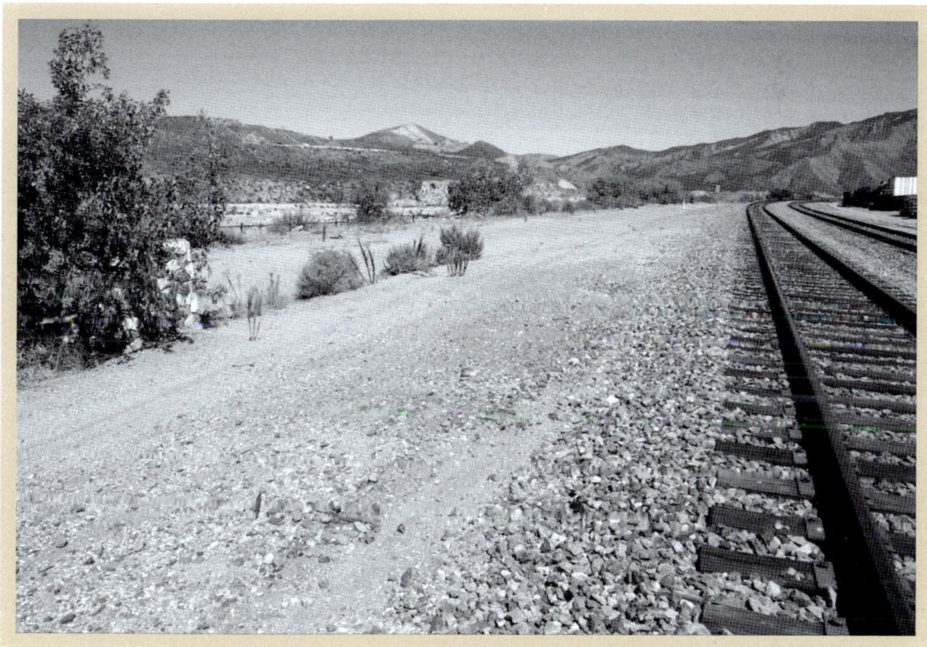

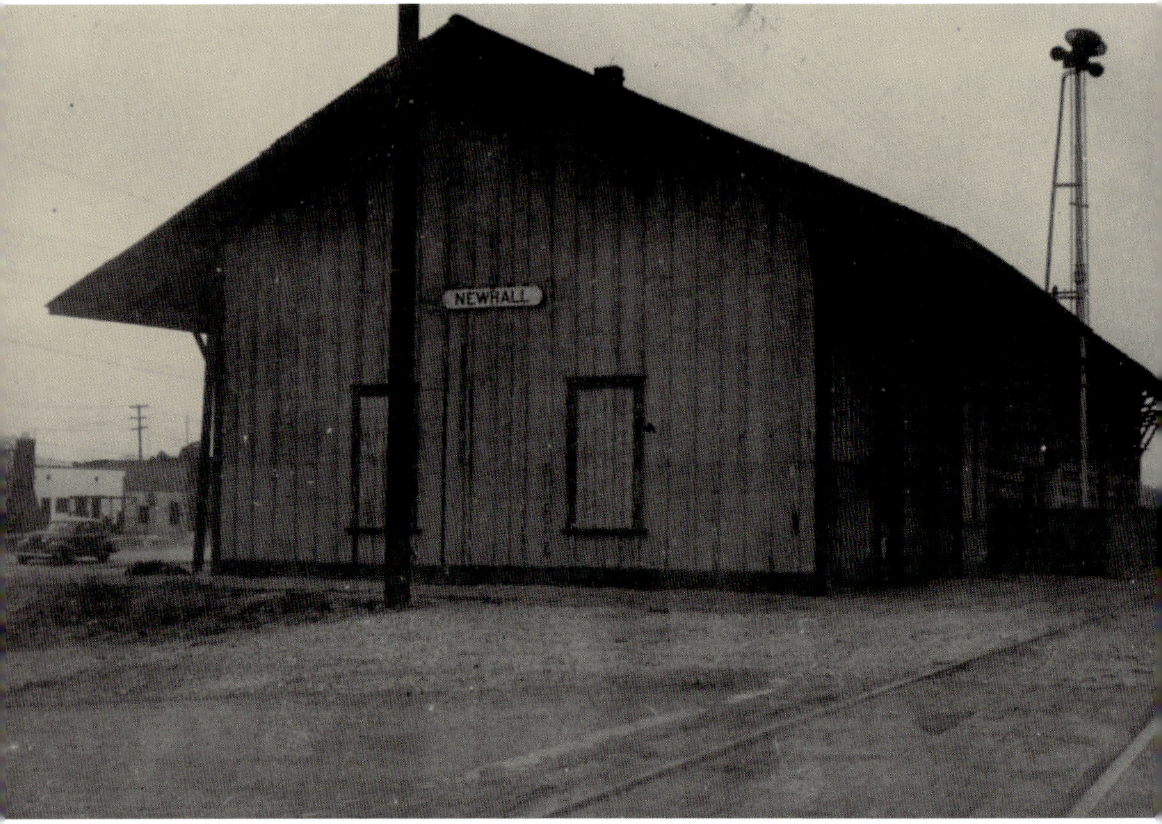

The Newhall depot was originally built in 1876 in present-day Saugus. Two years later, a lack of water forced the fledgling town and its depot to relocate two miles south to the corner of Railroad and Market Streets. The depot is seen here in 1939 at its new location. Opened in March 2000, the Newhall Metrolink Station now stands on the site of the former Newhall depot, continuing Newhall's long railroading tradition.

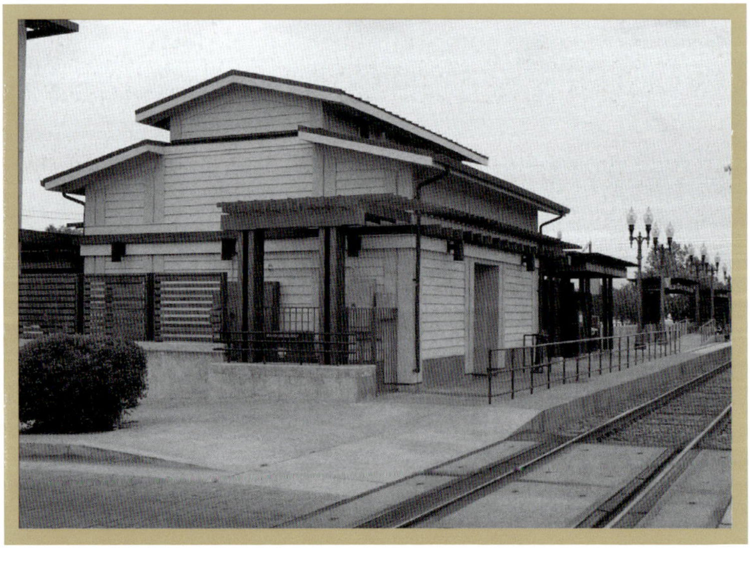

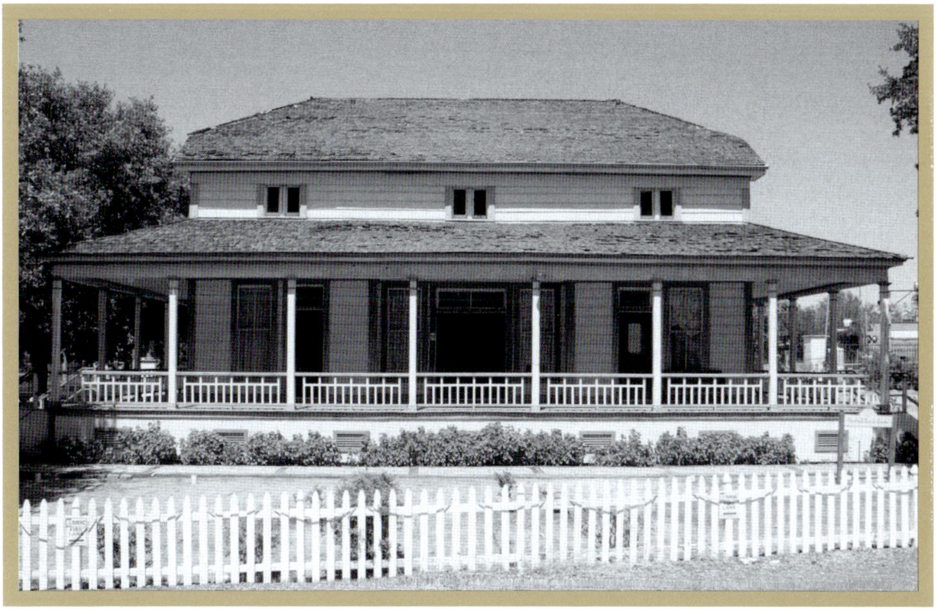

The Newhall Ranch House was originally located on what is now the employee parking lot of Valencia's Six Flags Magic Mountain amusement park. Sometime after 1875, the year Newhall founder Henry Mayo Newhall purchased the Rancho San Francisco, which comprised most of the present-day Santa Clarita Valley, the ranch house was transformed from a cabin into a 4,000-square-foot, two-story Victorian mansion. The mansion is pictured at its original site as well as its present location in Heritage Junction, Newhall, where it was moved in 1990.

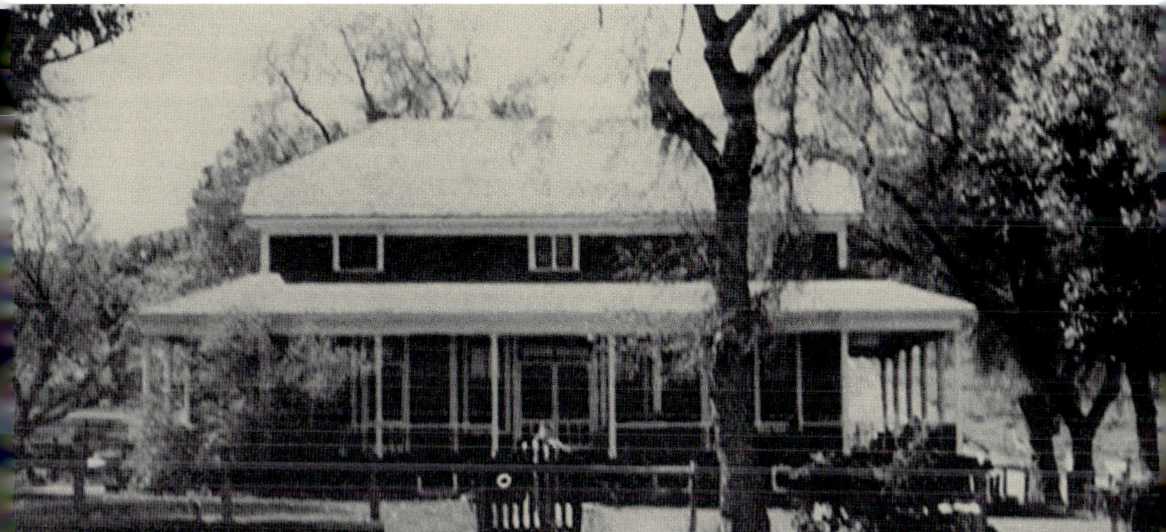

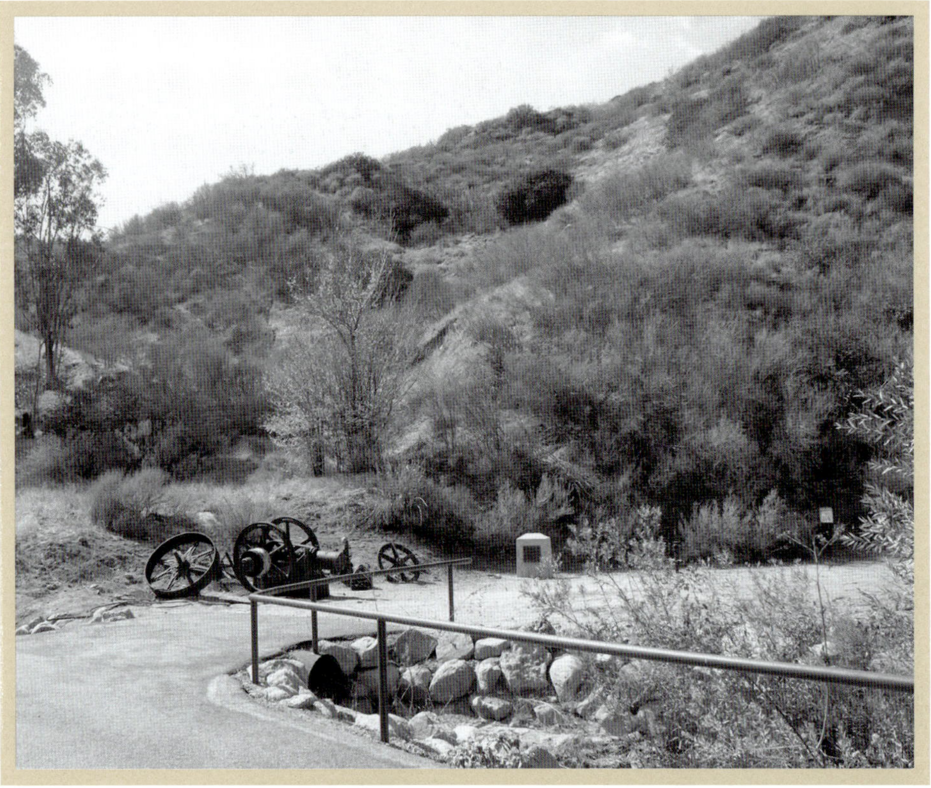

In the far reaches of Pico Canyon lies the site of the West's first commercially successful oil well. Demetrius G. Scofield established the California Star Oil Works in July 1876. He had purchased an oil claim the previous month from expert driller Alexander Mentry and convinced him to stay on with the new company. Mentry's fourth well in the canyon produced a gusher on September 26, 1876. Known as CSO (California Star Oil) No. 4, this well remained in operation until 1990.

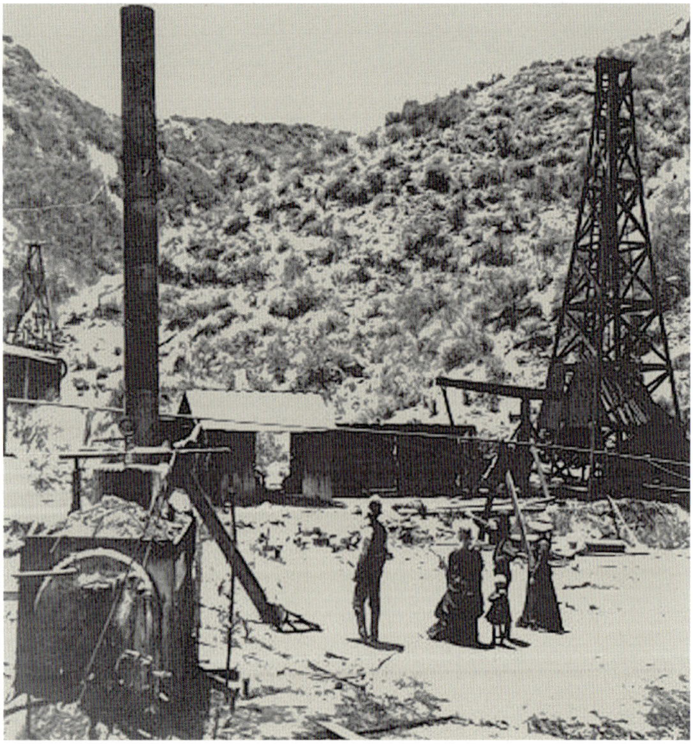

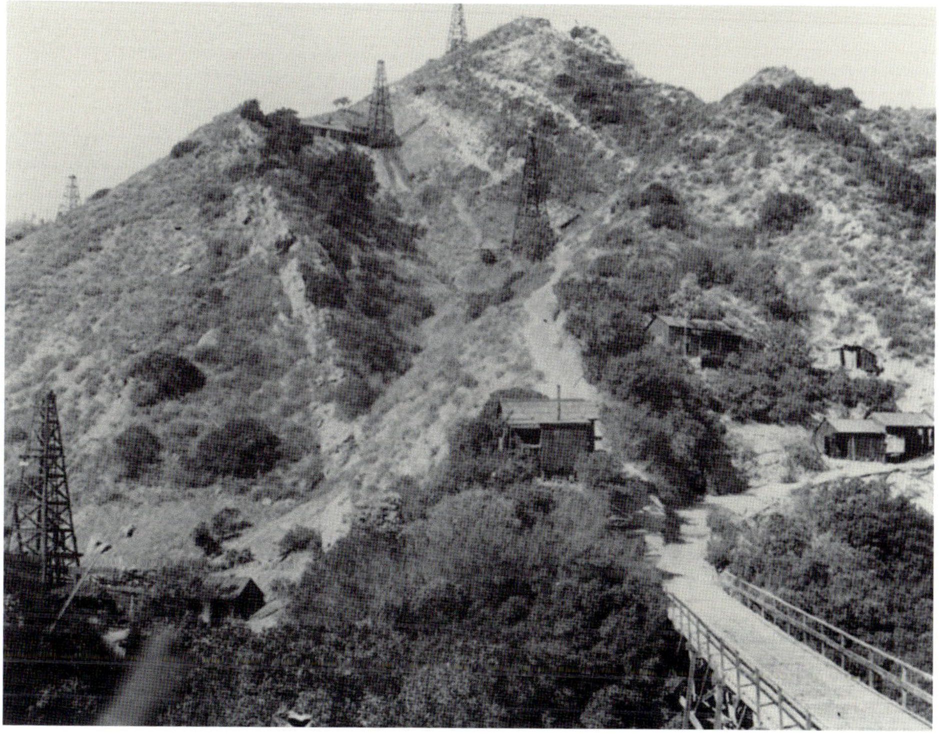

The hill behind the CSO No. 4 oil well was known as Christian Hill in reference to the pious oilman Lyman Stewart. Stewart and his partner Wallace Hardison sank five unsuccessful wells on the hill before drilling a productive well that they later sold. With the proceeds, Stewart and Hardison moved their operations to Santa Paula and formed a partnership with former Rancho San Francisco owner Thomas Bard, creating the Union Oil Company of California.

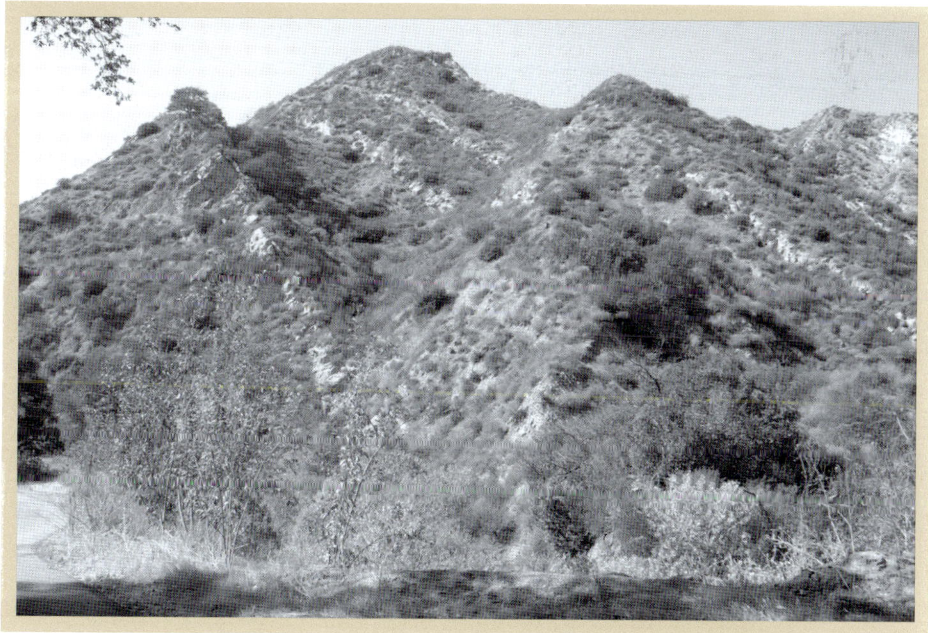

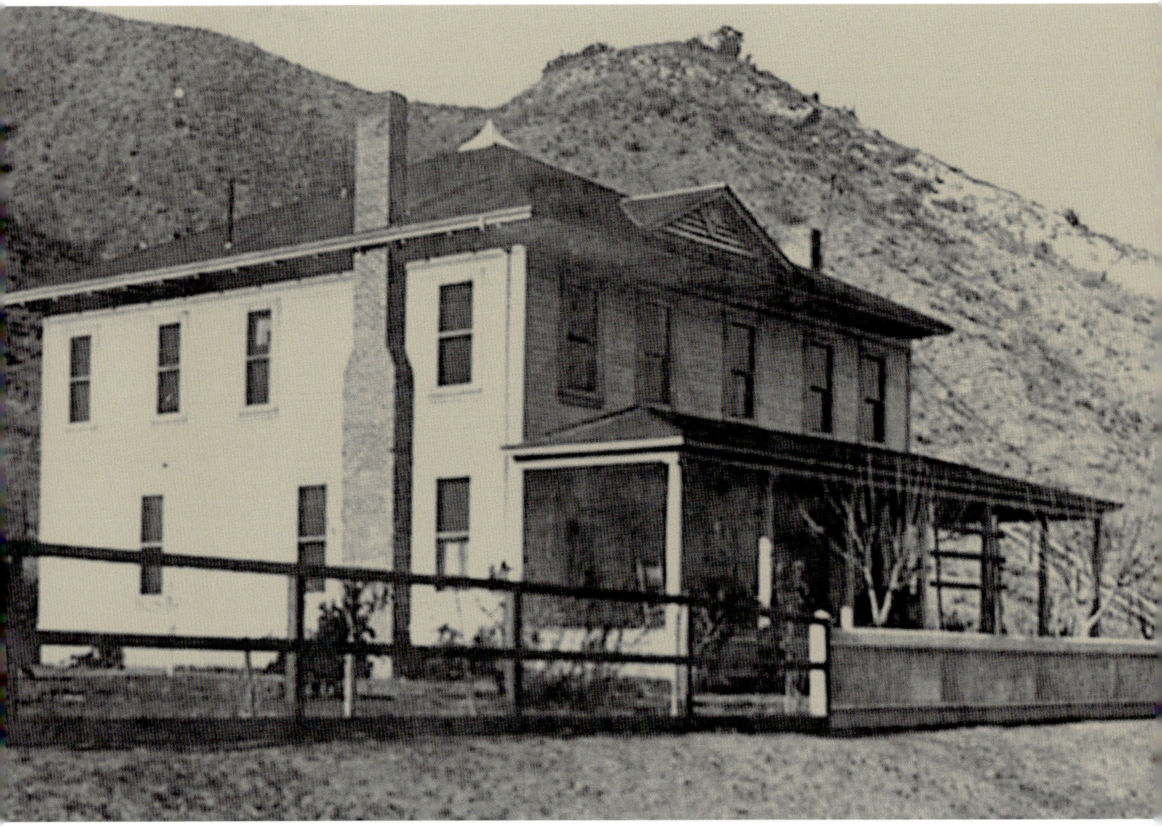

The "Pico Cottage" stands in the ghost town of Mentryville in Pico Canyon. This 13-room Victorian mansion, built in 1898, was the home of Charles Alexander Mentry. Mentry was an accomplished driller in the Pennsylvania oil fields who came to Pico Canyon in 1875. The following year, Mentry drilled the CSO No. 4 well, the first commercially successful oil well in the West. Mentry died in 1900 from typhoid fever.

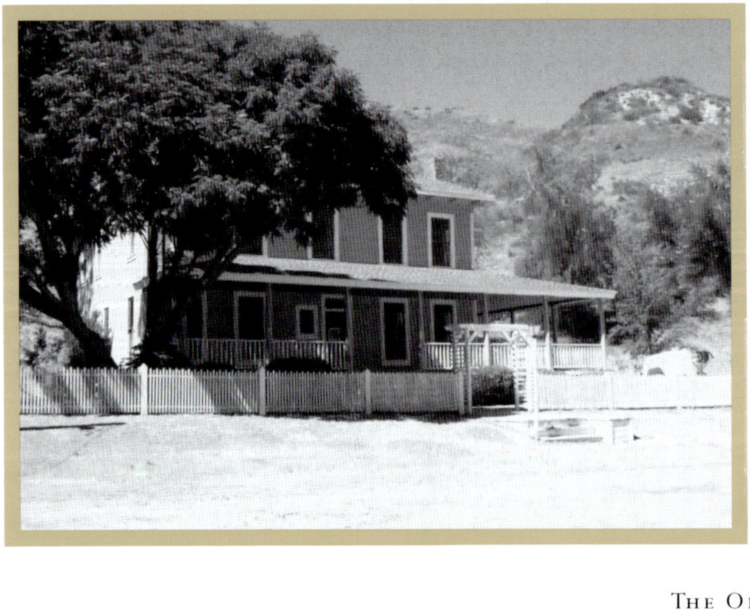

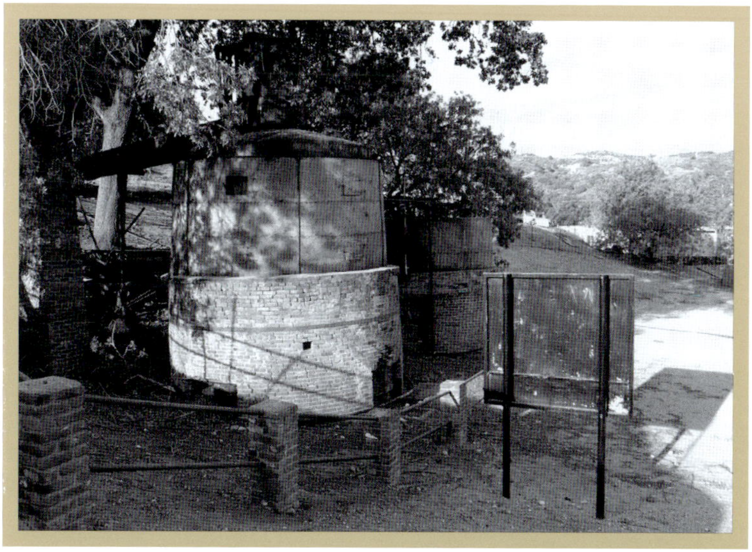

The Pioneer Oil Refinery, located on Pine Street in Newhall, was the first successful oil refinery in the West and is the oldest surviving refinery in the world. Completed in August 1876, the refinery produced benzene and illuminating oil for ships, railroads, factories, and mines for 12 years. Ownership of the abandoned refinery eventually passed to Chevron, which gifted the historic site to the City of Santa Clarita in 1997.

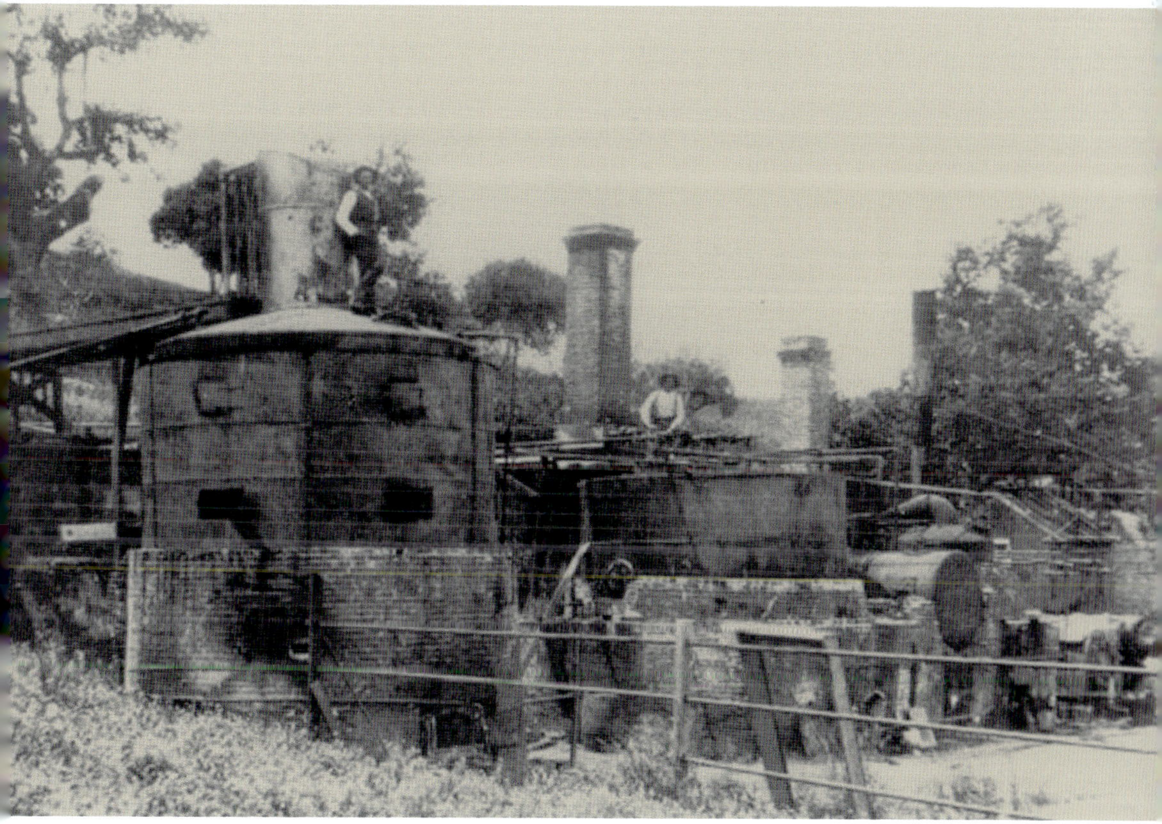

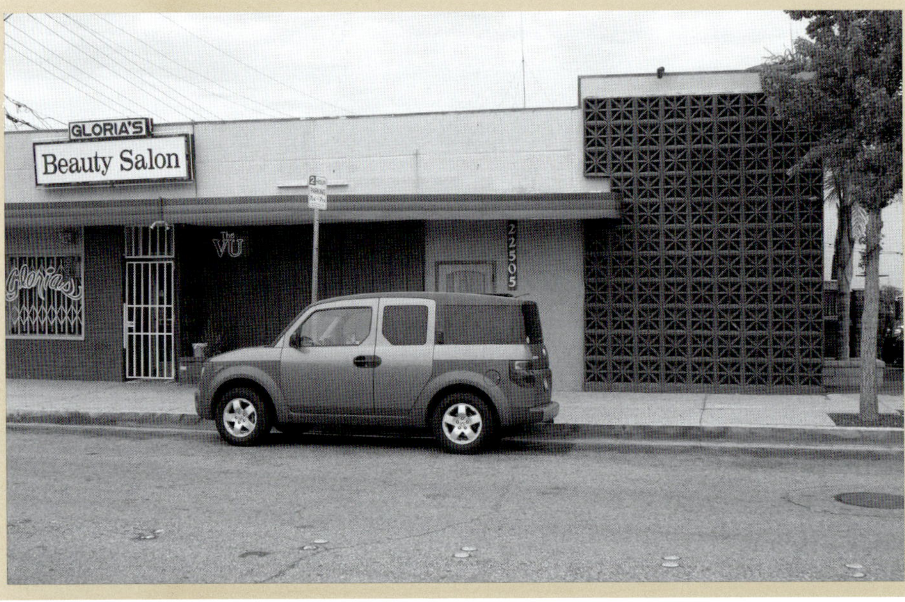

What was formerly a saloon is now a salon, as a portion of the site is now occupied by a beauty parlor.During Newhall's Wild West days, there were more drinking establishments than churches. One was the Derrick Saloon, located on Eighth Street and Railroad Avenue. The Derrick, built in 1878, was popular with oil workers living in the dry town of Mentryville in Pico Canyon. Emile Chaix took over operations in 1908. Today, the former saloon hosts the Vu Ultra Bar as well as a beauty salon.

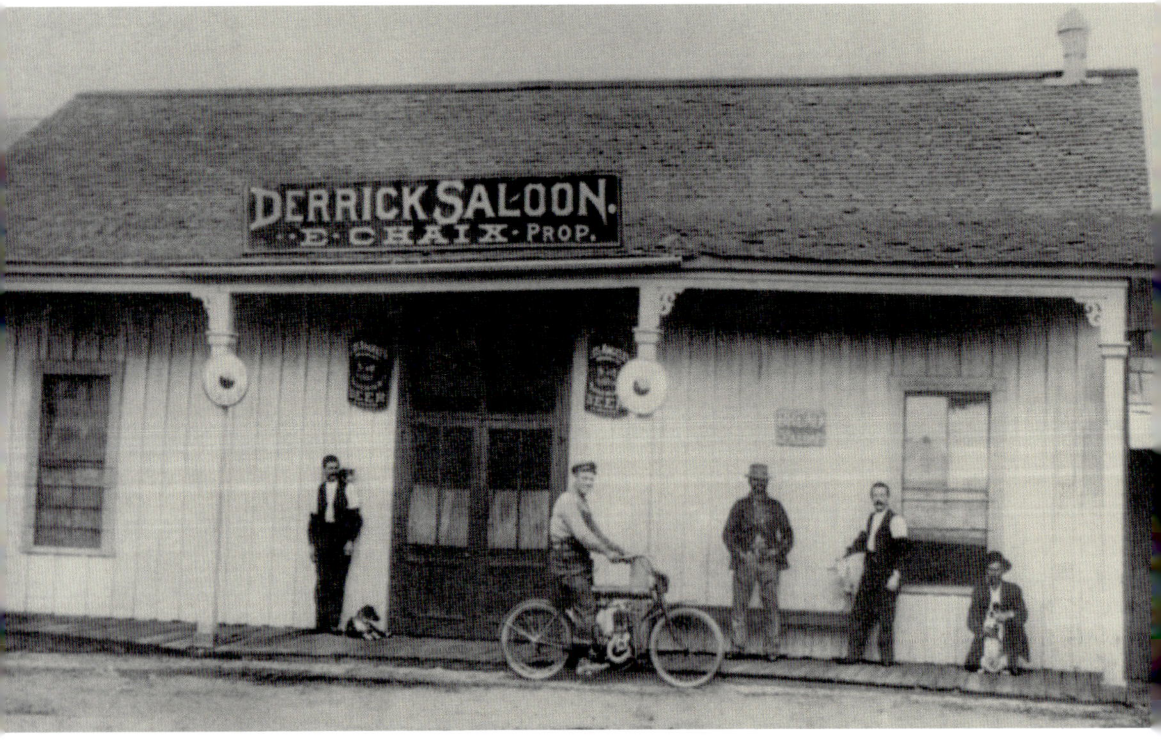

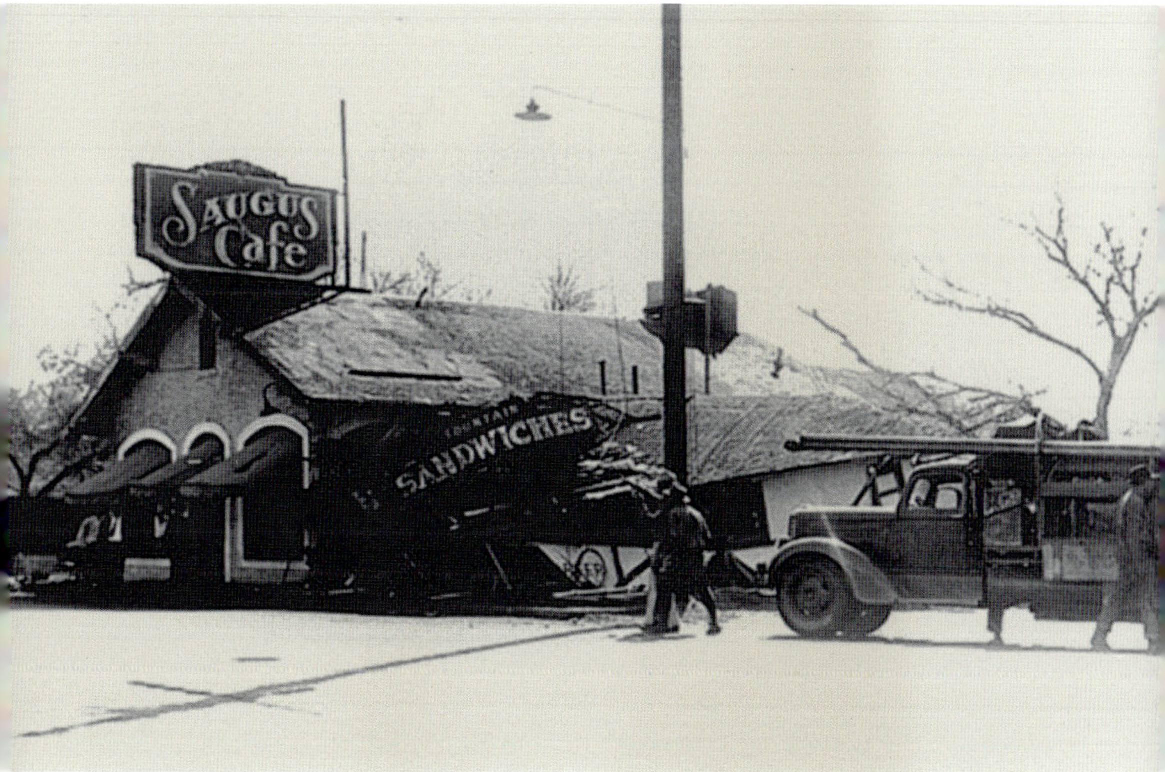

The Saugus Café began in 1887 as the Saugus Eating House in the north end of the Saugus Train Station. In 1905, Martin Wood moved it across the street to the location where it stands today on Railroad Avenue. As seen in the photograph from 1941, only one day after the remodeled restaurant reopened for business, an out-of-control trucker demolished the building. The café boasts the distinction of being the longest continually operated restaurant in Los Angeles County.

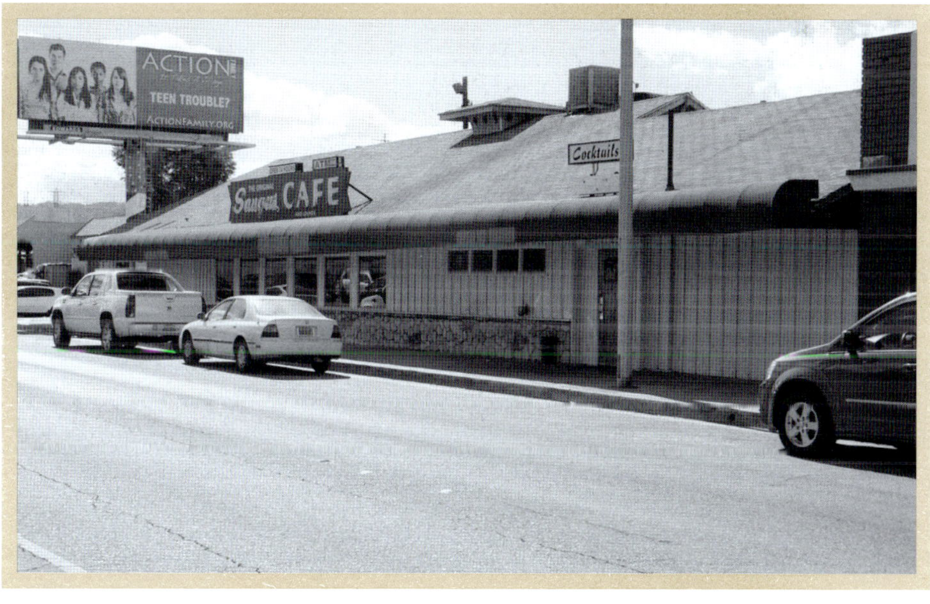

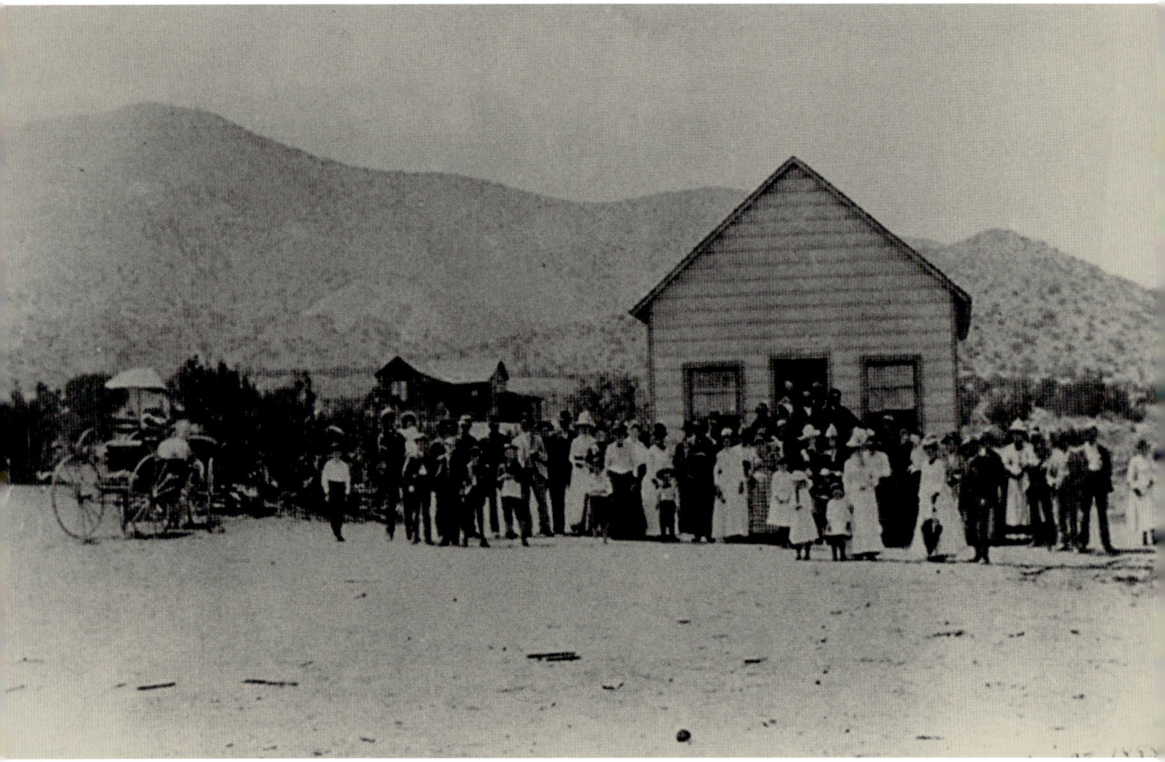

Members of the Union Moral and Religious Association of Acton pose in front of the Little White School, Acton's original schoolhouse. This one-room building was constructed in 1881 and was replaced by the brick Soledad School on the same site in 1890. It was used until the 1930s, when it was converted into a farmhouse that still stands today. Rudolph Nickel, the founder of Acton, took the vintage photograph on August 25, 1889.

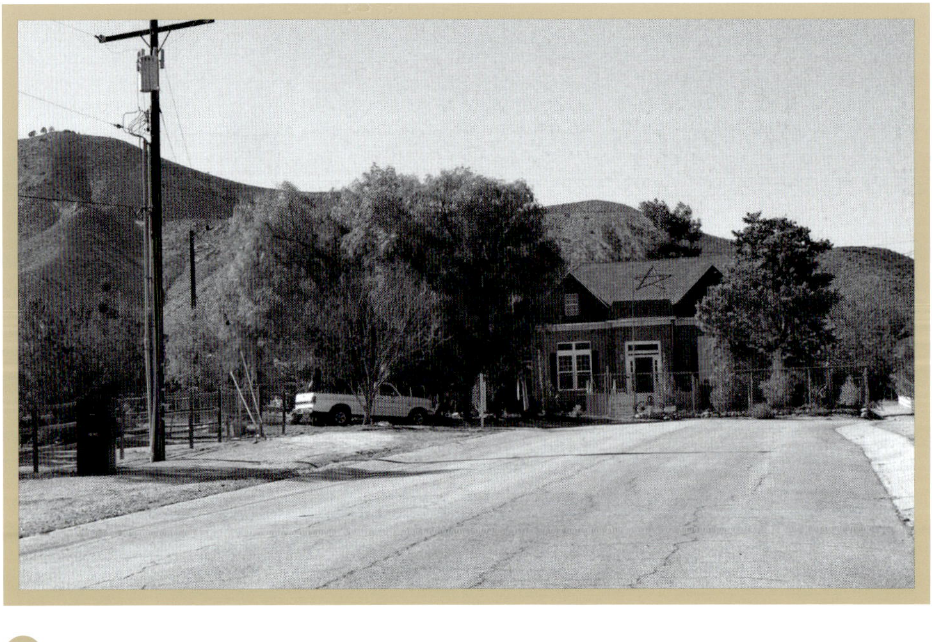

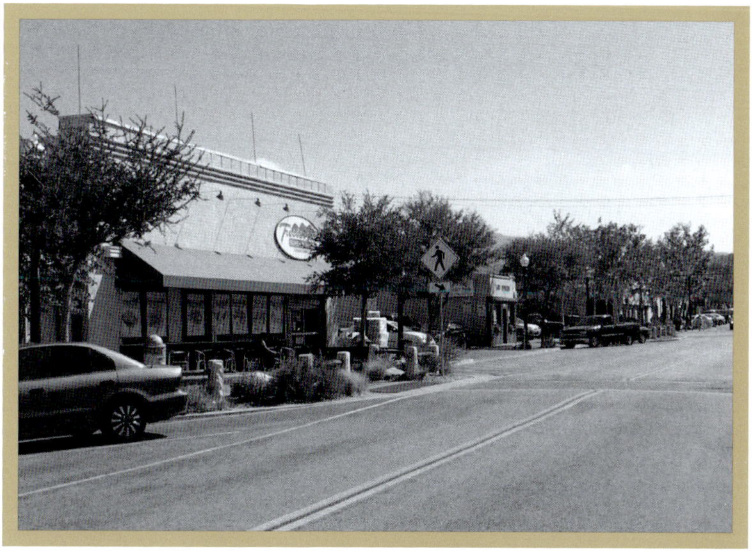

Ed Pardee established the Newhall livery stable on Spruce Street (today's Main Street) in 1887. Around the same time, the elegant Southern Hotel across the street burned to the ground. The vintage photograph show the livery stable (left) and the Second Southern Hotel, which was built on the site of its predecessor. Until 2014, the site of the livery stable was occupied by Tresierras grocery store. Today, the El Trocadero restaurant sits on the site of the Second Southern Hotel.

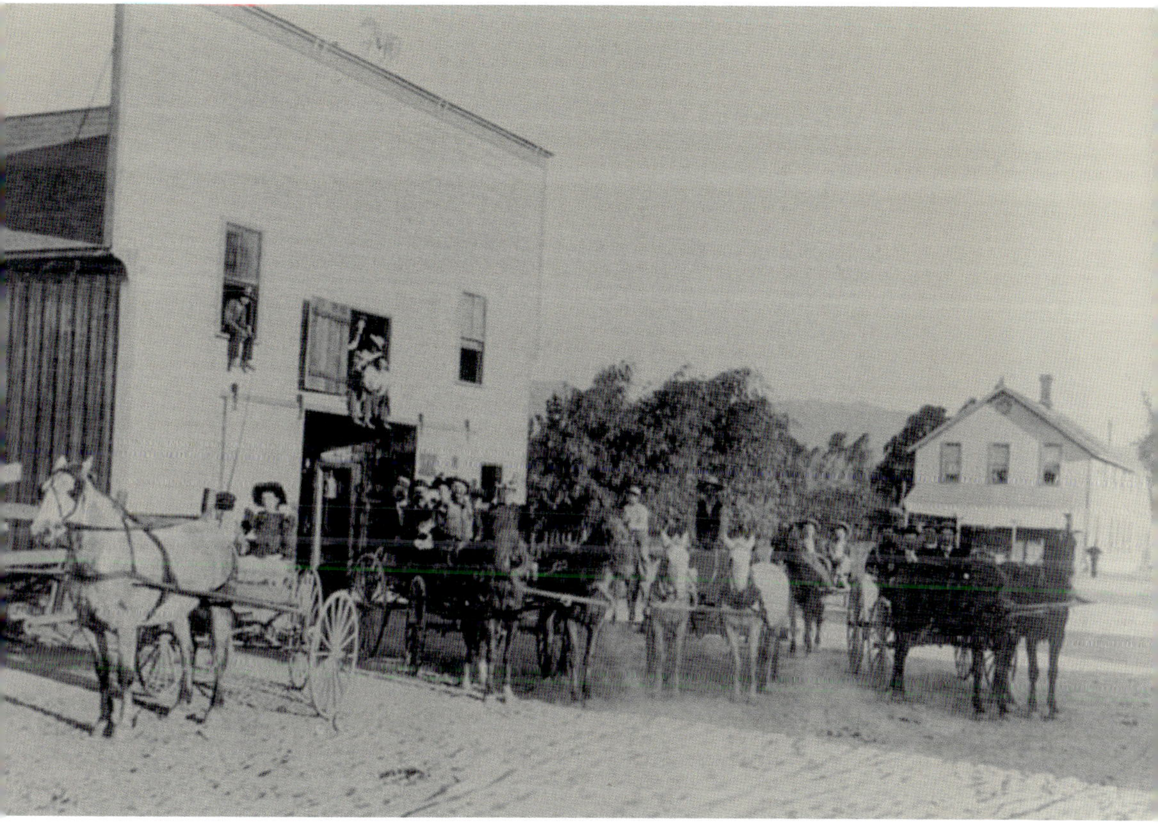

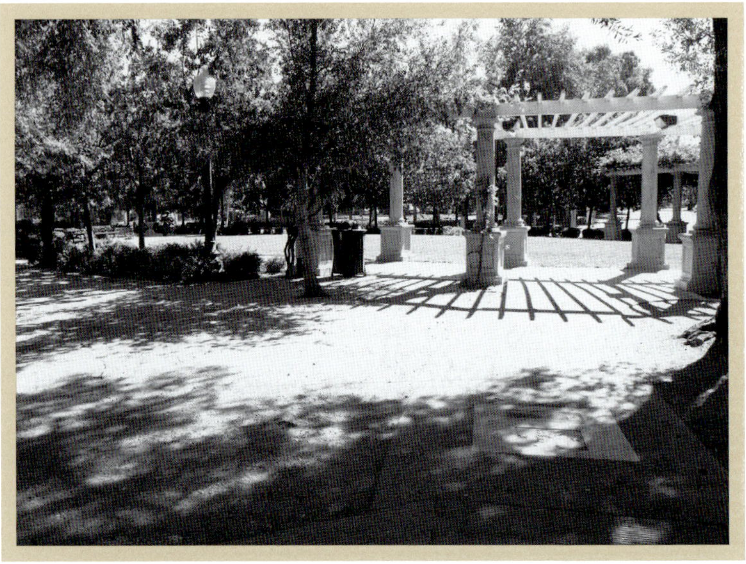

Ed Pardee purchased the Good Templar's Hall in 1893 and moved it from Pine Street to the corner of Market and Walnut Streets. The building would later serve the Pacific Telephone exchange, Santa Clarita Valley Boys Club, and, as pictured here in 1977, the Newhall-Saugus-Valencia Chamber of Commerce. The house was moved to its present location in Heritage Junction in 1992. Today, the triangular plot of land where the house once stood is home to the Veteran's Historical Plaza.

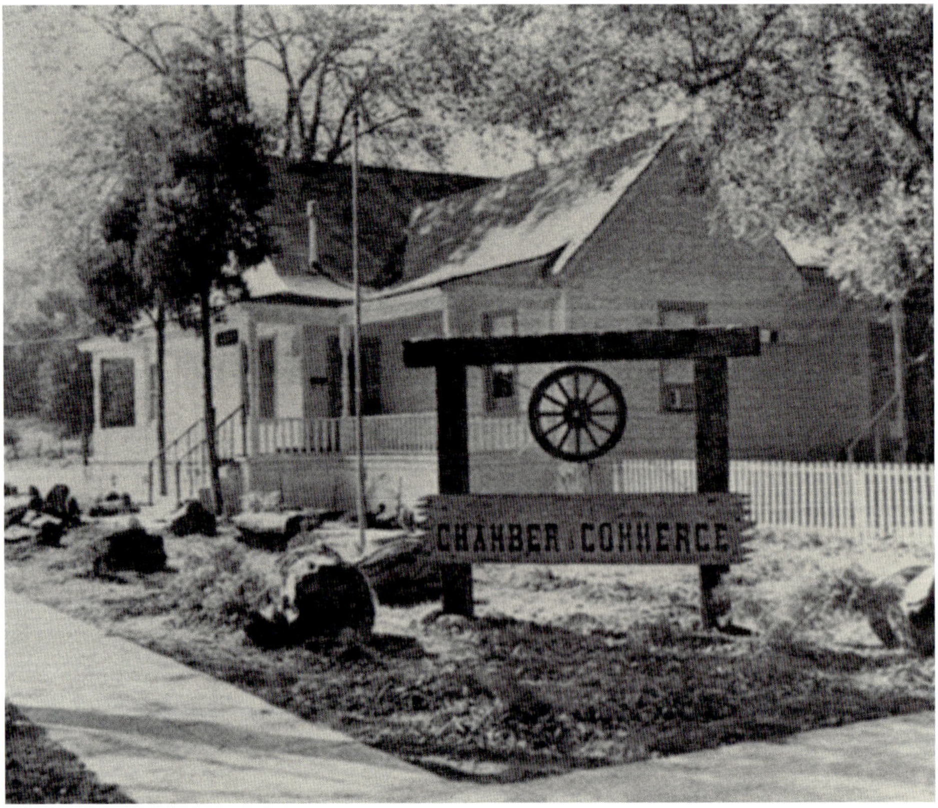

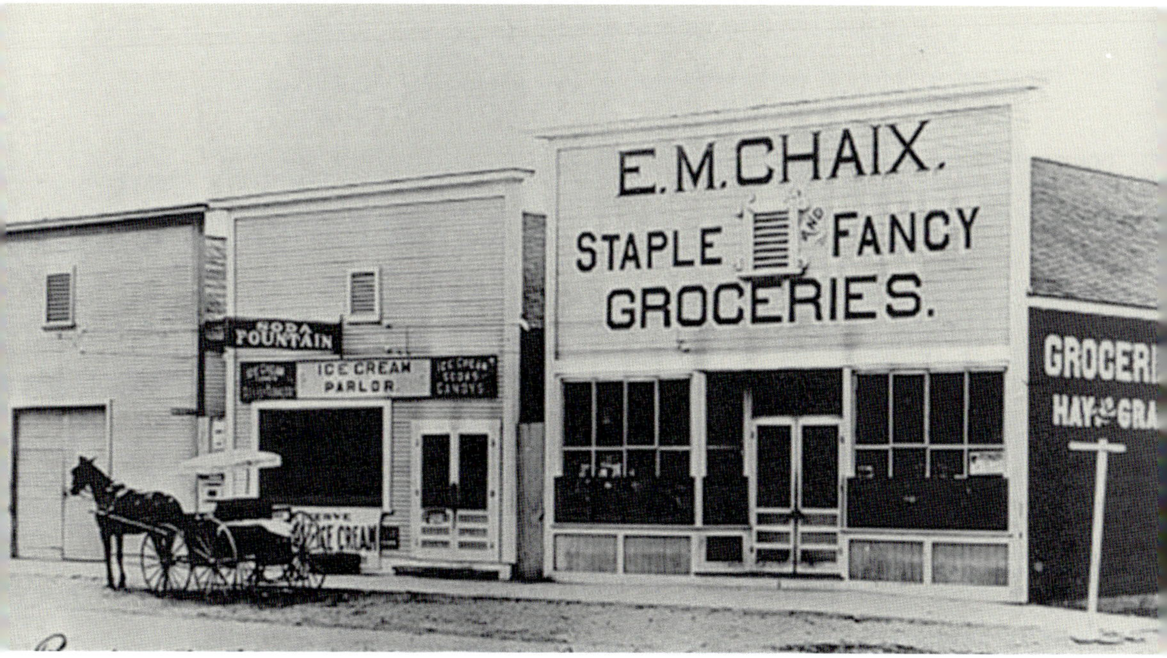

Emile Chaix opened a grocery store in 1898 at the southwest corner of Spruce (now Main) and Eighth Streets. Chaix had previously owned the Derrick Saloon, just down the street on Railroad and Eighth Streets, which he purchased in 1892. The grocery store was converted to a restaurant in 1913 and then a tire shop in 1924. The photographs show Chaix's grocery store around 1900 and the vacant building today, which was formerly the location of the Newhall Plaza.

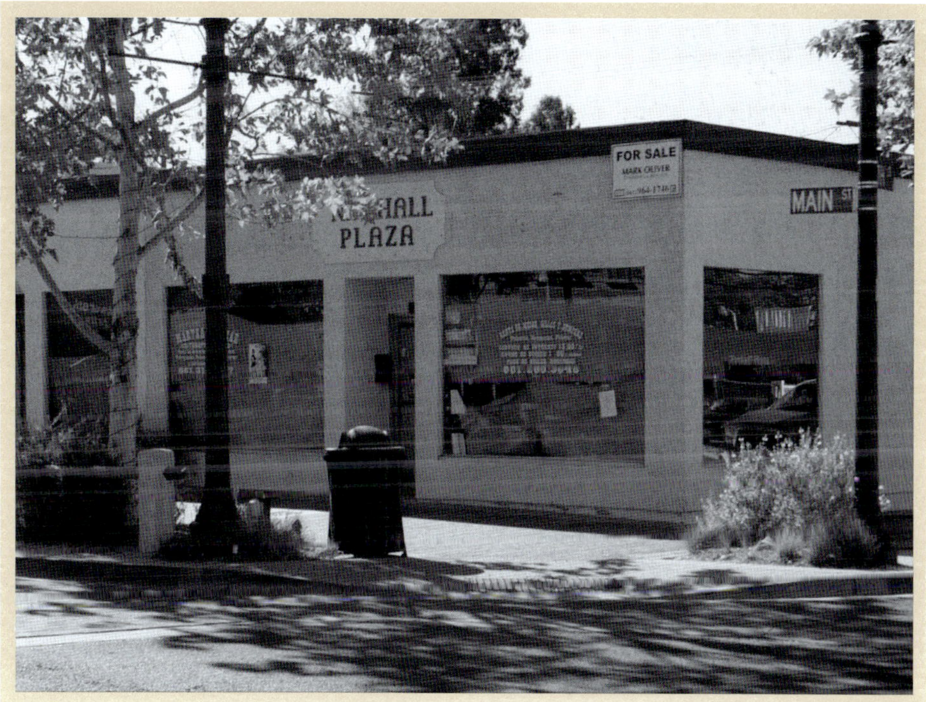

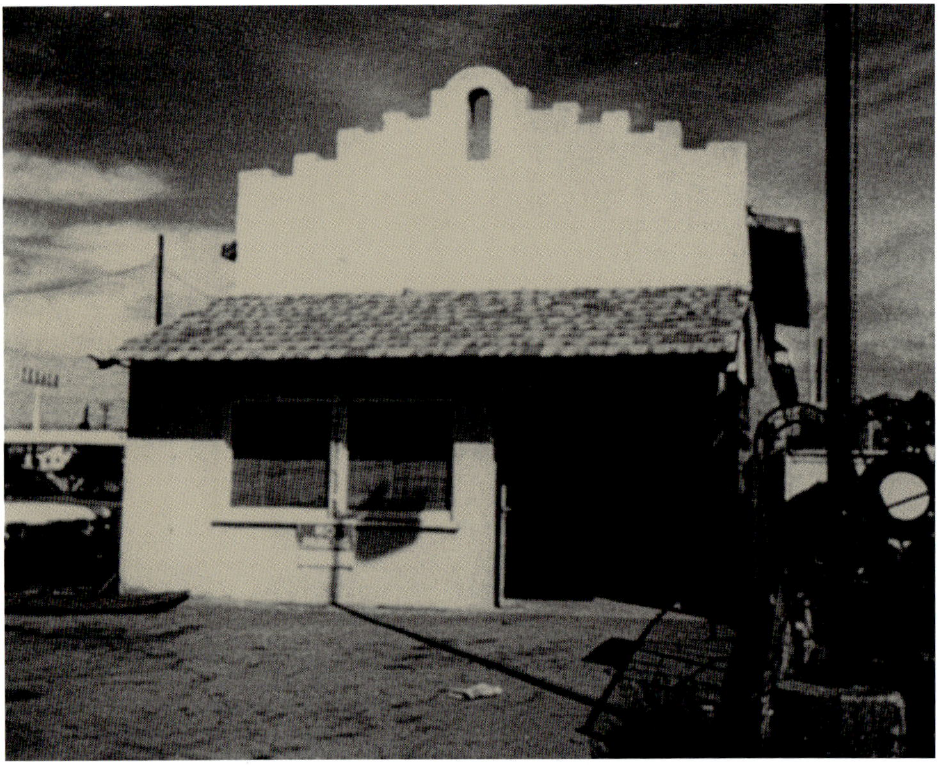

In May 1906, this jailhouse, with 12-inch-thick cement walls, was constructed at a cost of $2,200. The *Los Angeles Times* reported that "Newhall has a new jail, break-proof from the inside out; dangerous from the outside in." Earlier, a jail constructed from wooden railroad ties was built on the site, which proved too porous to secure inmates. The new jail housed prisoners until 1939. Today, the building can still be seen in the parking lot of the Old Town Newhall Library.

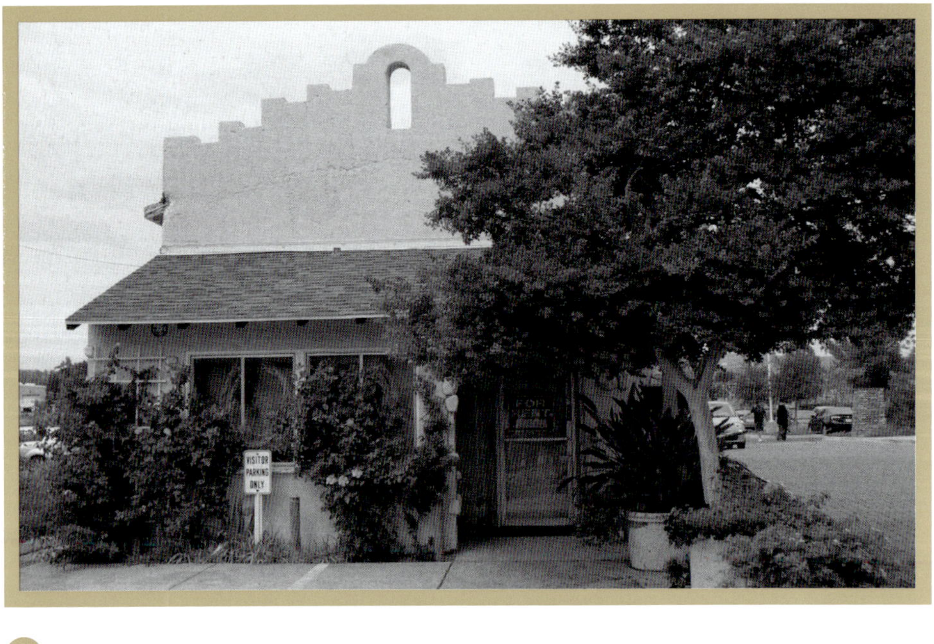

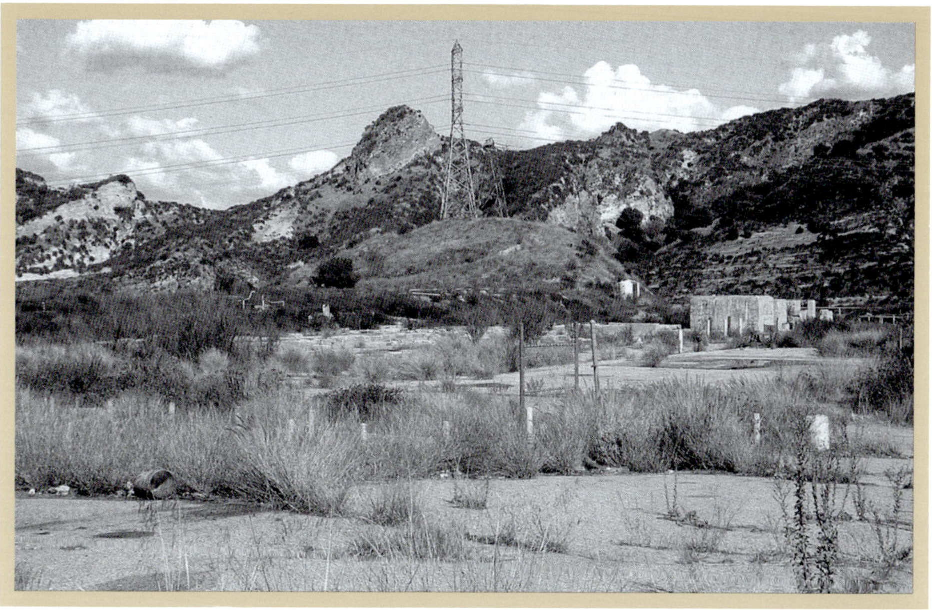

This 1908 postcard shows oil wells in the Newhall Pass. The Newhall Refinery opened at this same location 22 years later and supplied gasoline to 69 service stations in California by 1939. The refinery was purchased by its employees in 1942 and destroyed by fire two years later. It was rebuilt, and over the following decades, it survived several accidents and a major earthquake before spiraling environmental protection costs forced its closure in 1989.

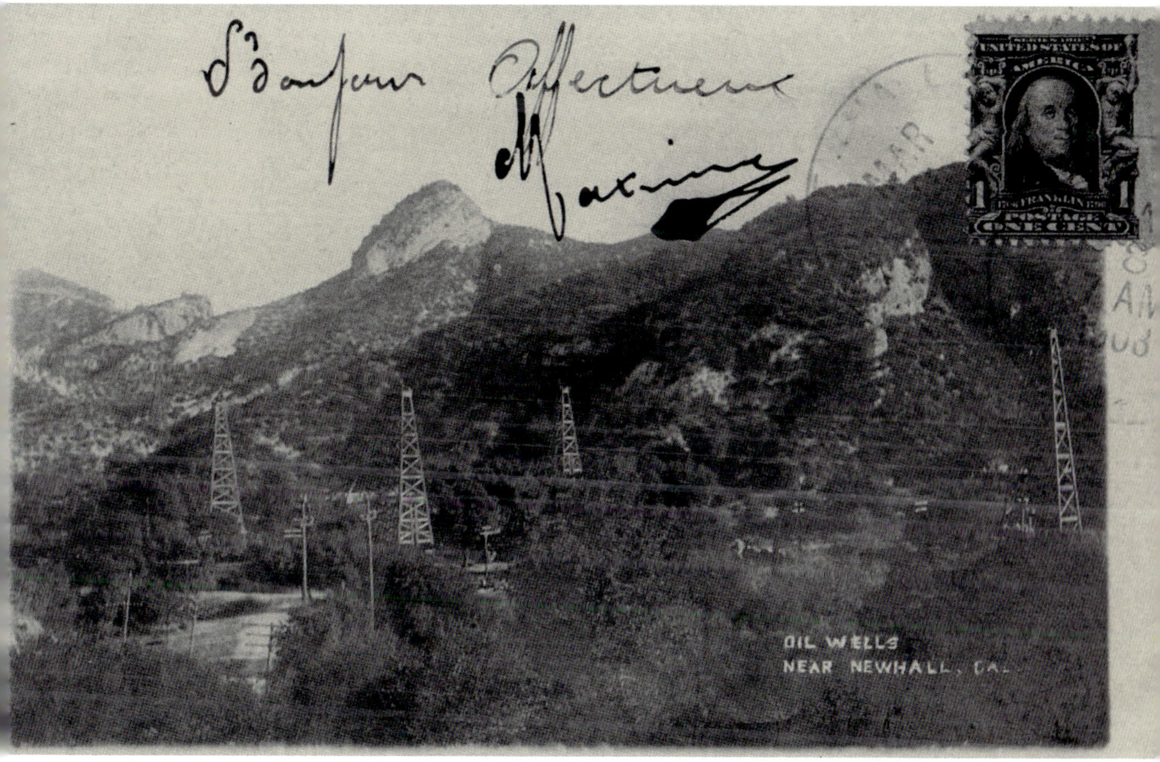

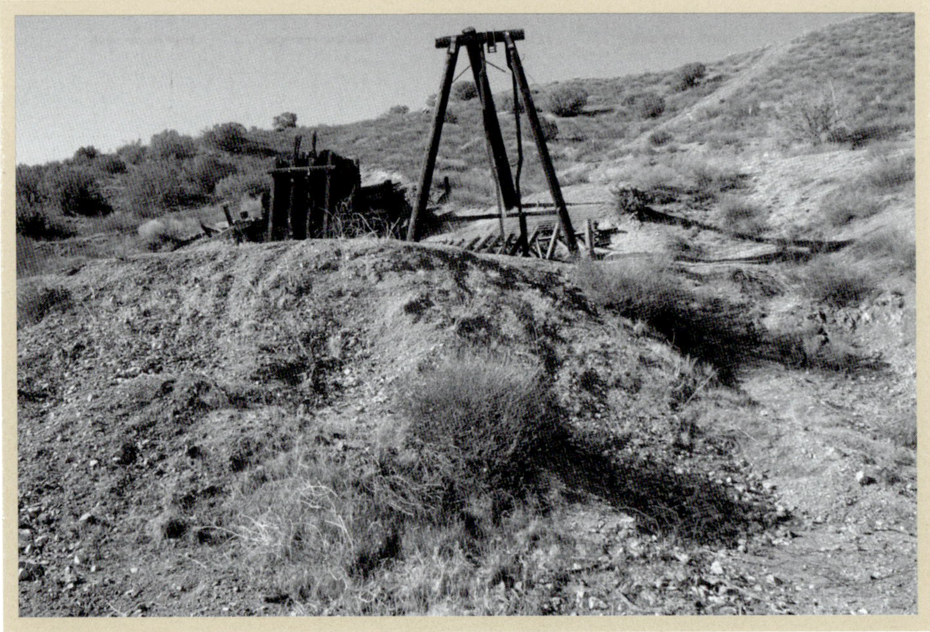

For several years, California governor Henry T. Gage (1899–1903) owned four lucrative gold mines in the Acton area. One was the Red Rover Mine. The photograph from 1911 shows its mill, assay office, boardinghouse, and leaching plant. In the foreground is Paris Brough, son of mine superintendent Ed Brough. Today, the remains of the Red Rover Mine can still be seen just south of the intersection of Red Rover Mine Road and Escondido Canyon Road.

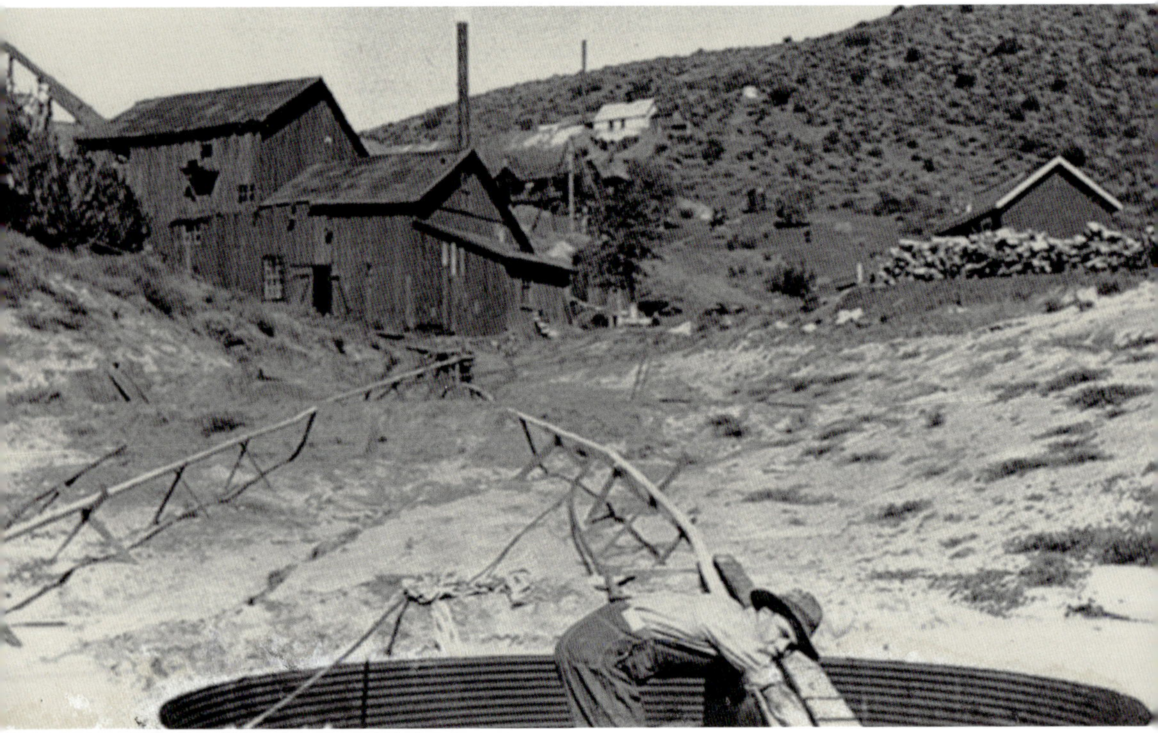

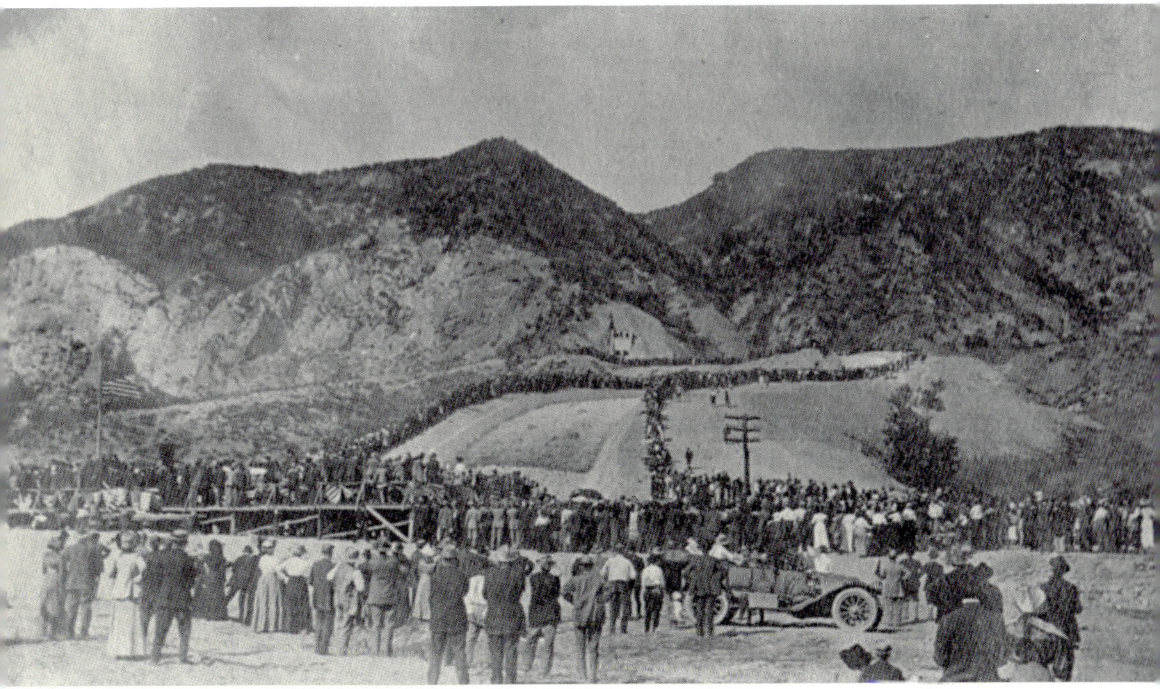

On November 5, 1913, 40,000 people gathered at the southern end of the Newhall Pass to celebrate the opening of the Los Angeles Aqueduct. On that day, Los Angeles water czar William Mulholland uttered the words "There it is, take it," as water imported (some say "stolen") from the Owens Valley first rushed down the cascade. Today, there is an additional cascade, built in 1970 as part of the Second Los Angeles Aqueduct. The modern photograph was taken on November 5, 2013, the aqueduct's 100th birthday.

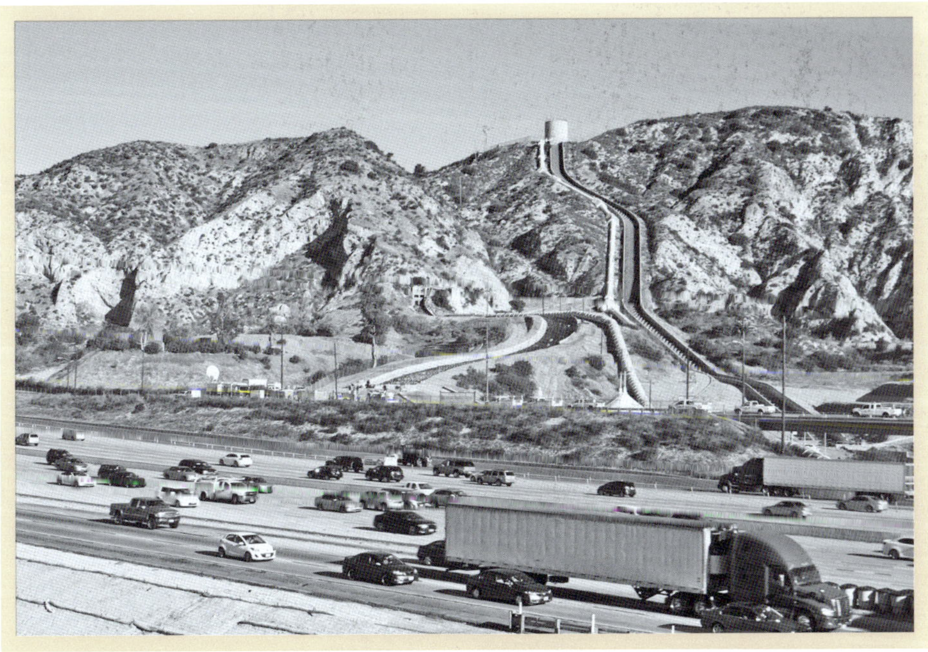

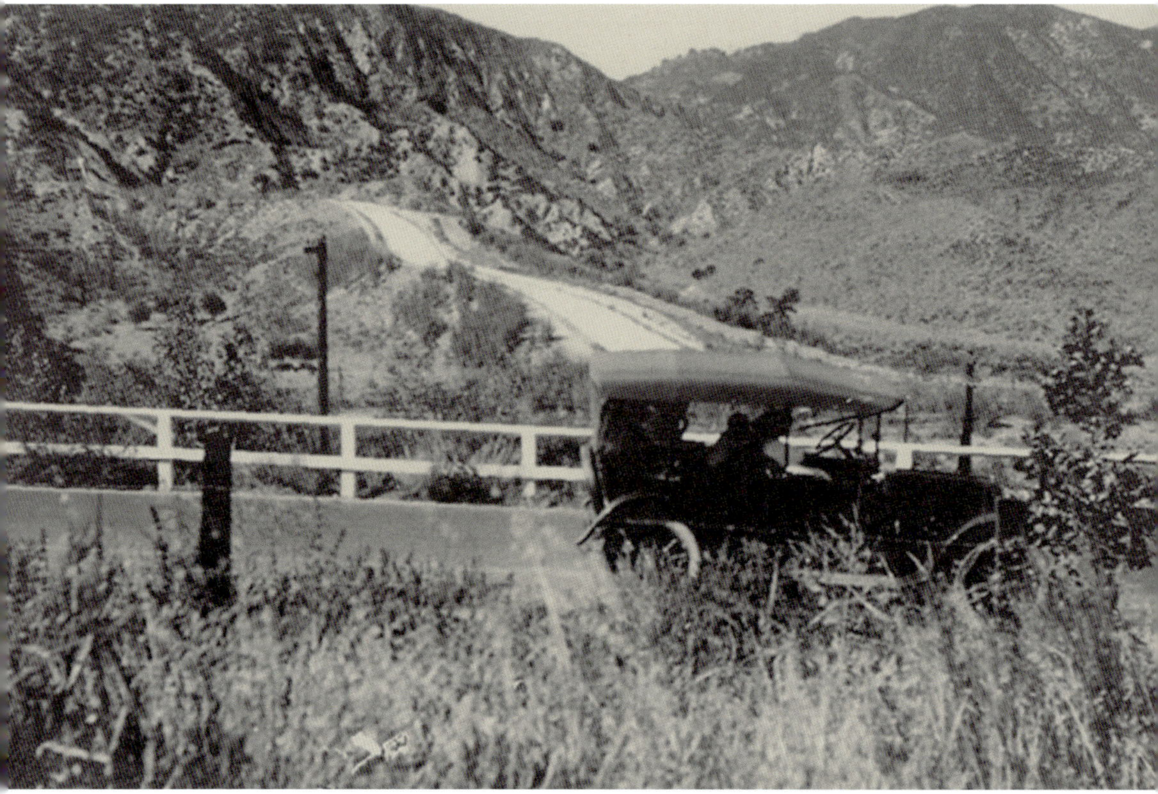

Los Angeles could not have developed into the megalopolis of today if not for William Mulholland's Los Angeles Aqueduct. The aqueduct brings water 233 miles from the Owens Valley, through the Santa Clarita Valley, to its terminus in the San Fernando Valley. The cars passing in front of the cascade along Foothill Boulevard have changed greatly between 1915 and today.

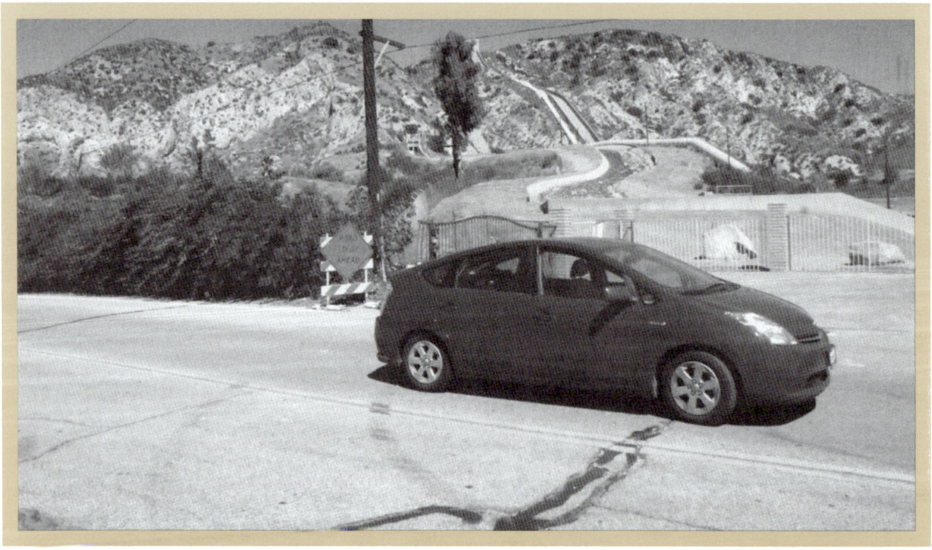

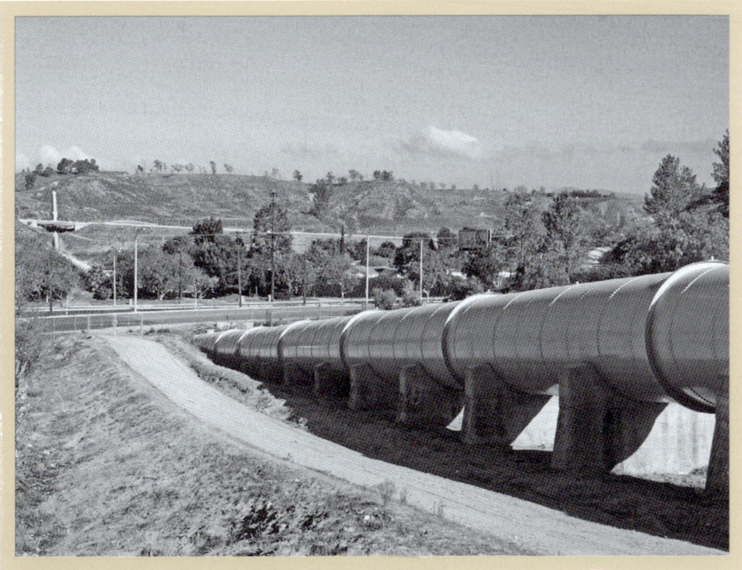

The Los Angeles Aqueduct, constructed between 1908 and 1913 by legendary Los Angeles water chief William Mulholland, brings water 233 miles from California's Owens Valley south to the San Fernando Valley. After leaving San Francisquito Canyon, the aqueduct passes through Santa Clarita before crossing over the Newhall Pass to its terminus at the cascades in Sylmar. In the early-1910s photograph, the aqueduct is seen passing under Soledad Canyon Road. The present-day photograph shows the same site with the new Cross Valley Connector roadway traversing the aqueduct in the distance.

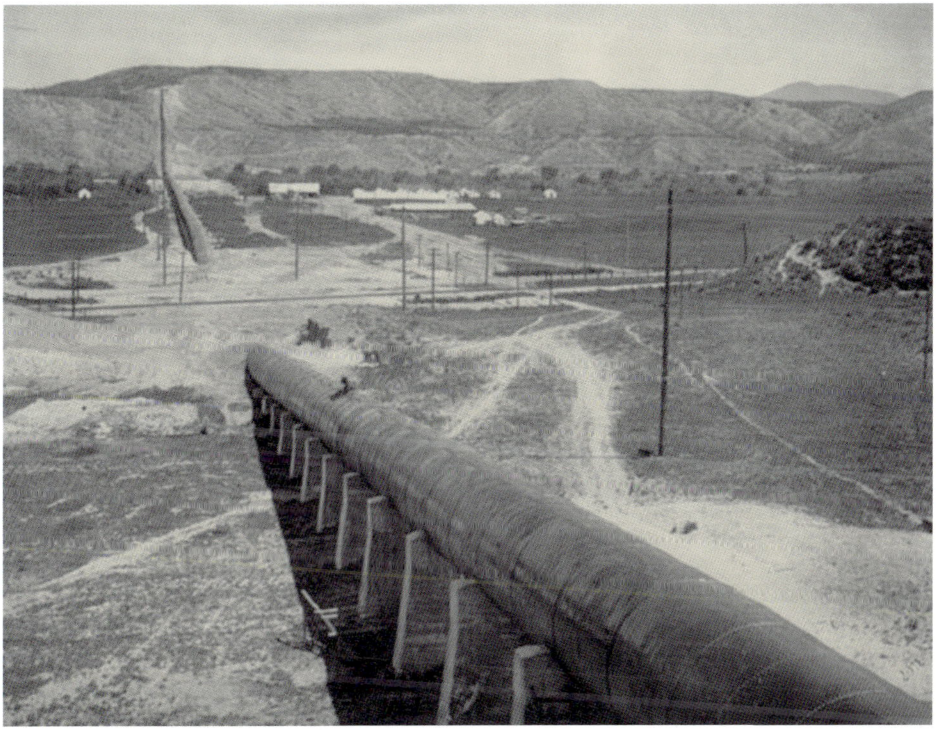

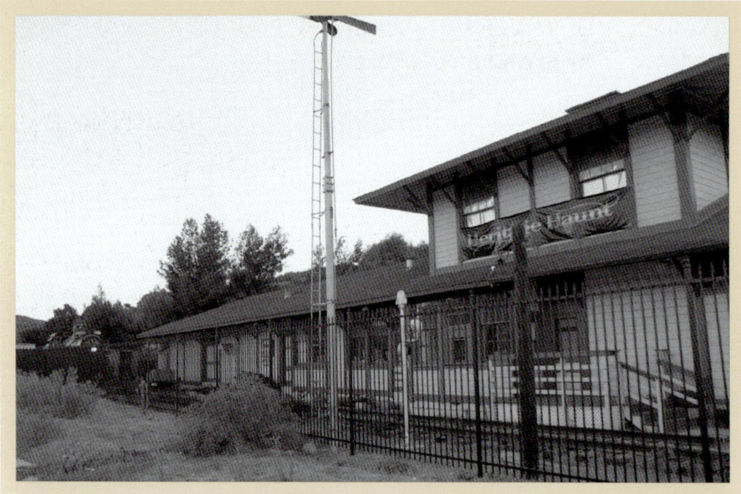

Three young men proudly pose in 1914 in front of the Saugus Train Station, which, at the time, was an outlet of Wells Fargo & Company Express, whose sign is displayed to the right of the men. The last passenger train stopped here in 1971, and the depot closed for good on November 15, 1978. After a successful fundraising effort led by Ruth Newhall, the station was moved to its present location at Newhall's Heritage Junction in 1980.

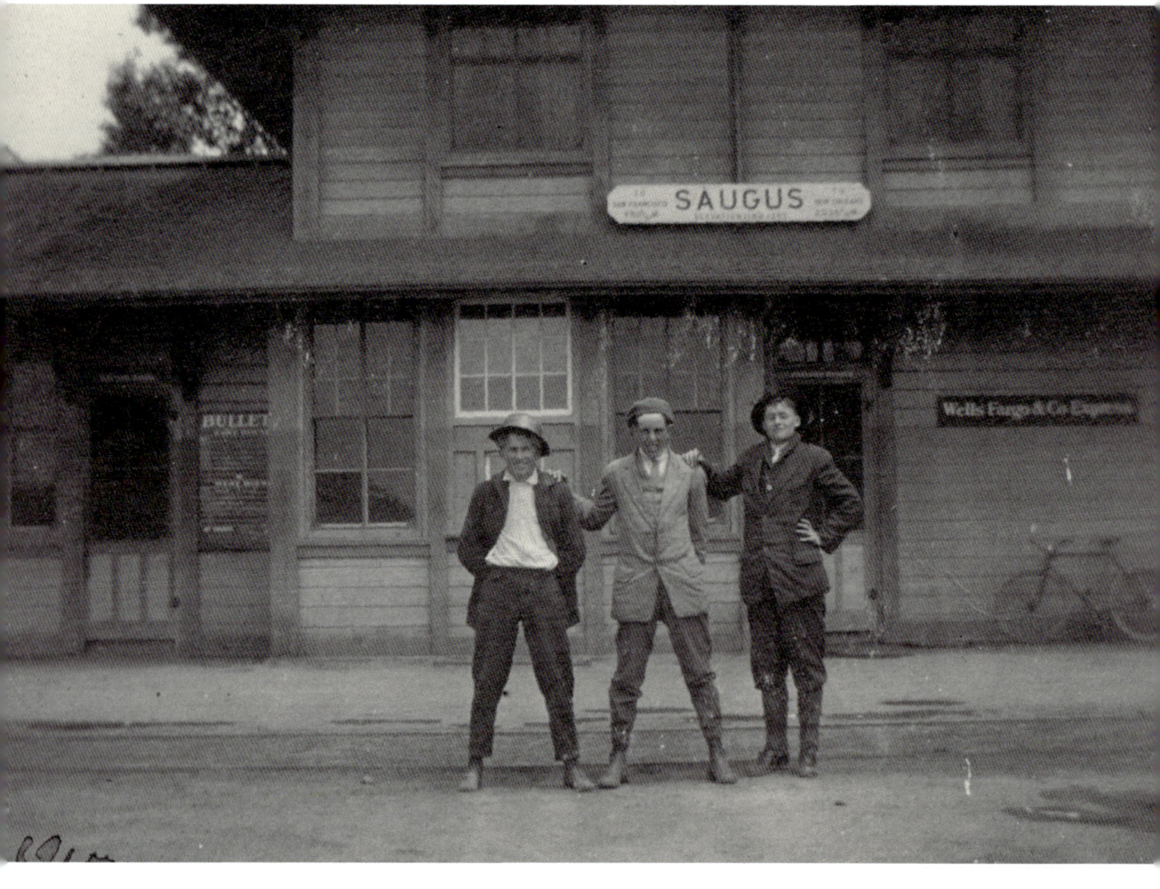

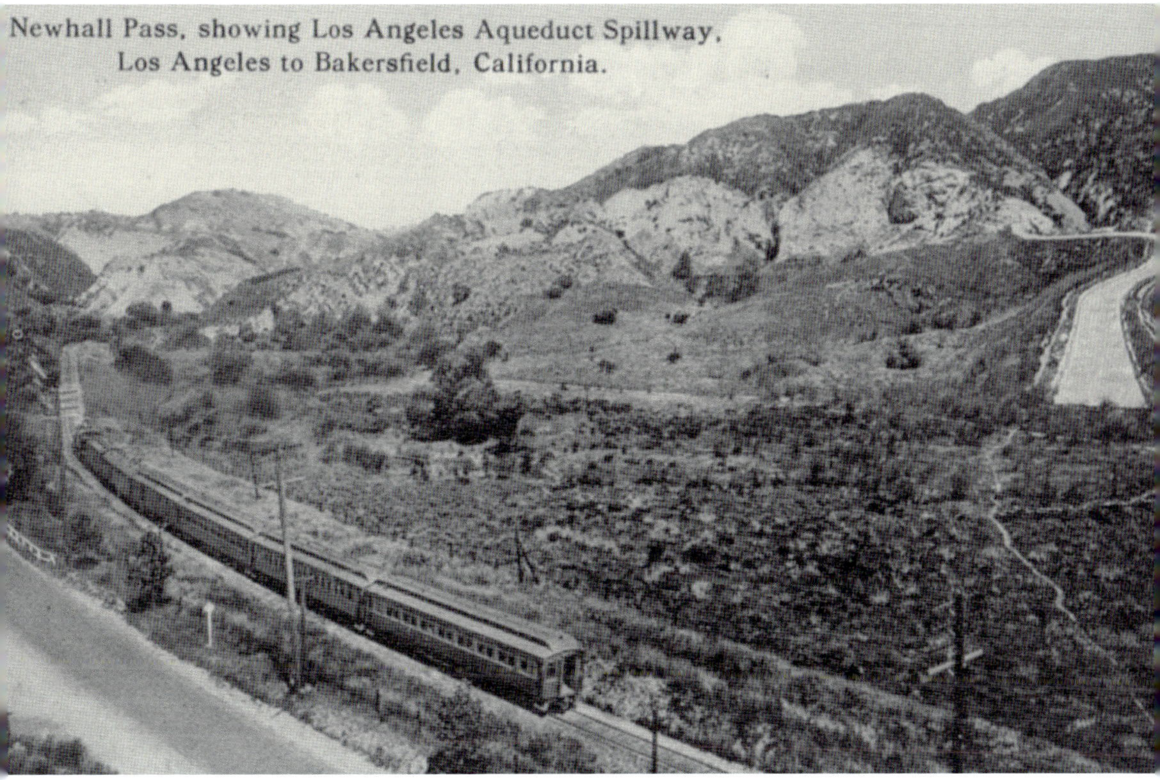

At the time of this postcard from the 1920s, only a small two-lane highway, now called the Old Road (previously Route 99), and a Southern Pacific rail line traversed the Newhall Pass. On the right are the original cascades of the Los Angeles Aqueduct, completed the previous decade. The chaparral-covered pass in the postcard has since been replaced by bustling Interstate 5, the main north-south thoroughfare through Los Angeles, Santa Clarita, and the Pacific Coast states.

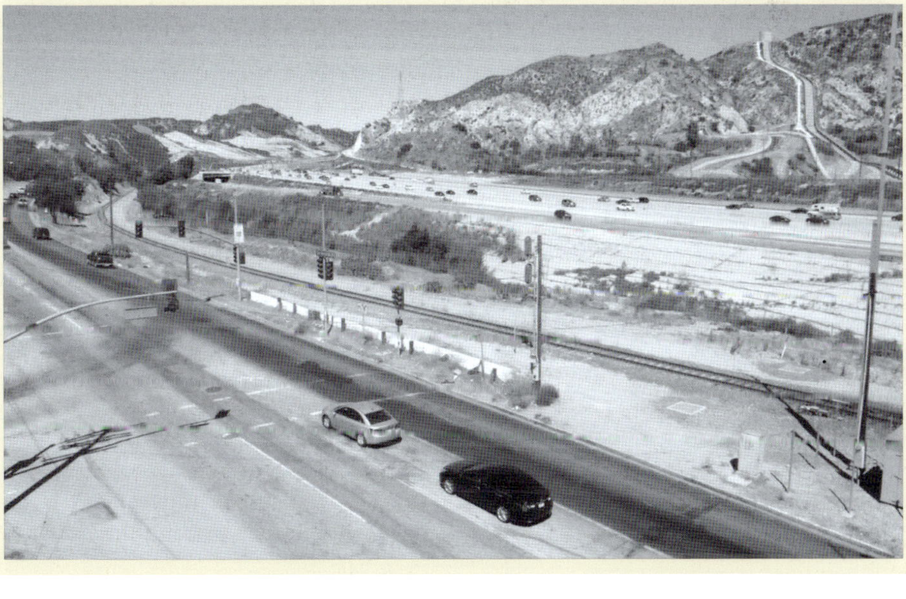

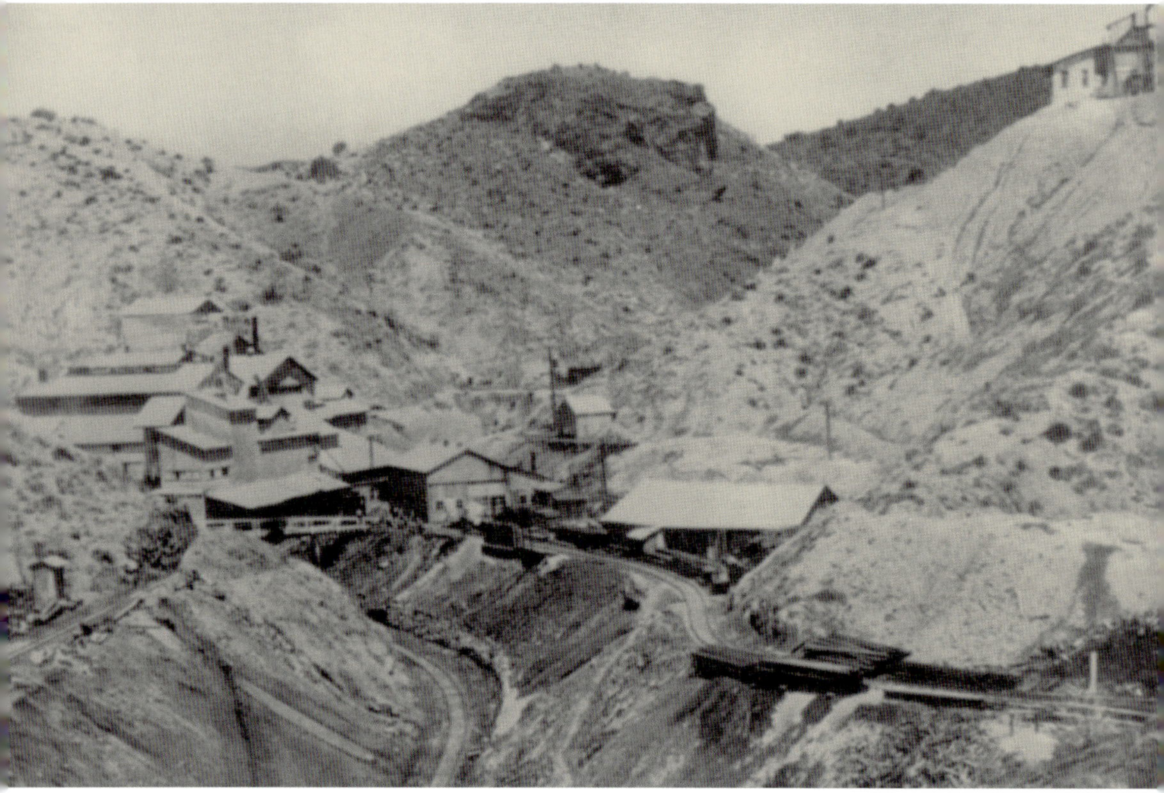

Thomas Thorkildsen and Stephen Mather started the Sterling Borax Mine in Tick Canyon in 1908. The mine earned both men fortunes until its demise in 1921. Thorkildsen became a renowned Hollywood playboy and died penniless. The more prudent Mather served as the first director of the National Park Service. The complex is pictured during its heyday. Today, only a few mine tailings are still visible along Davenport Road near Agua Dulce.

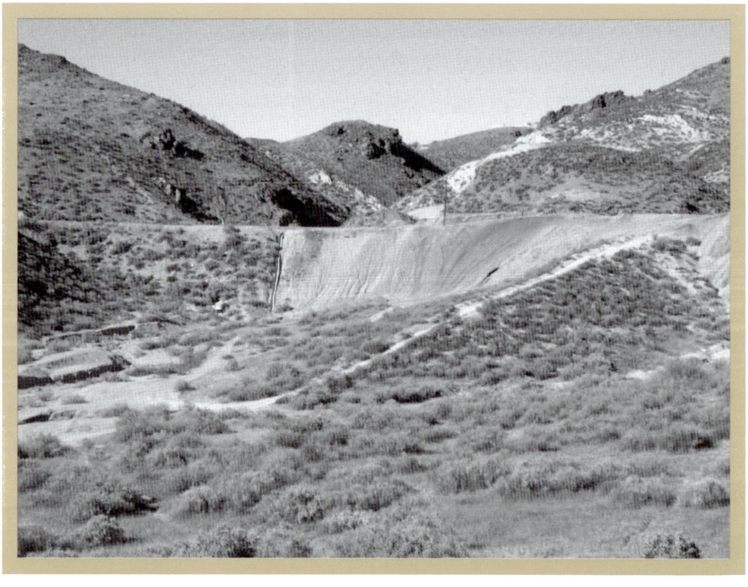

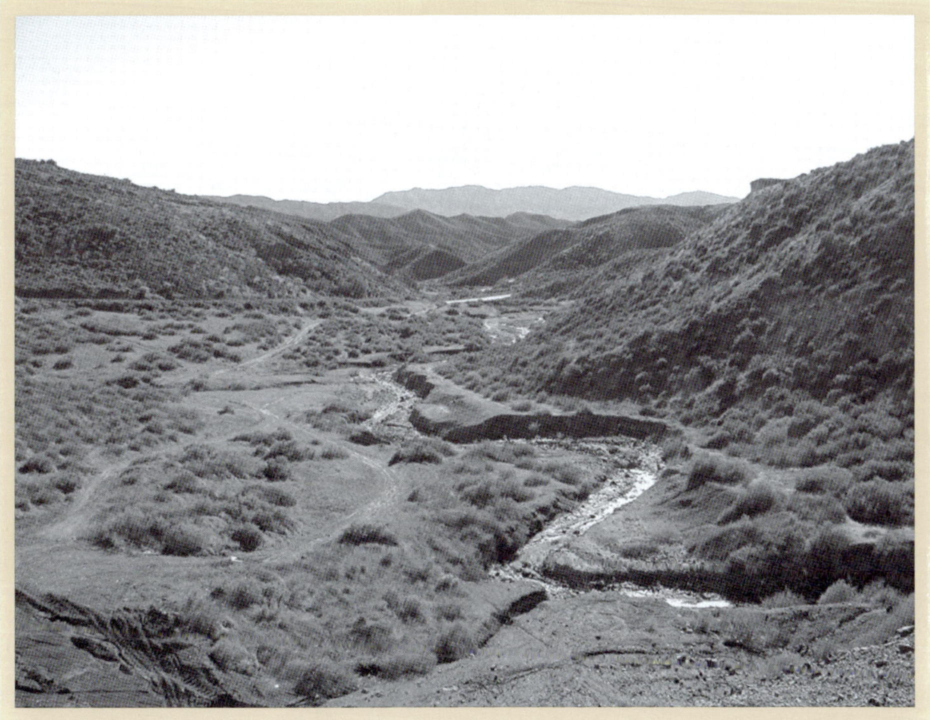

The Sterling Borax Mine operated in Tick Canyon between 1908 and 1921. A narrow-gauge railroad was built between the mine and the railhead at Lang station, a few miles to the southwest. During the active years of the mine, a small community sprouted in the canyon below, housing the mine workers. The town, called Lang, disappeared after the mine closed down in 1921.

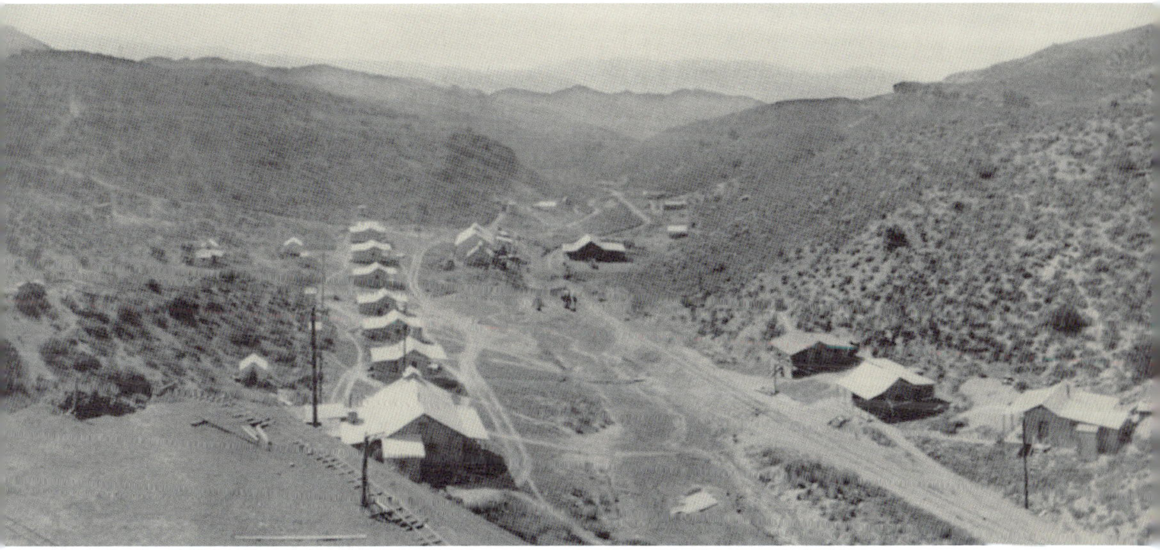

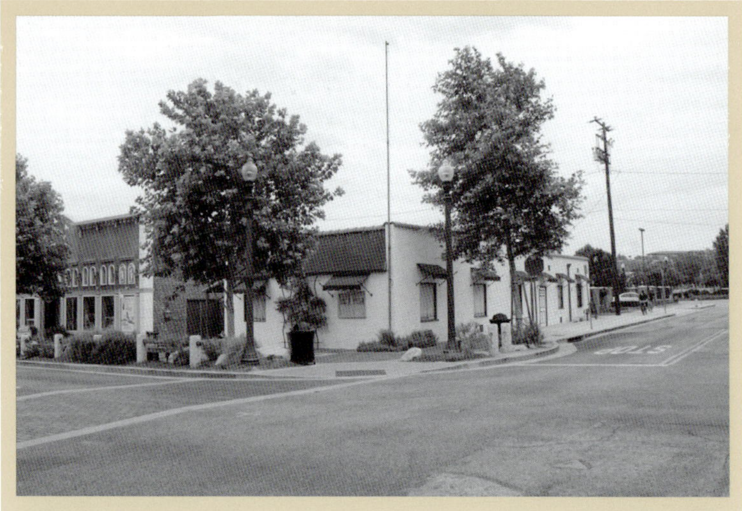

Located at Sixth and Spruce Streets, Sheriff's Substation No. 6 was built in 1926 to replace the 20-year-old Newhall Jail. In the 1970s, the building became the headquarters for the *Newhall Signal* newspaper. The Canyon Theatre Guild (CTG) currently occupies the former substation and the adjacent building. The CTG is a community theater and was based for many years in a remote building on Sierra Highway that had once been part of an amusement park called Robert Callahan's Old West Indian Village.

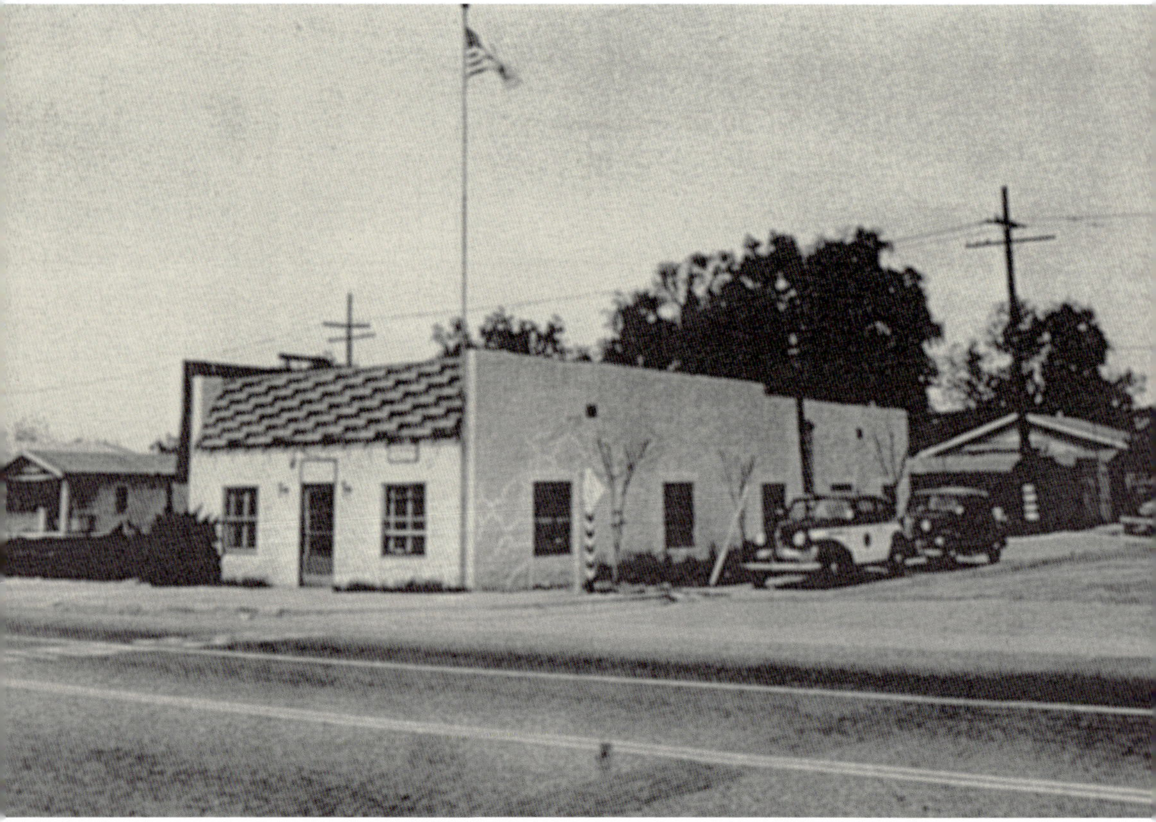

CHAPTER 2

THE NEW WEST

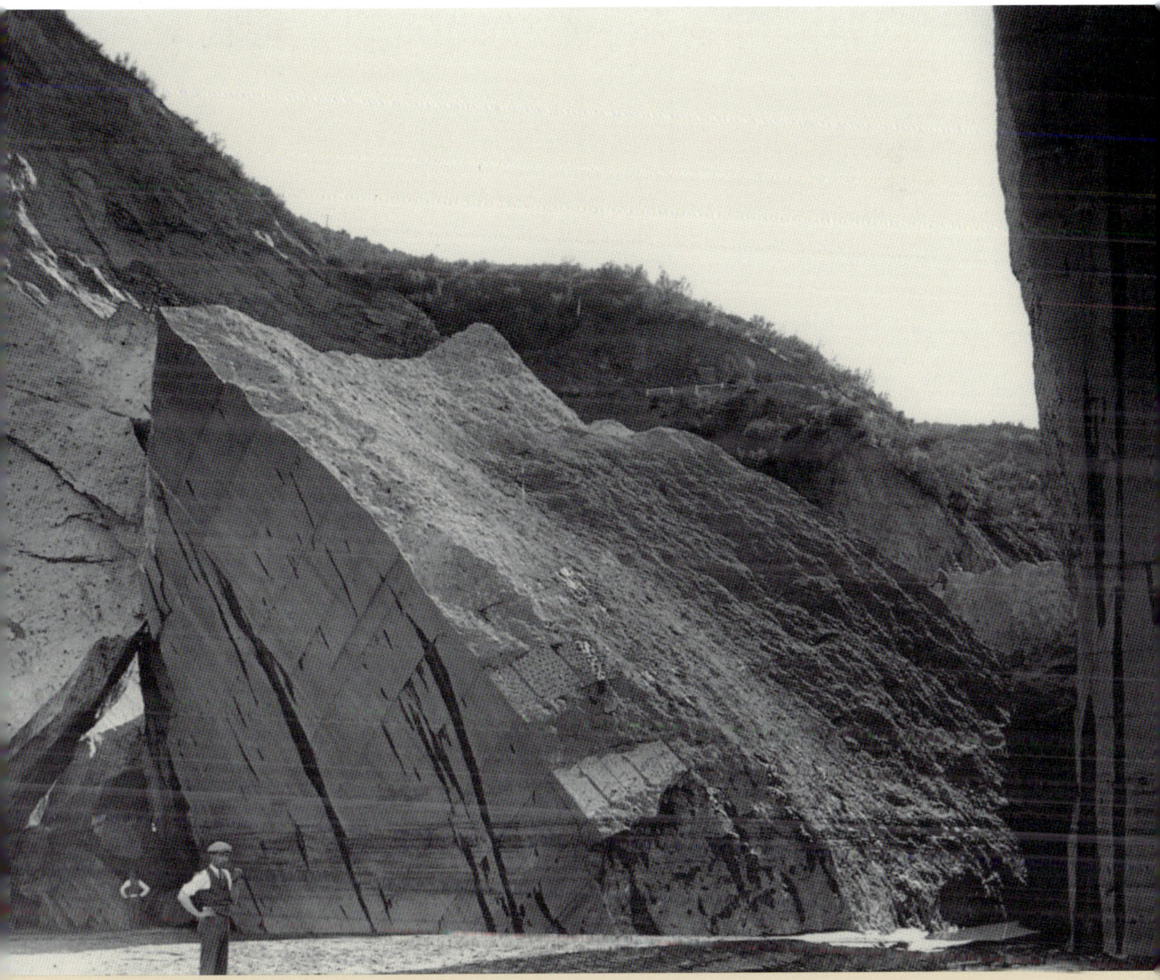

Just before midnight on March 12, 1928, the mighty 205-foot St. Francis Dam collapsed, sending a sea of debris crashing along a 53-mile path of destruction to the Pacific Ocean. Over 400 people perished that night. Here, two men are dwarfed by a huge chunk of the dam shortly after the disaster.

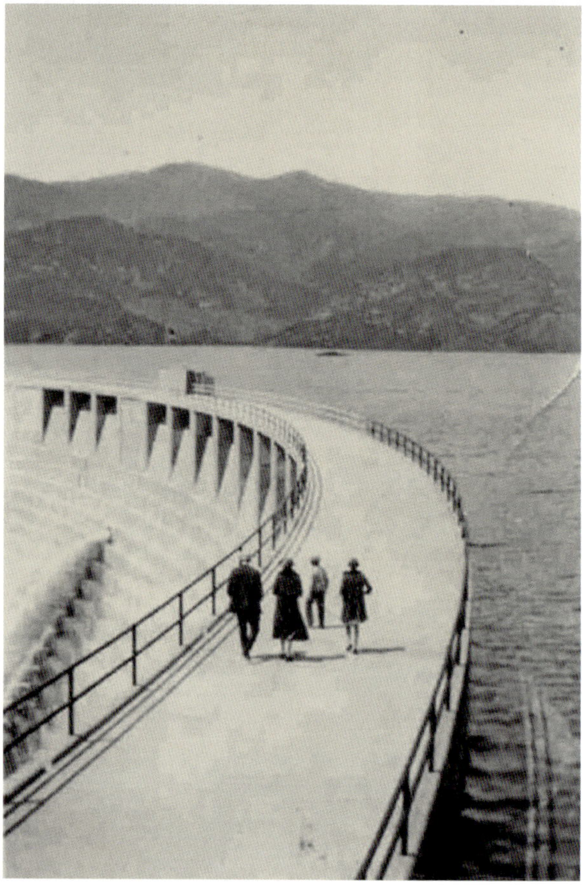

In the old photograph, a family walks across the ill-fated St. Francis Dam shortly before its collapse. The dam was built between 1924 and 1926. For the next two years, water filled the reservoir, which reached capacity just days before its collapse on March 12, 1928. The historical photograph was taken from the eastern abutment, where a waterlogged ancient landslide gave way, setting off a chain of events that resulted in the dam's collapse.

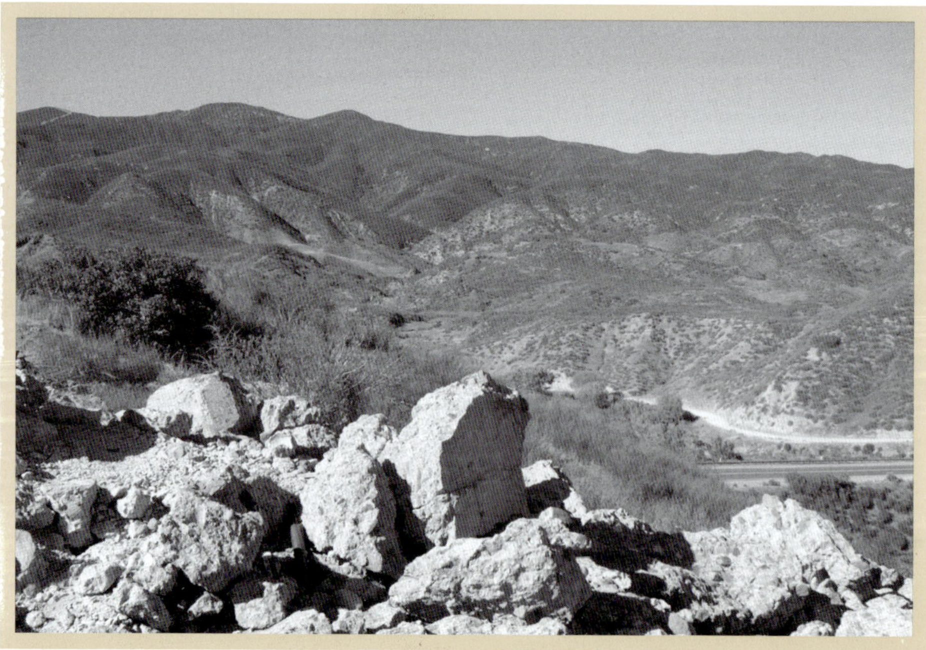

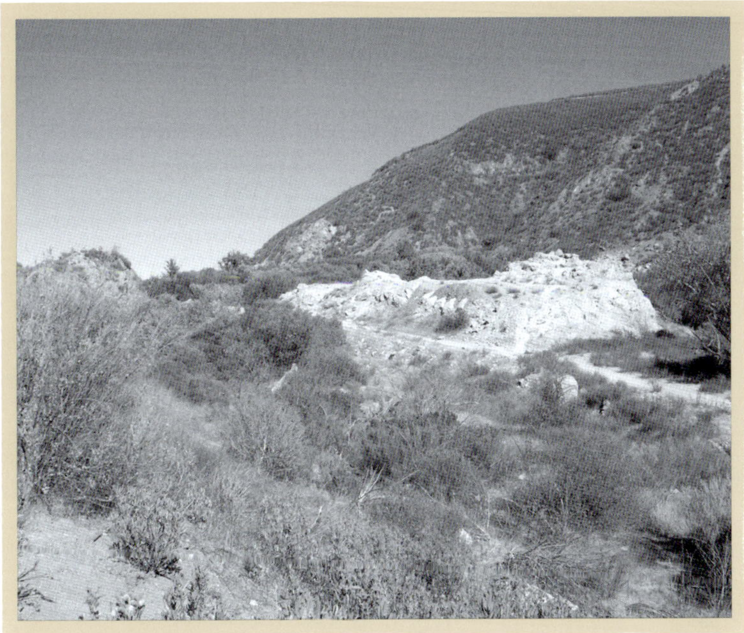

The shattered remains of the foundation of the St. Francis Dam can still be seen today in San Francisquito Canyon. Pictured in this photograph from 1928 is the center section of the dam that remained standing after the collapse. It was christened "the tombstone." A year after the dam disaster, a young boy was killed after falling from the top of the structure. The tombstone was then demolished, leaving only the pulverized foundation today.

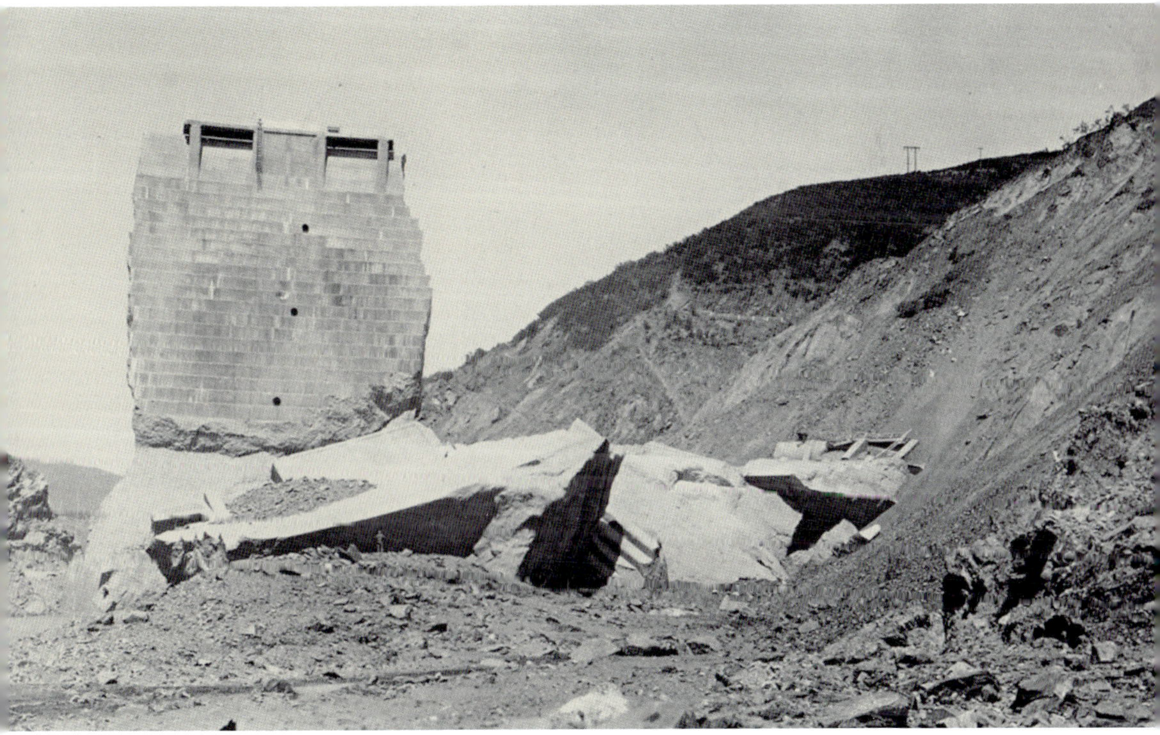

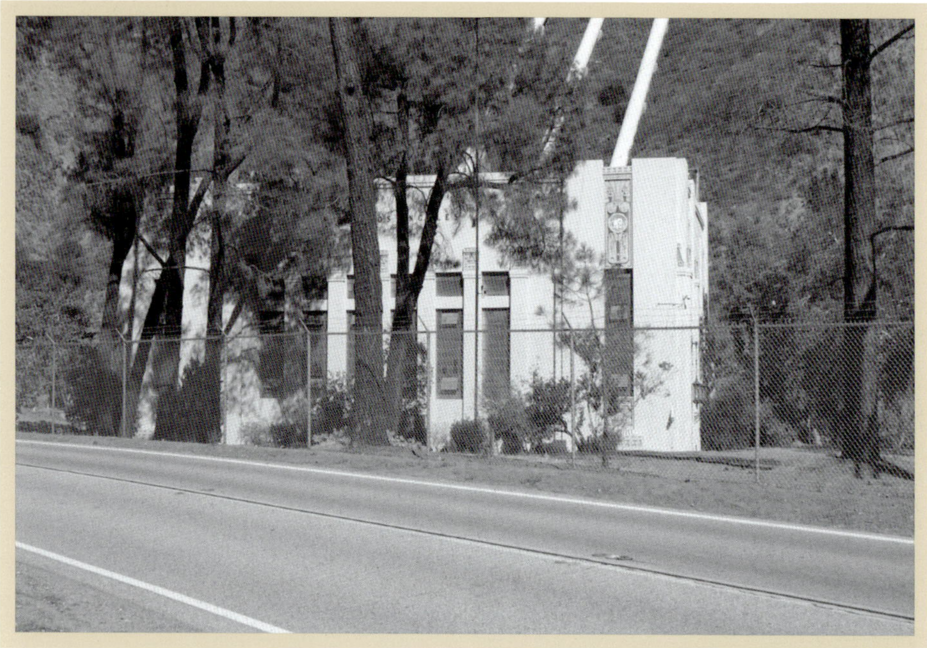

As part of the Los Angeles Aqueduct, the city built two power stations in San Francisquito Canyon. Powerhouse No. 1 was constructed in 1917, followed by Powerhouse No. 2 in 1920. Minutes after the dam collapsed, a 100-foot wall of water decimated Powerhouse No. 2, leaving only the generators pictured here. By November 1928, the plant was rebuilt and back in service. It continues to provide electricity for the city of Los Angeles today.

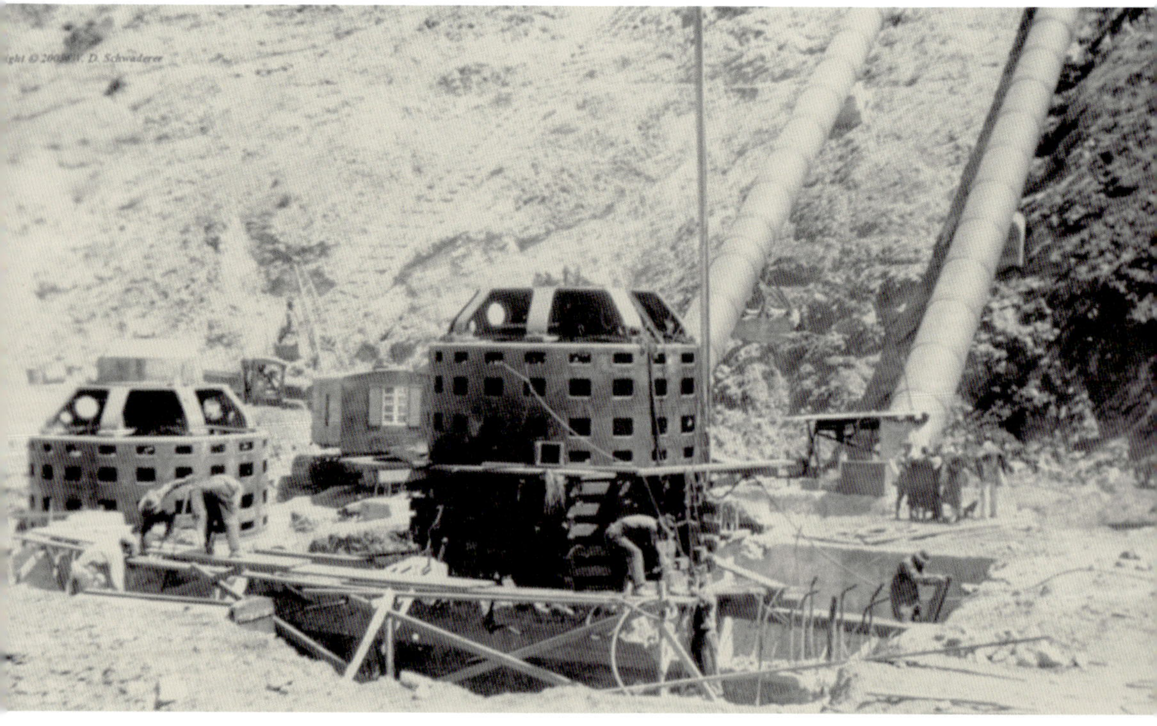

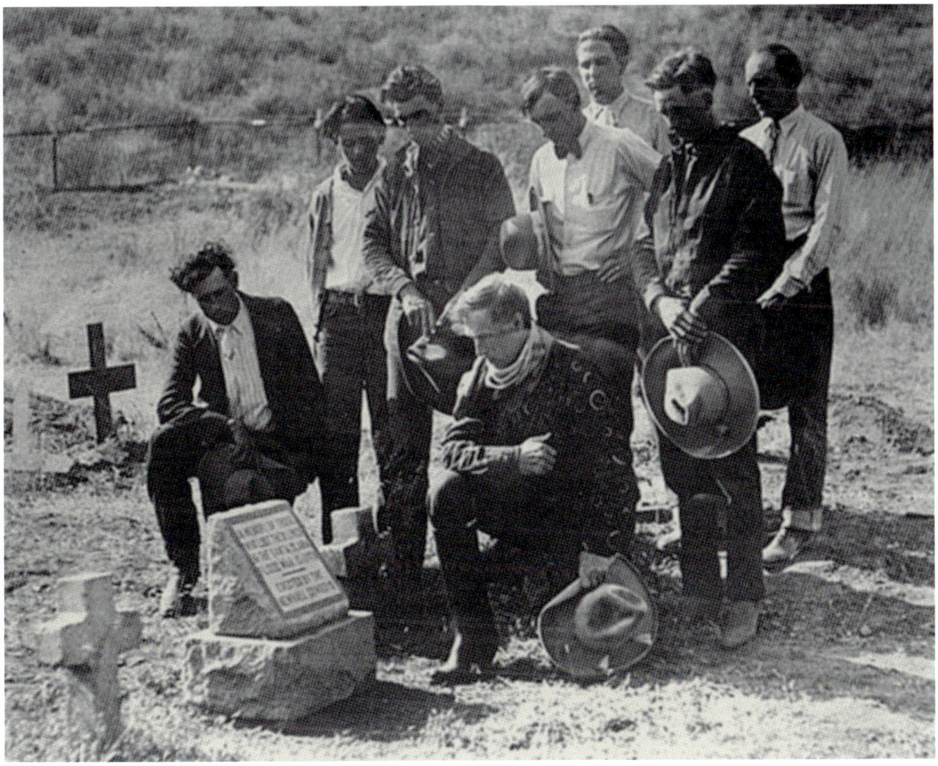

Soon after the St. Francis Dam break, silent Western star and local Newhall resident William S. Hart and a group of his cowboy friends erected this stone marker dedicated to the memory of the victims of the disaster. Among the dead were eight members of the Ruiz family of San Francisquito Canyon. The memorial marker and graves of the unfortunate Ruiz clan can still be viewed today in the Ruiz Cemetery, just a few miles downstream from the former dam site.

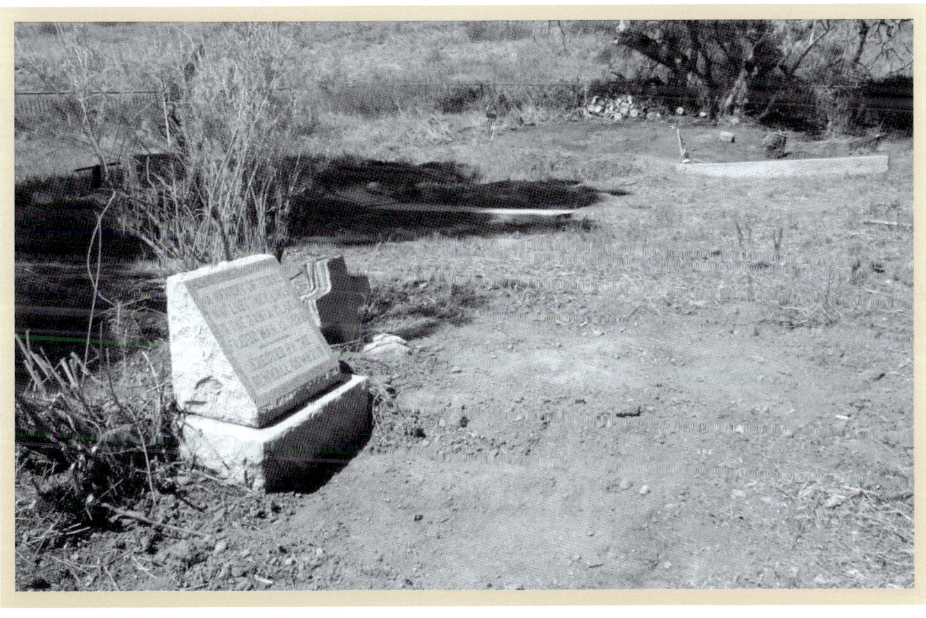

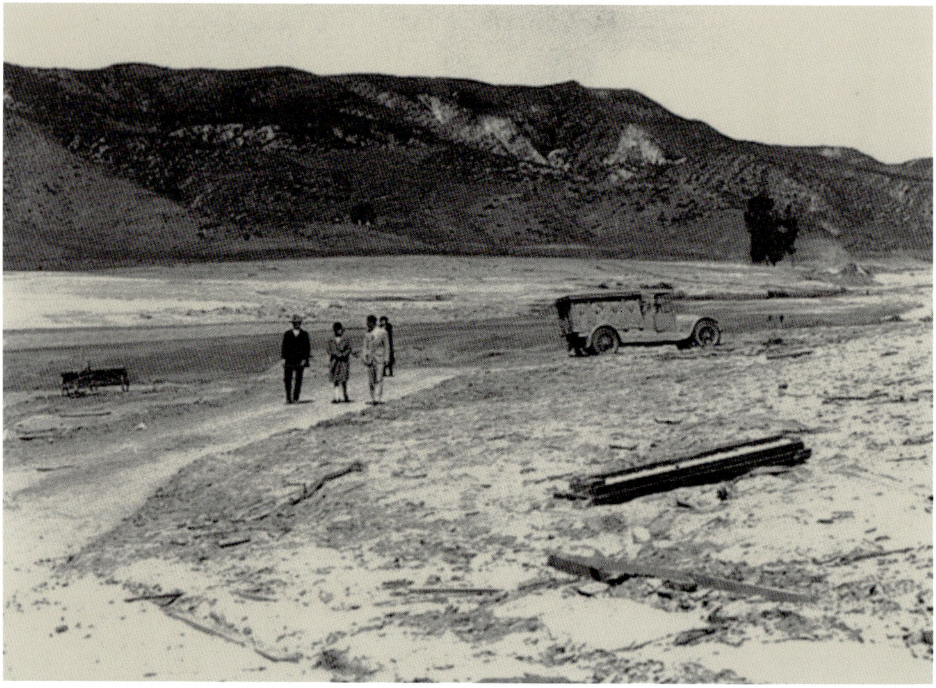

Over 400 lives were lost in the St. Francis Dam disaster. The Ruiz family of San Francisquito Canyon was one of the hardest hit, losing eight members. Their family cemetery rests on a distant hill. In the vintage photograph, taken shortly after the disaster, four people walk past the remains of a piano keyboard in the foreground. The modern photograph was taken on March 12, 2013, the 85th anniversary of the one of the worst man-made disasters in California history.

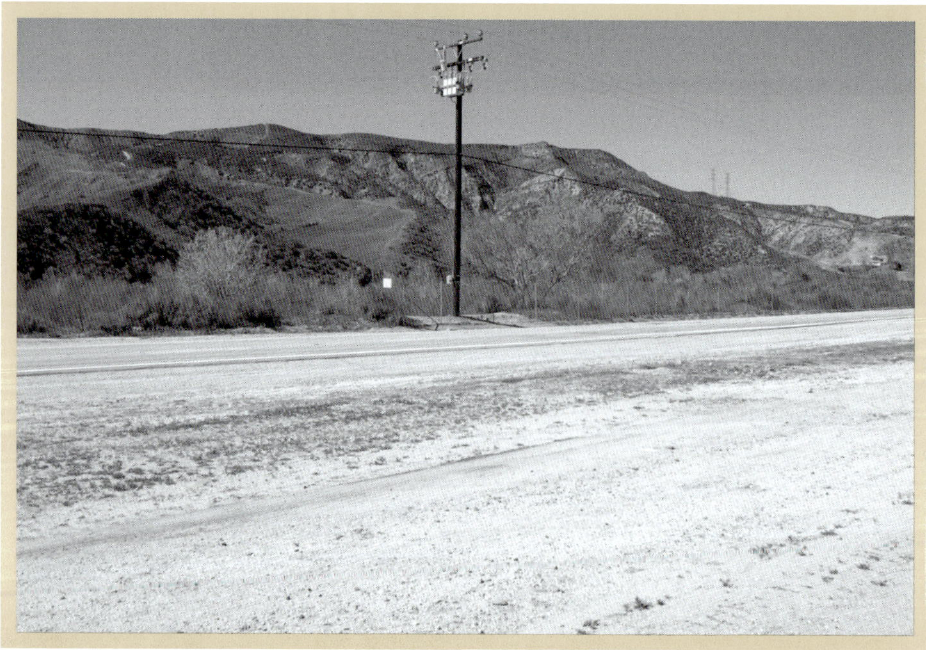

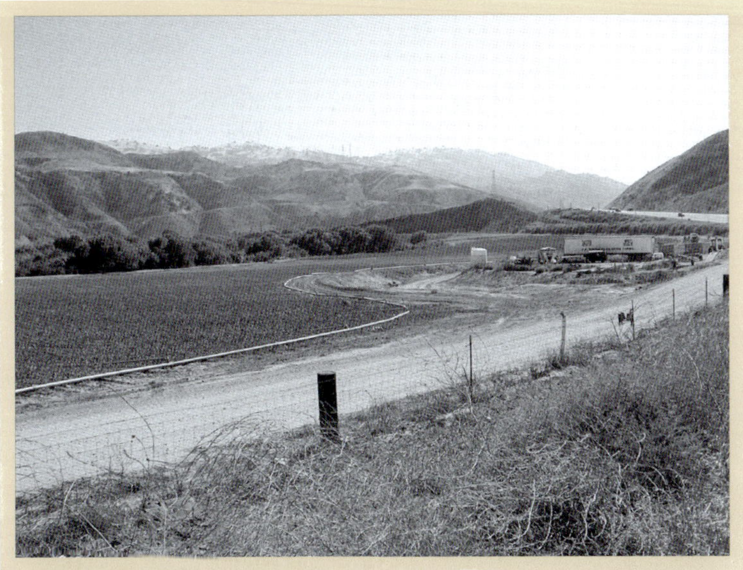

When the St. Francis Dam ruptured on the night of March 12, 1928, a group of Edison workers were asleep in a tent camp near the Ventura County line. Night watchman Ed Locke saved many of them before perishing along with 84 of the workers, as a whirlpool formed here at an outcropping called Blue Cut. Most of the survivors had their tents zipped up, which allowed them to float to safety. Today, Highway 126 passes by the site.

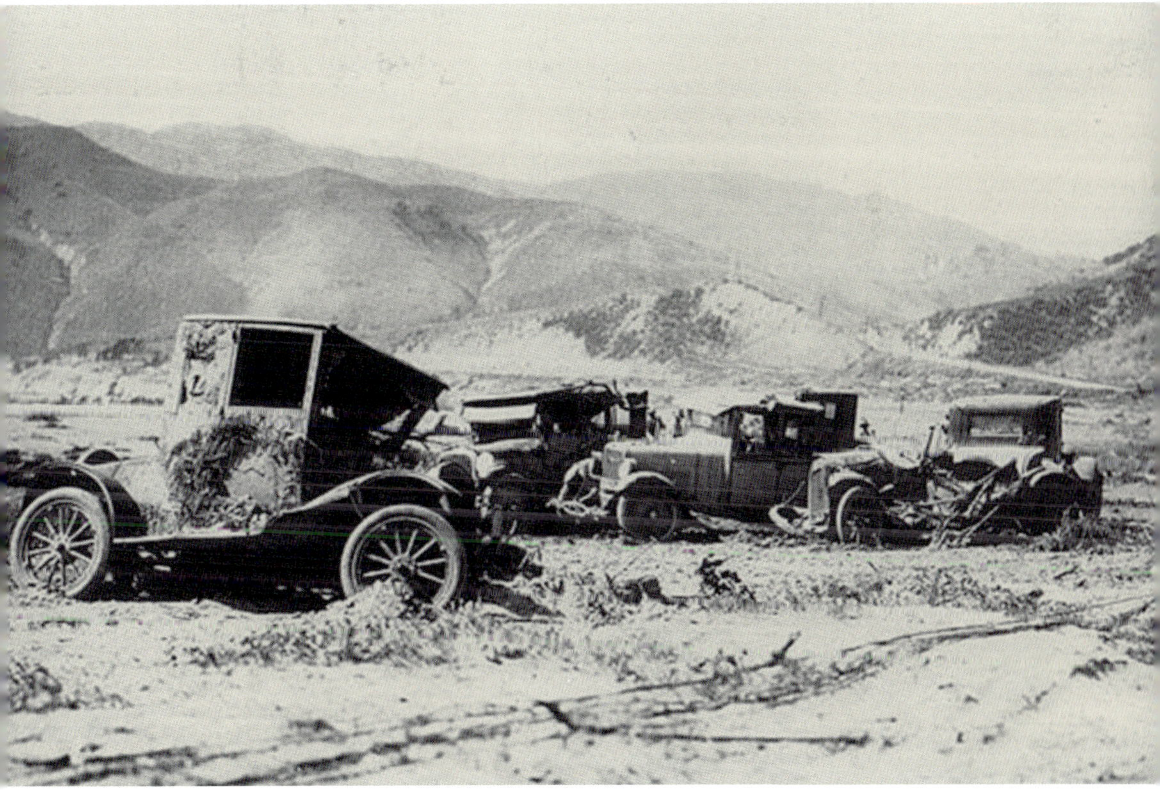

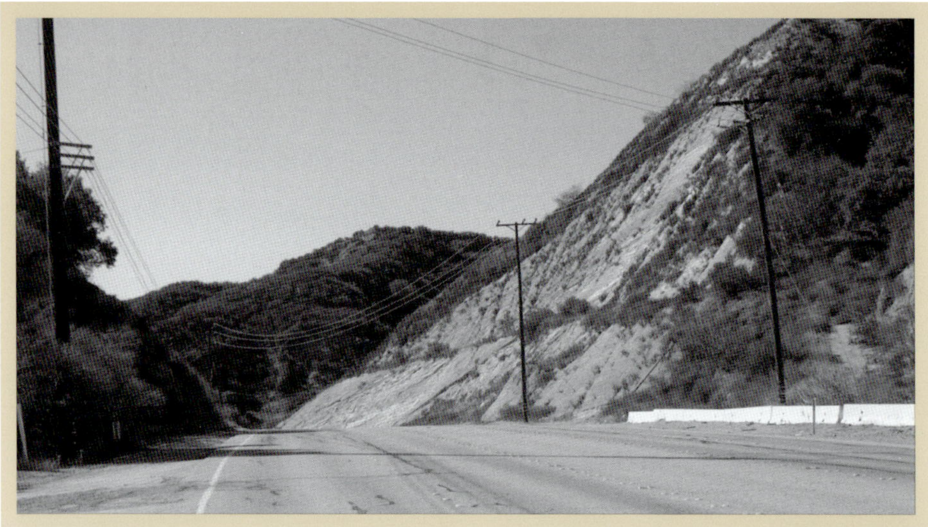

Beale's Cut had been the main passageway between the Santa Clarita and San Fernando Valleys since 1864, but the age of the automobile rendered it obsolete. In 1910, the 435-foot Newhall Auto Tunnel was constructed a quarter-mile to the northwest of Beale's Cut. It too would quickly prove inadequate, and in July 1938, the mountain above was blasted away and a four-lane road was built over the site of the former tunnel. Originally part of US 6, the road is now called Sierra Highway.

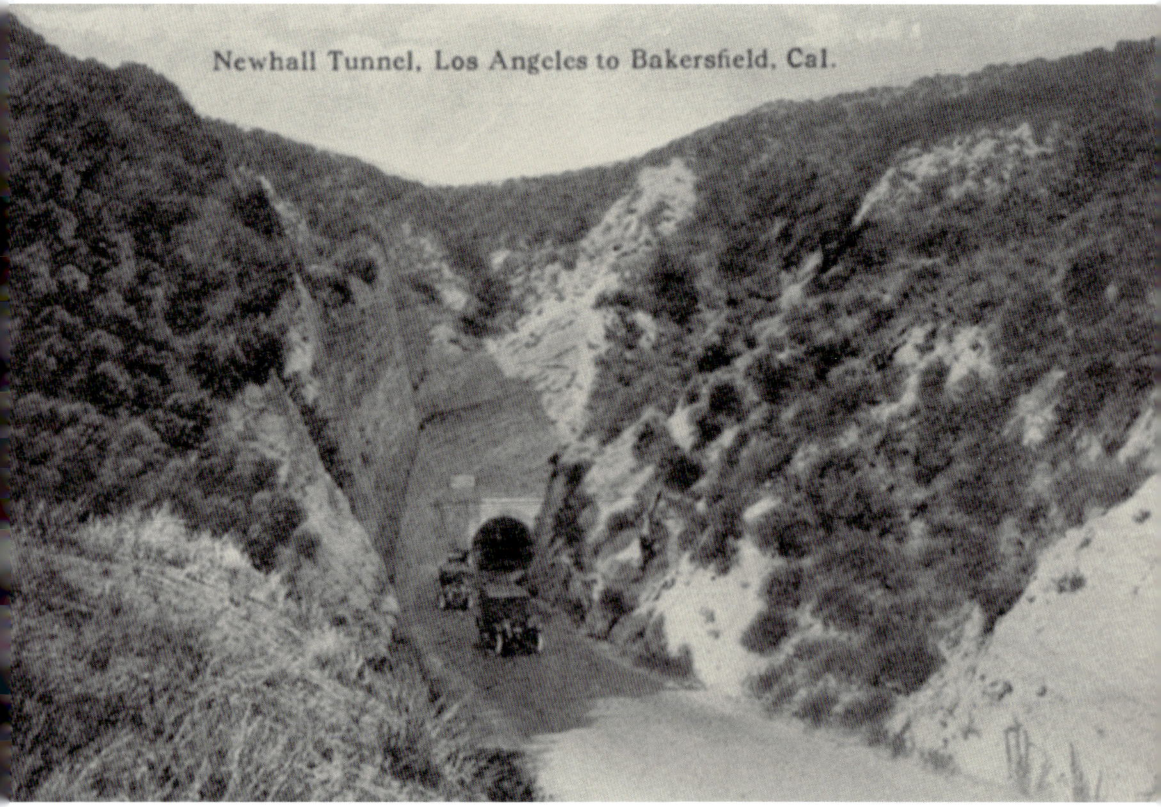

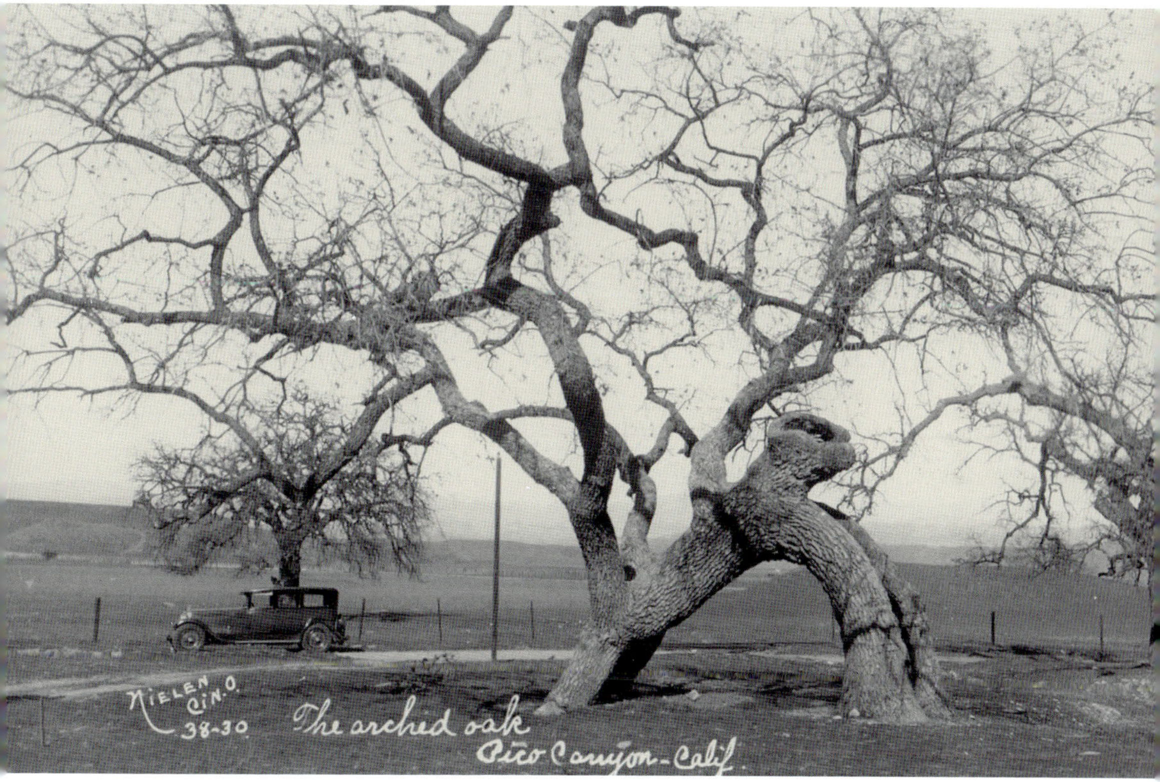

Back in the 1930s, this arched oak tree was truly out in the middle of nowhere. Situated at the mouth of Pico Canyon, the tree was said to have been bent by Native Americans as a sapling to be used as a directional marker, although evidence to support this theory is flimsy at best. The tree still stands on Pico Canyon Road just west of the Old Road, nestled between a Coco's Restaurant and an Extended Stay America Hotel.

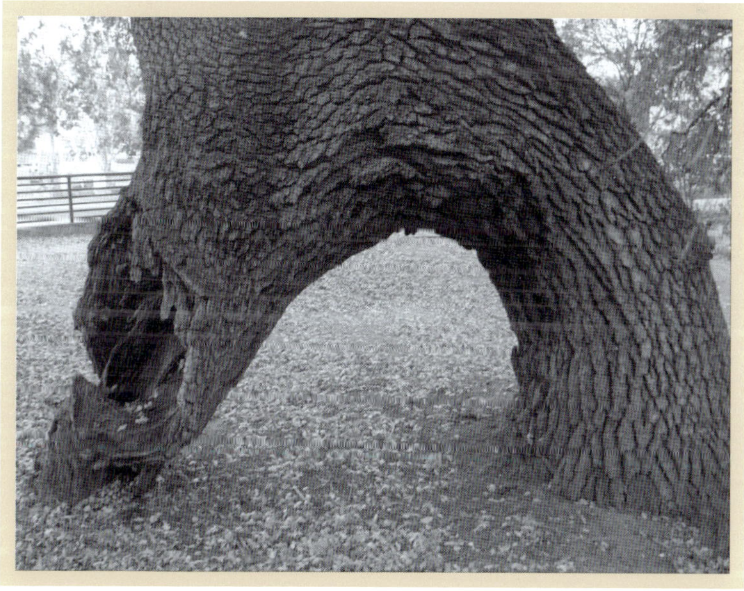

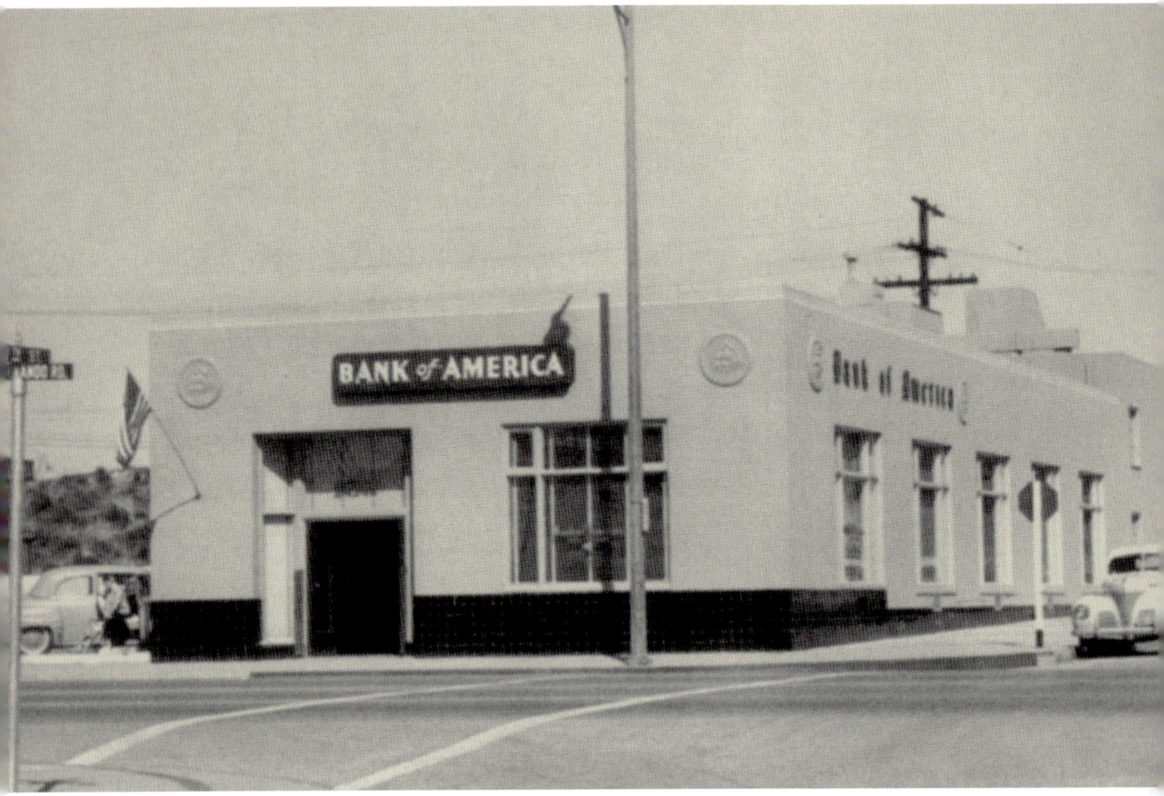

The Bank of Italy, once located on the northeast corner of San Fernando Road and Eighth Street, became the Bank of America in 1931. It was here in November 1940 that Newhall resident and Western film star William S. Hart deeded the property for the American Theatre to the American Legion Post No. 507. The American Theatre was the first movie house in the SCV. The old bank building is now occupied by a church.

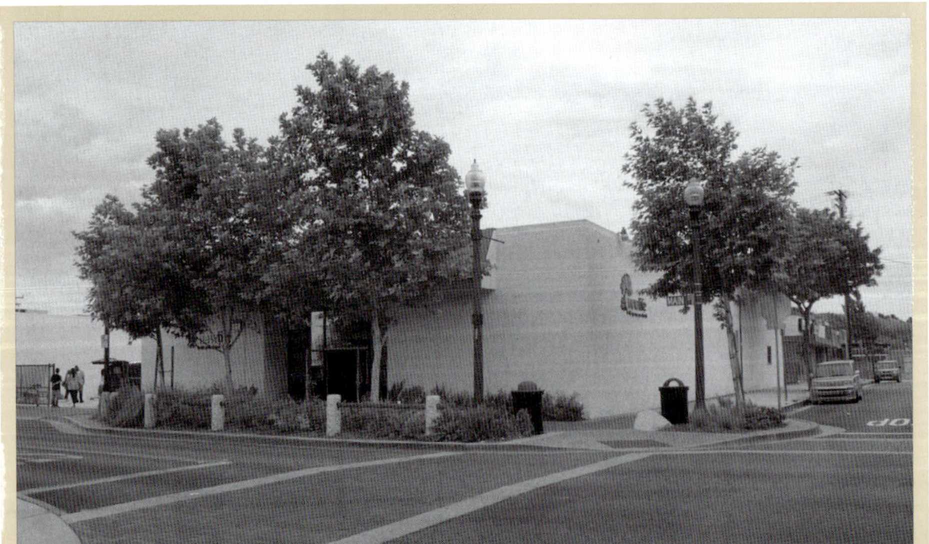

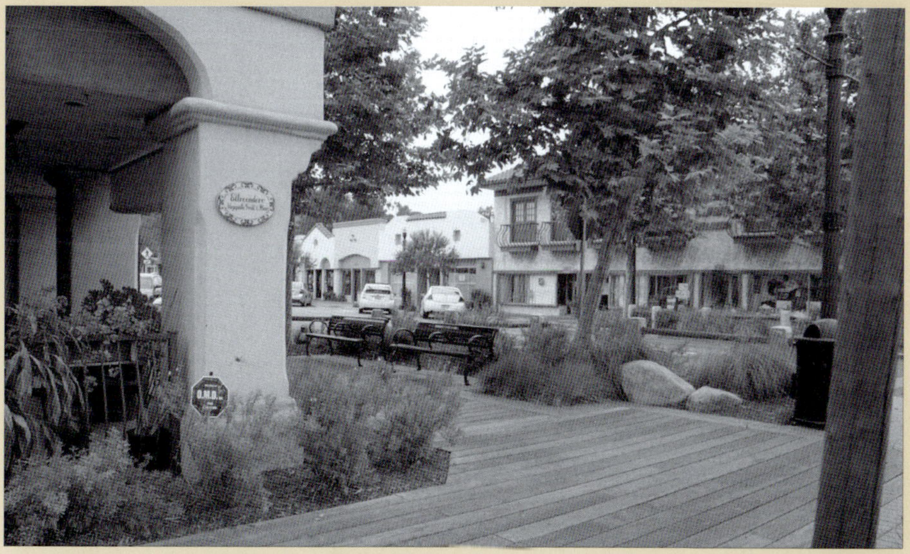

It rarely snows in Newhall, but here is proof that it happened at least once in 1931. A Willys-Knight automobile sits in front of what appears to be a gas station at the southeast corner of Spruce Street (now Main Street) and Market Street. Today, this same spot is home to Old Town Newhall's popular Mexican restaurant, El Trocadero. Main Street in Old Town Newhall has been revitalized between 2010 and 2012 with Western-themed landscaping and sidewalks.

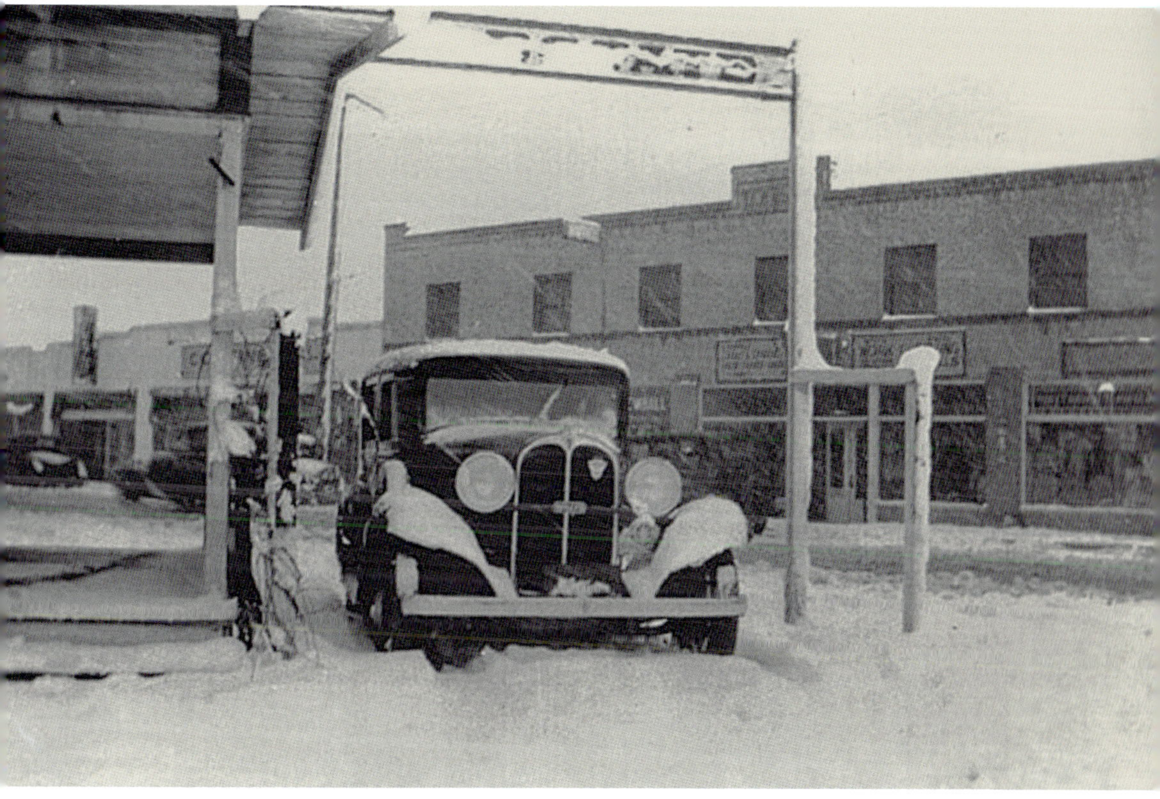

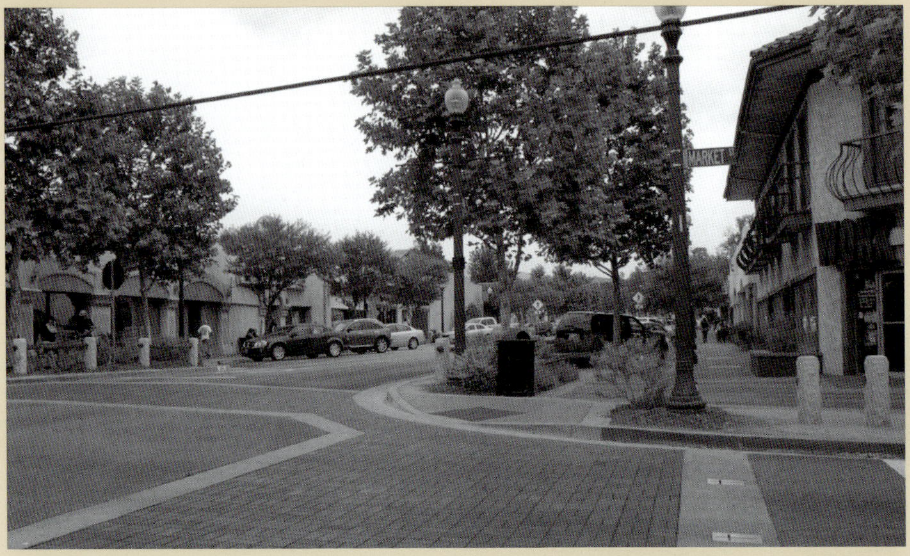

The Swall Hotel stood on the southwest corner of Spruce (now Main Street) and Market Streets before the Sylmar earthquake destroyed it in 1971. The same corner was the former site of the Southern Hotel. The hotel was widely considered the finest between Los Angeles and San Francisco before burning down around 1887. Today, a mural of the hotel, painted by local artist and historian Frank Rock, can be found on Market Street.

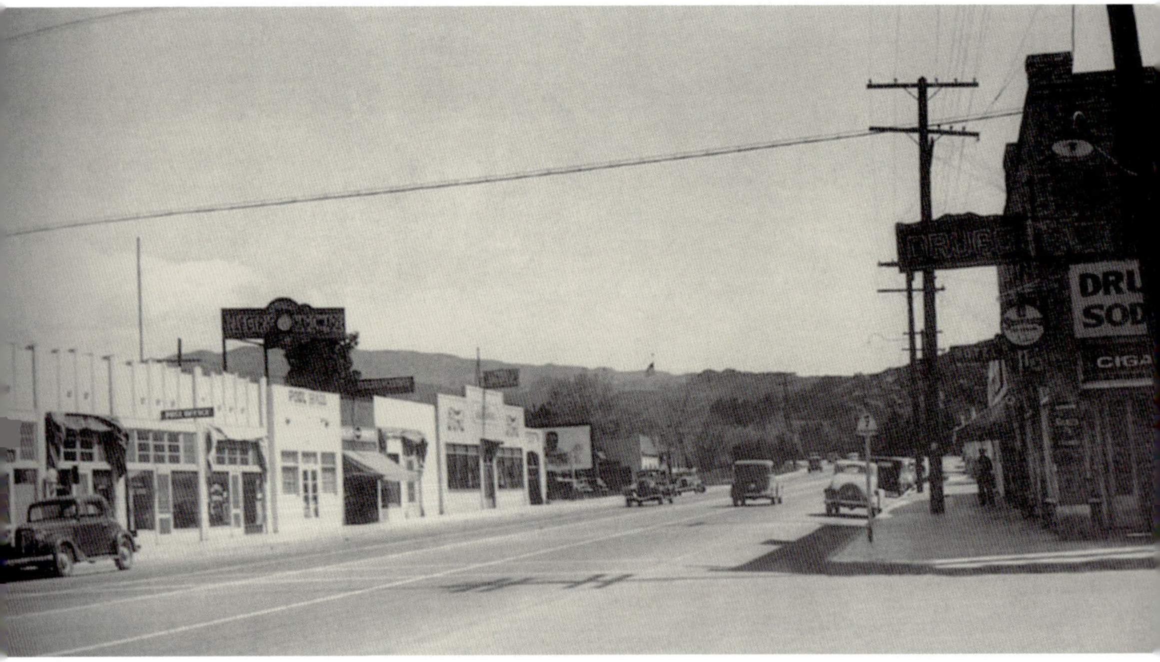

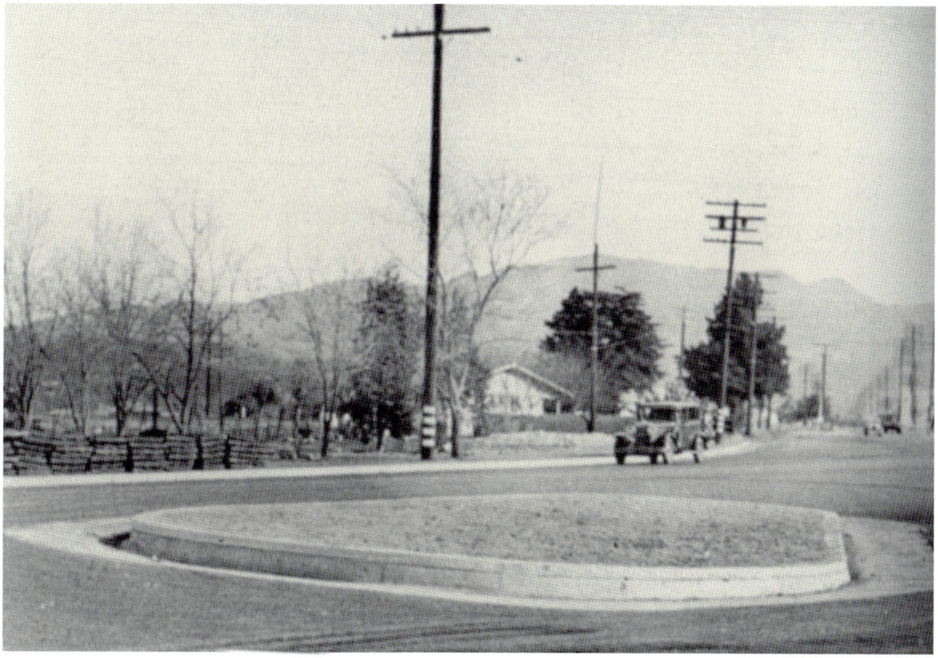

Old Town Newhall got a new traffic roundabout near the entrance to William S. Hart Park in 2014. But as can be seen in this photograph from the 1930s, it was not the first roundabout at this location. The new roundabout was constructed near the southern end of the Walk of Western Stars, a city-supported project honoring the rich history of Western movie production in the SCV.

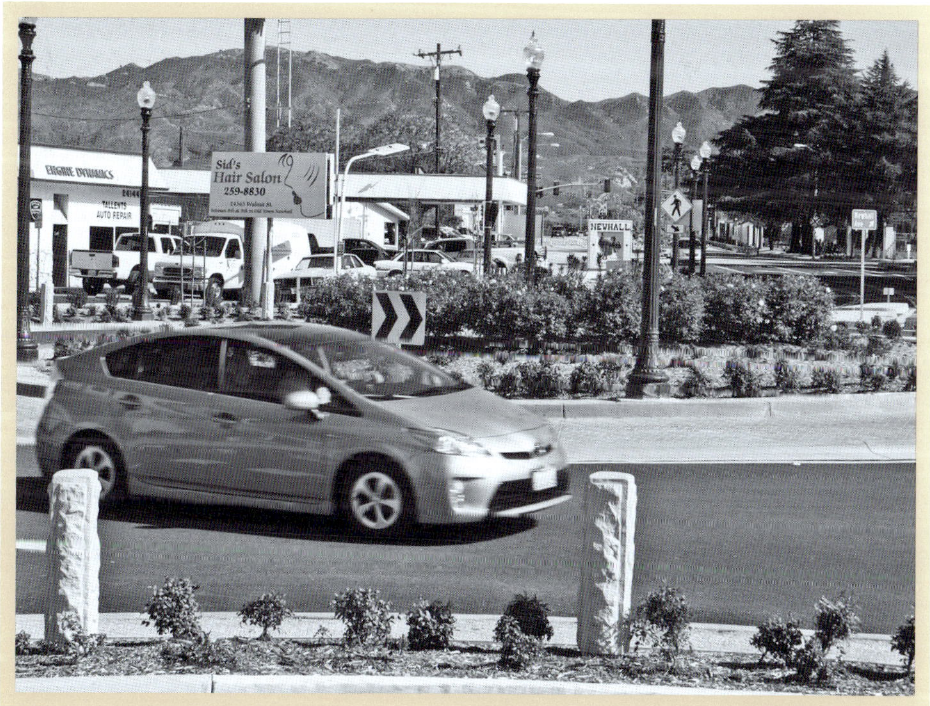

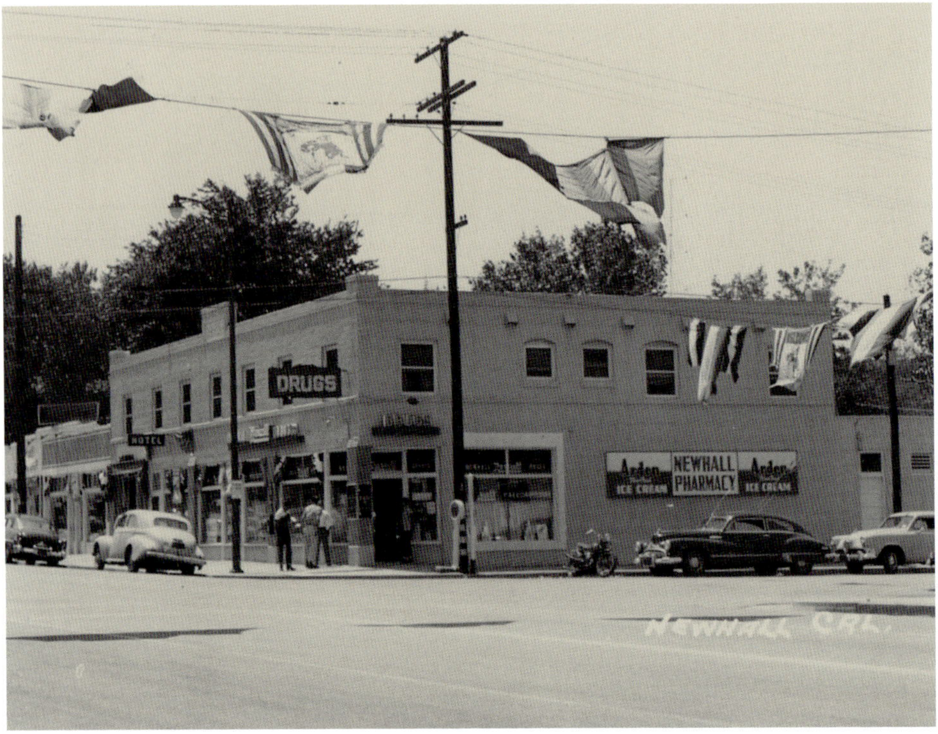

This photograph from the 1930s looking south from Market Street along Spruce Street (today's Main Street) shows the Swall Hotel and Newhall Pharmacy on the right side of the street. Albert Swall originally ran a meat market on Railroad Avenue before moving to this location in 1914 after the owner raised his rent. Most of the Railroad Avenue merchants followed him to Spruce Street, creating a new business district.

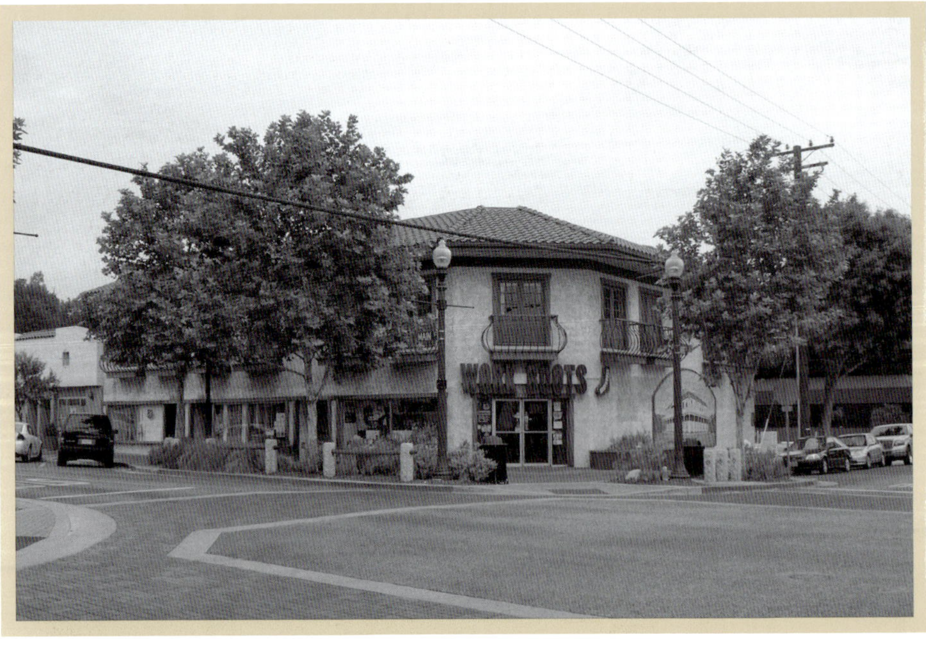

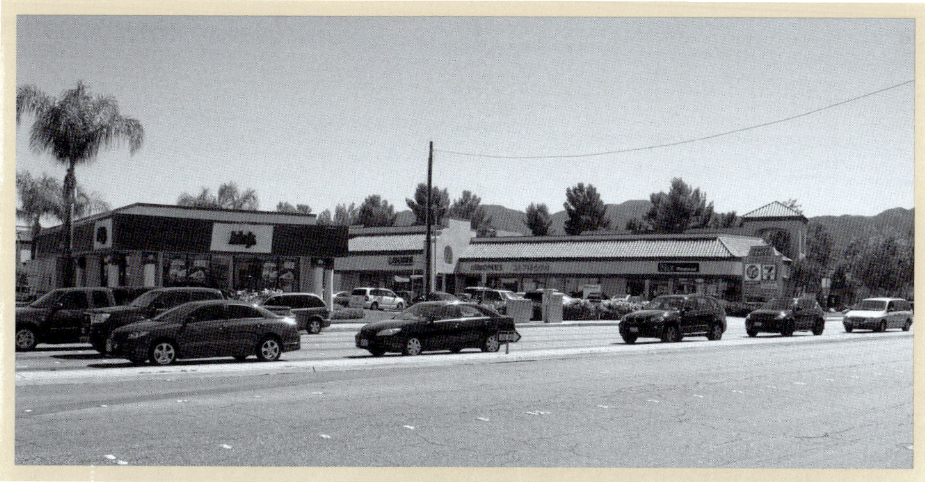

The Solemint Store, which was located on the southeast corner of Soledad Canyon Road and Mint Canyon (now Sierra Highway), was opened by Alfred Clark in 1938. It was considered one of the most unusual general stores in America, featuring a variety of hard-to-find and comical items. The vintage photograph shows the store in 1951. Today, a mini mall and an Arby's restaurant occupy the site of the Solemint Store.

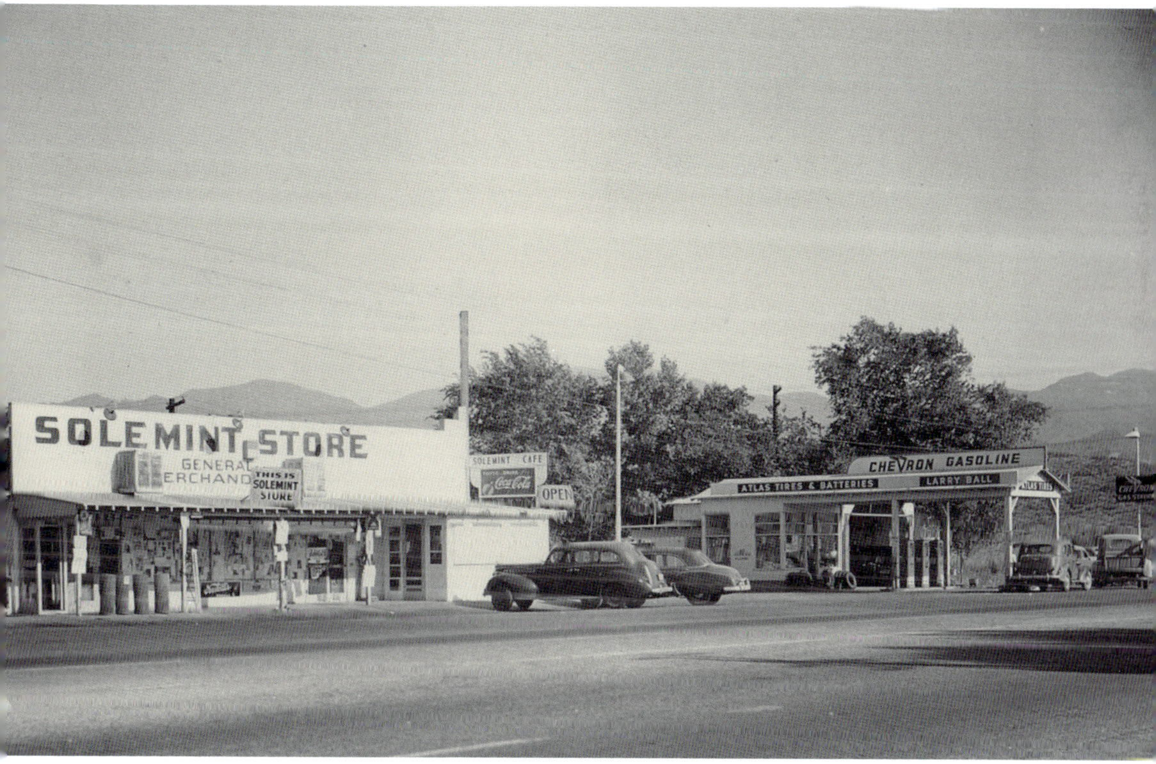

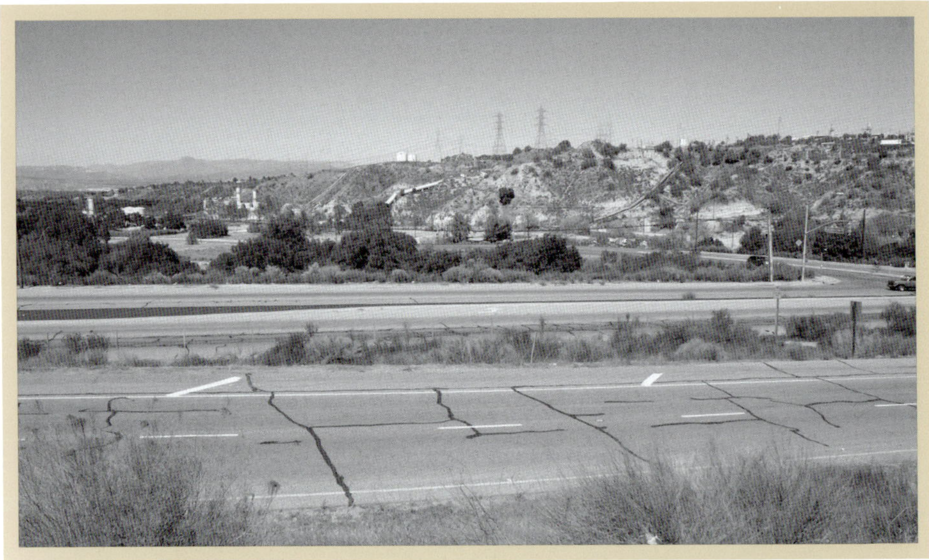

This 1940s postcard highlights the importance of gold, oil, and water to the history of Placerita Canyon. The pipeline in the photograph is the Los Angeles Aqueduct, which has traversed the canyon since 1913. A number of structures related to the oil industry surround the pipeline, which remains active in Placerita Canyon to this day. The caption on the postcard alludes to Francisco Lopez's discovery of gold nearby in 1842 (possible 1841), the first strike in California history.

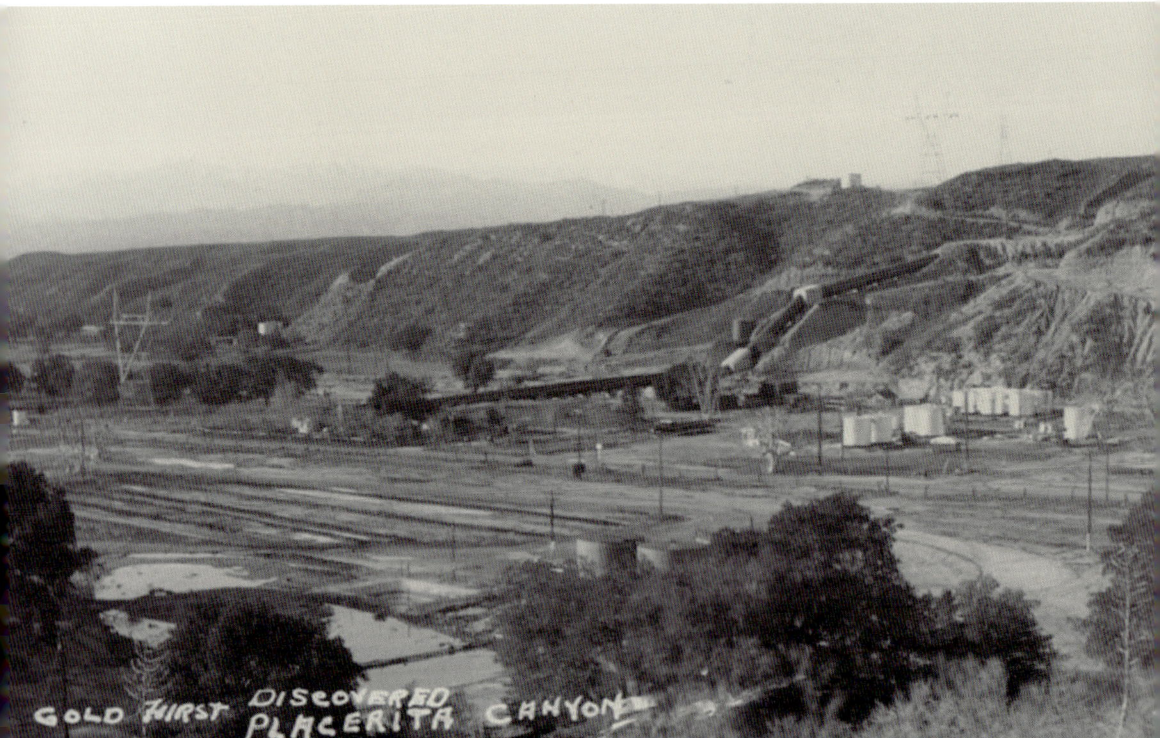

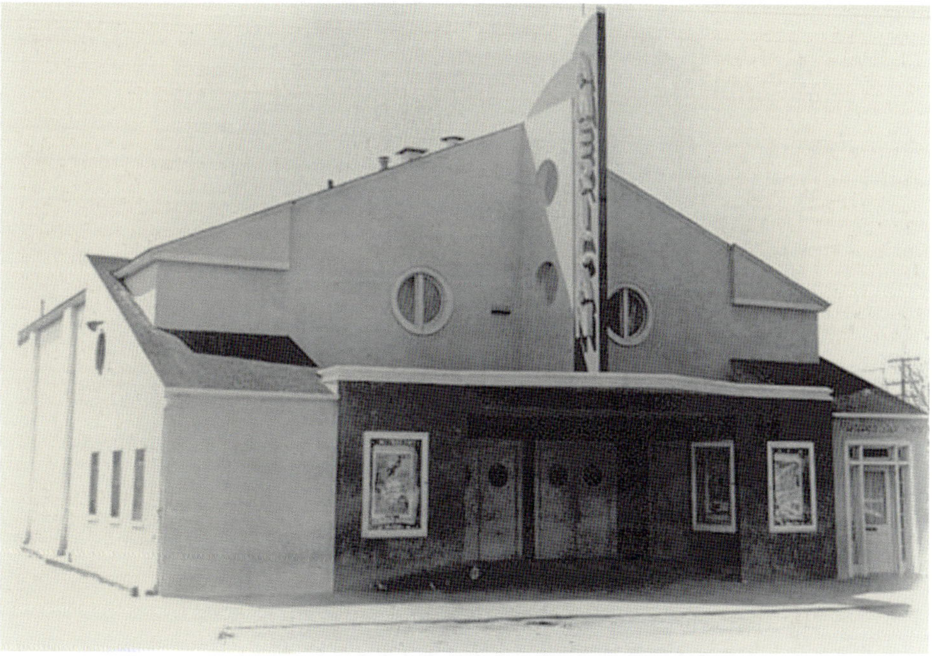

Although the town was frequently called "Hollywood's backlot," Newhall residents had no movie theater of their own until silent Western star William S. Hart donated the land at the corner of Spruce and Eleventh Streets. The American Theater opened on May 23, 1941, with a screening of Hart's popular final film, *Tumbleweeds*. The theater closed in 1965, but the building still stands today as American Legion Post No. 507 and is adjacent to the Old Town Newhall Library.

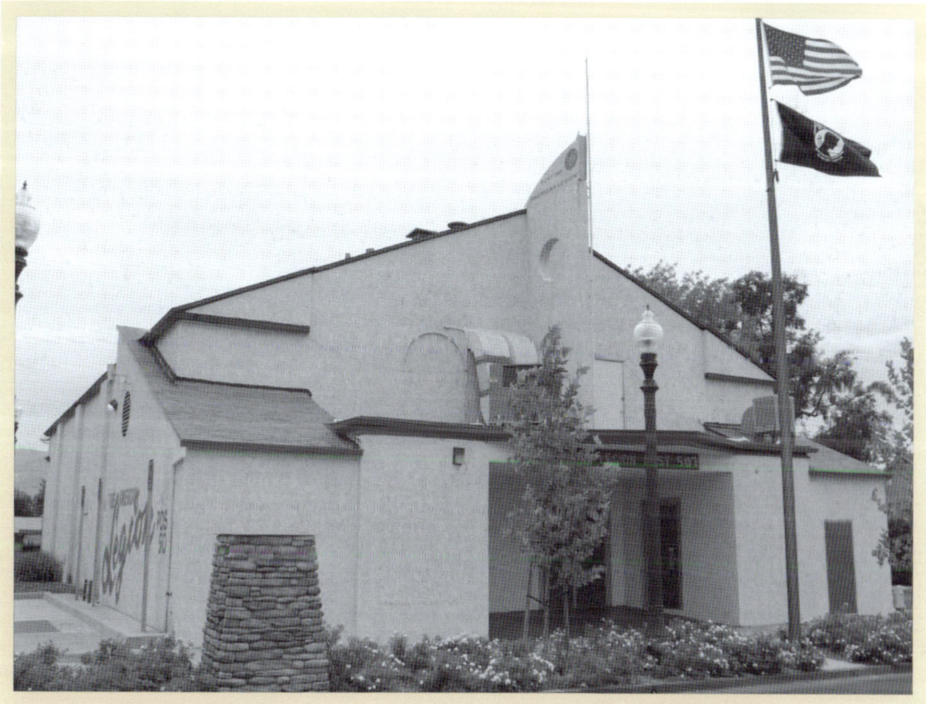

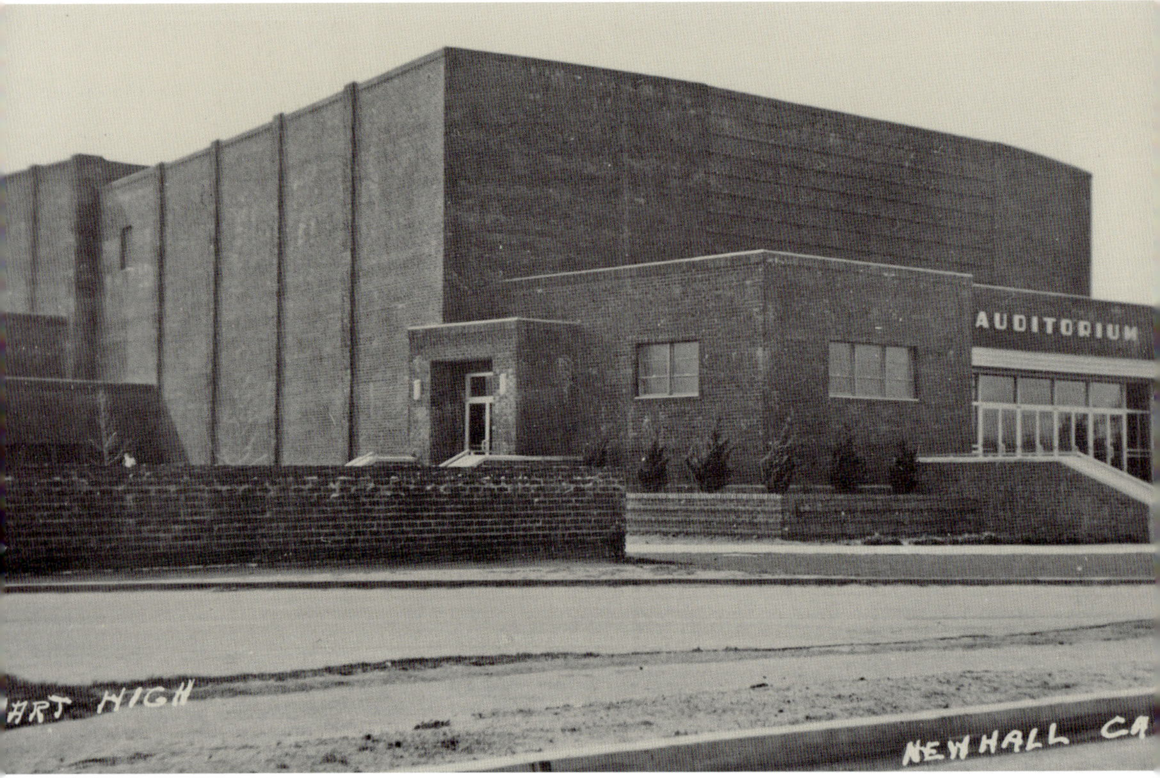

The Santa Clarita Valley's first high school opened in 1946 and was named after its chief benefactor, silent movie star William S. Hart, who had died three months earlier. The Hart Auditorium, originally called the Henry Mayo Newhall Auditorium, opened on September 12, 1952. It was heavily damaged in the 1994 Northridge earthquake and did not reopen until 2000. The auditorium, with its Art Deco lettering, still stands on Newhall Avenue near Fourteenth Street.

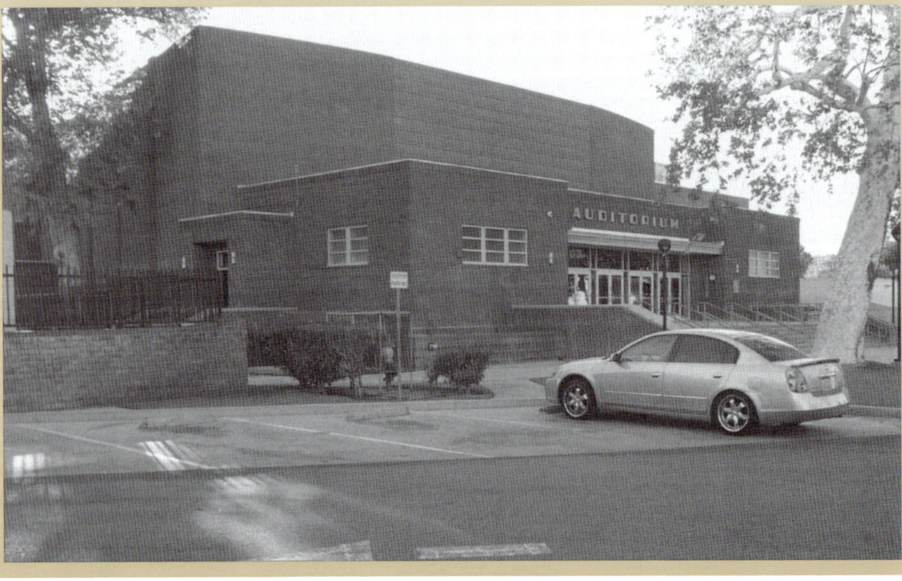

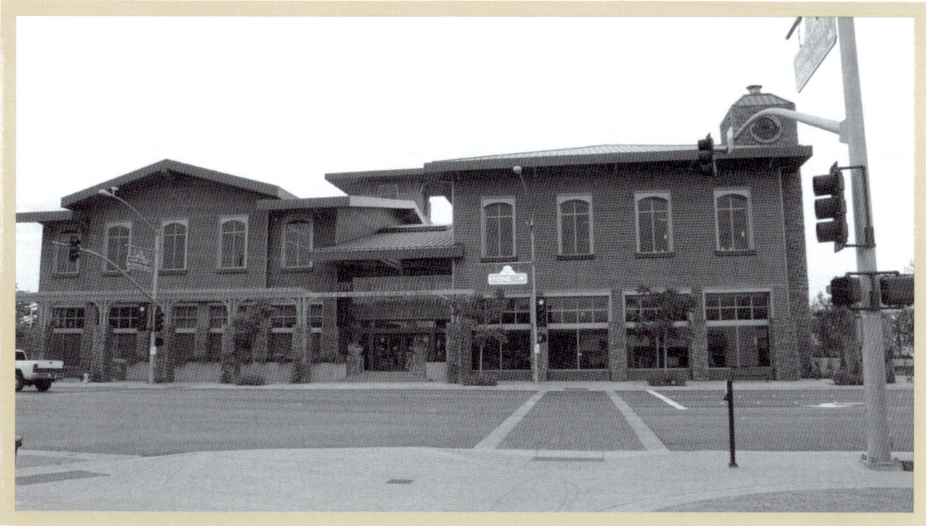

This photograph from the 1950s shows a Union 76 gas station on the corner of Lyons Avenue and San Fernando Road. Today, the Old Town Newhall Library resides on the spot. A grand opening celebration was held on the streets of Newhall for the new library on September 29, 2012. San Fernando Road (now Main Street) was rerouted to accommodate the new library, creating a more intimate experience for visitors to the Old Town Newhall area.

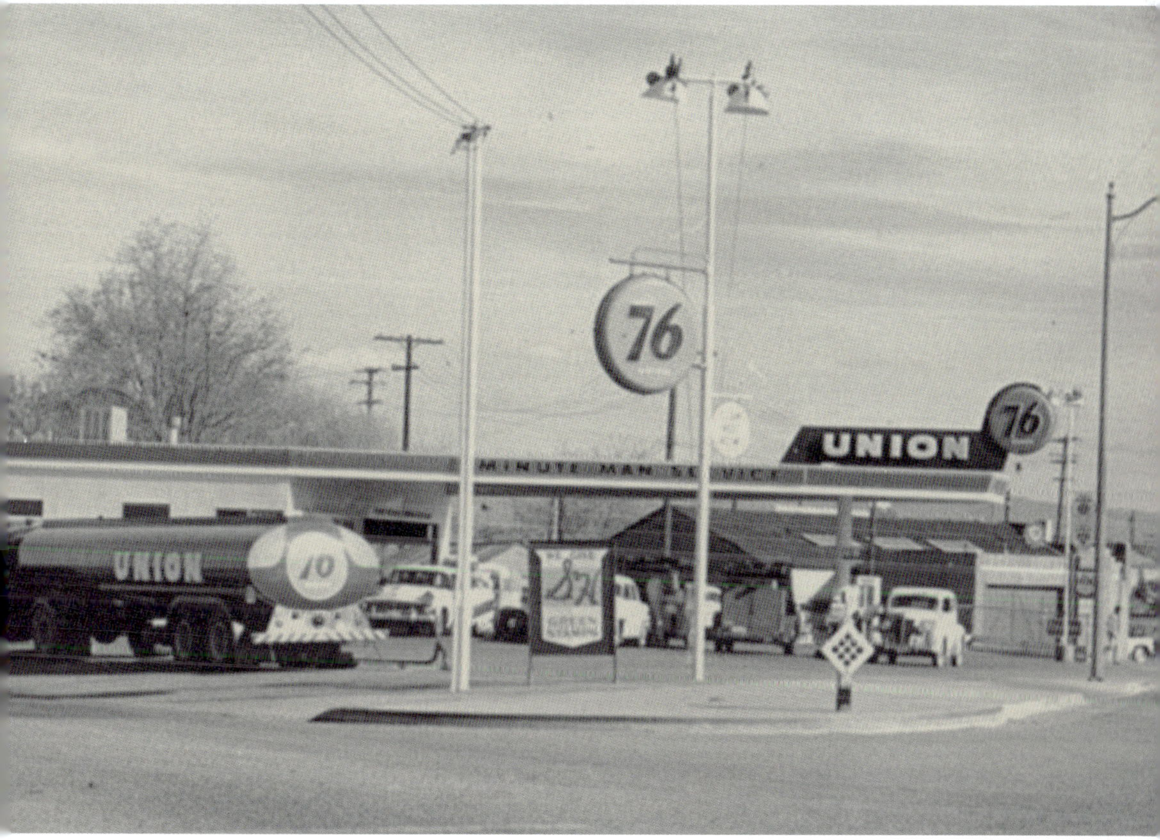

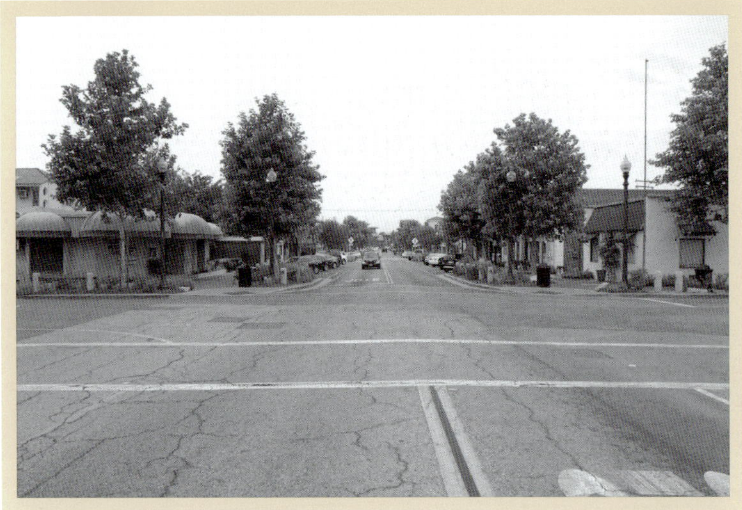

This postcard from the 1950s shows San Fernando Road (now Main Street), looking north from Sixth Street. To the left is the Newhall Community Hospital, which began life as a doctor's office in 1926 and served as one of a few small hospitals in the SCV until Henry Mayo Newhall Memorial Hospital opened in 1975. Previously, Main Street was the primary thoroughfare through Newhall. Today, it ends in front of the Old Town Newhall Library, which can be seen in the distance.

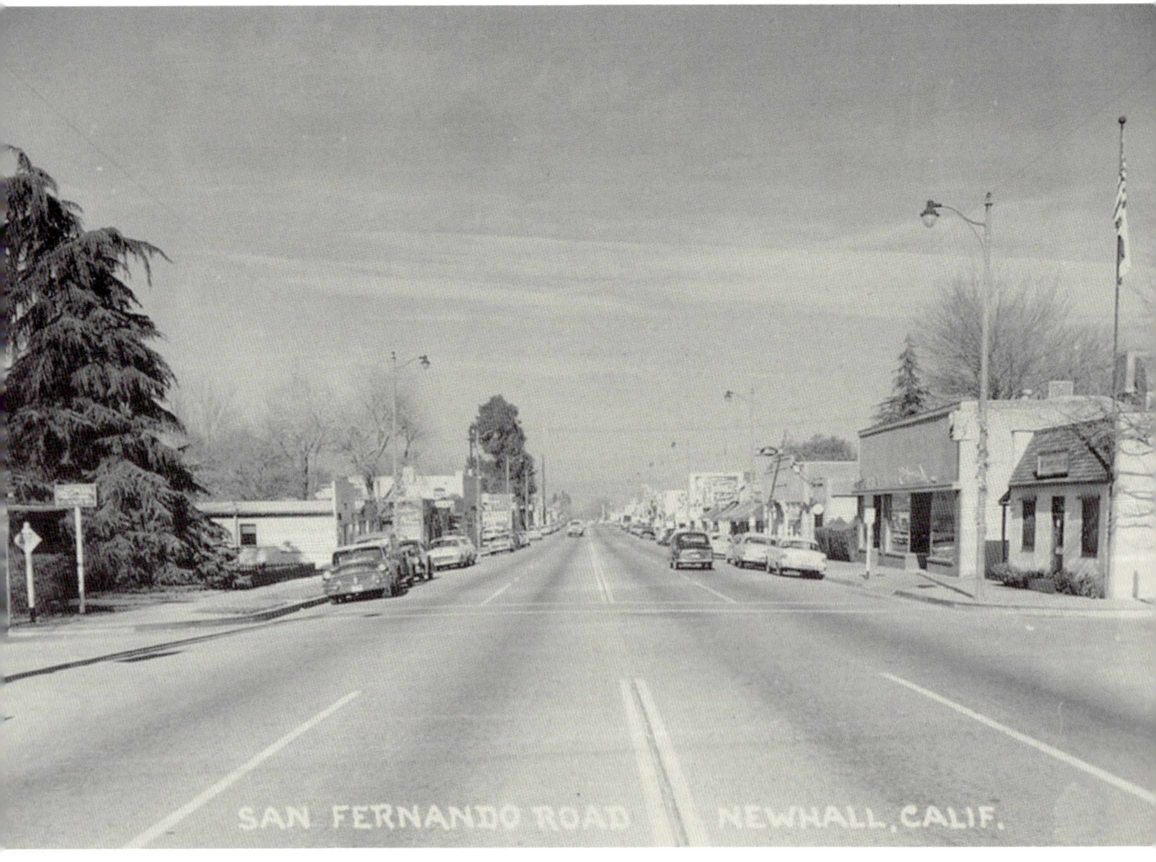

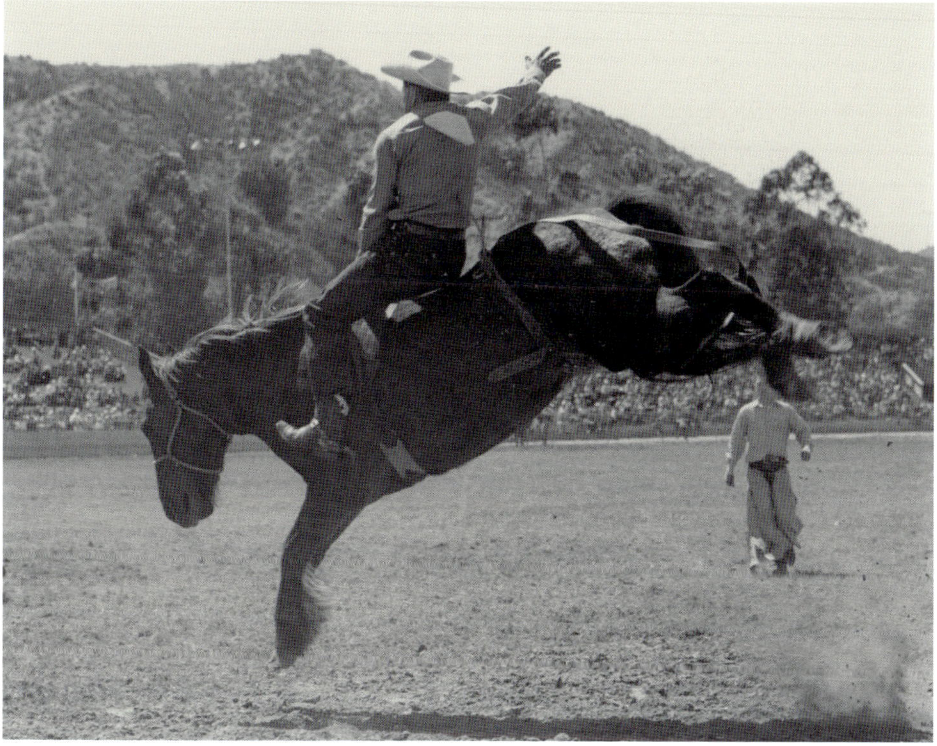

The Saugus Speedway, which today hosts the Saugus Swap Meet, began as a rodeo arena built by Roy Baker in 1927. The arena changed ownership three times in the 1930s, first passing to Western movie star Hoot Gibson in 1930, then to Paul Hill in 1934, and finally, to William Bonelli in 1938. Bonelli Stadium began hosting auto races in 1939 and continued featuring rodeos into the 1960s. Rodeo star Bob Yanez is seen riding a bucking bronco at a 1953 rodeo.

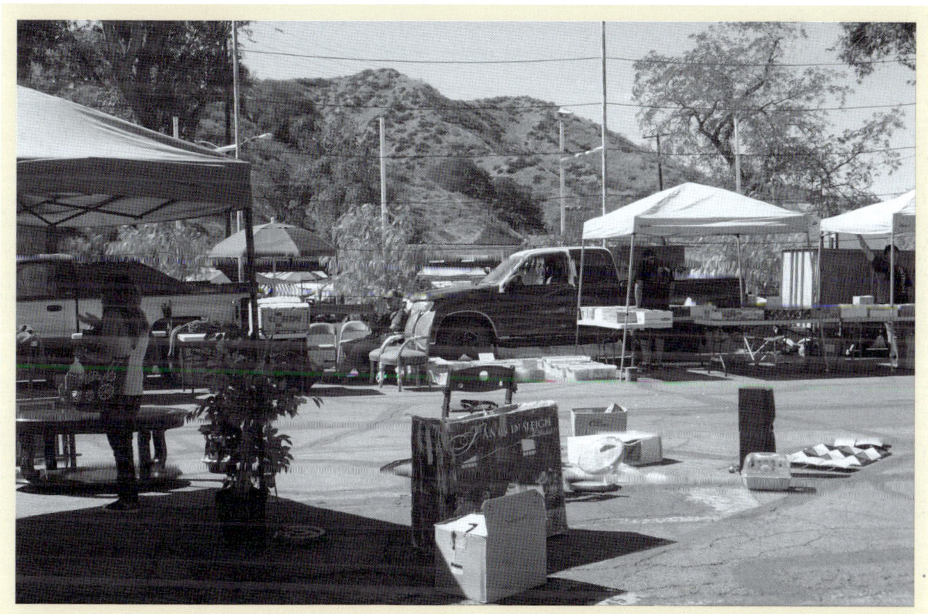

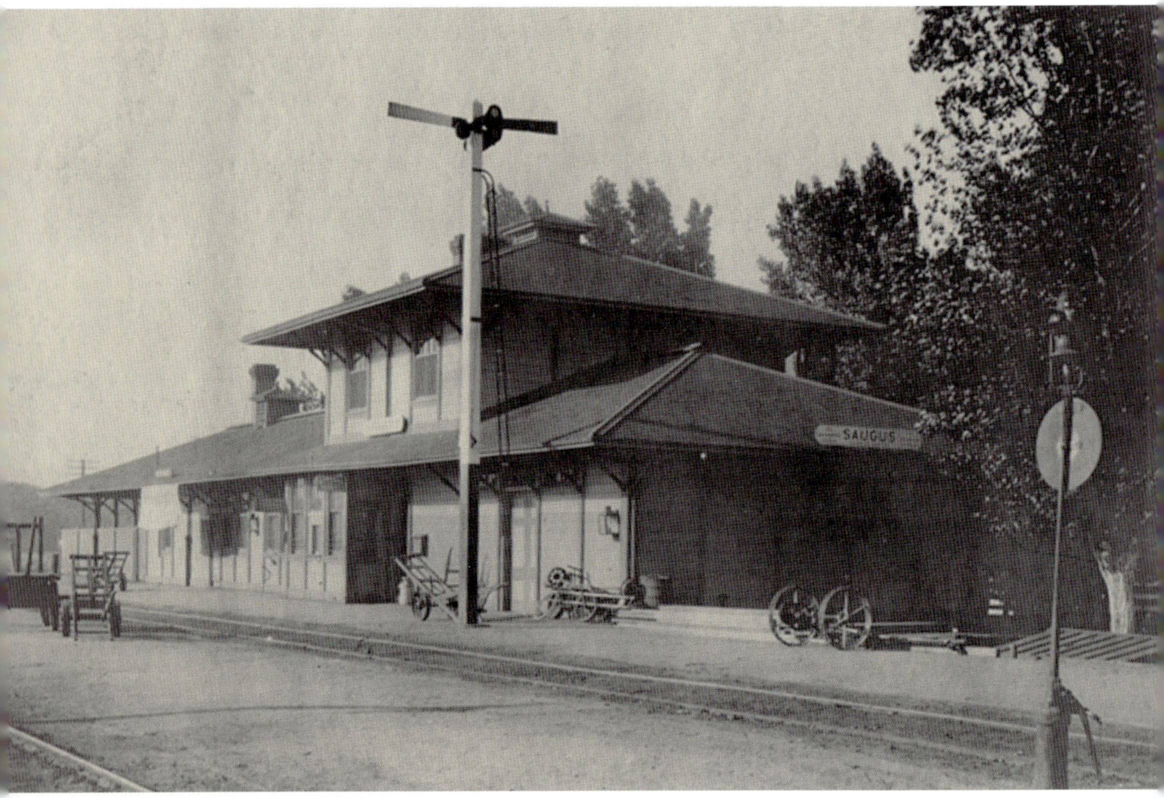

In 1887, the Southern Pacific Railroad completed a branch line from Saugus to Santa Barbara. That same year, it built the Saugus Train Station, pictured here in the 1930s or 1940s, alongside the main line near its junction with the new branch line. The station was moved in 1980 to Heritage Junction in William S. Hart Park, where it can still be seen today. The Stock Building Supply Company on Railroad Avenue now occupies its original site, across from the Saugus Café.

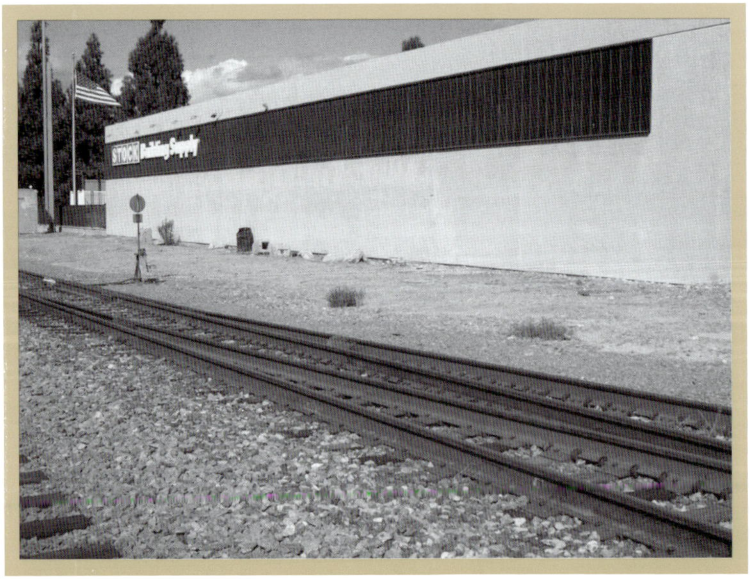

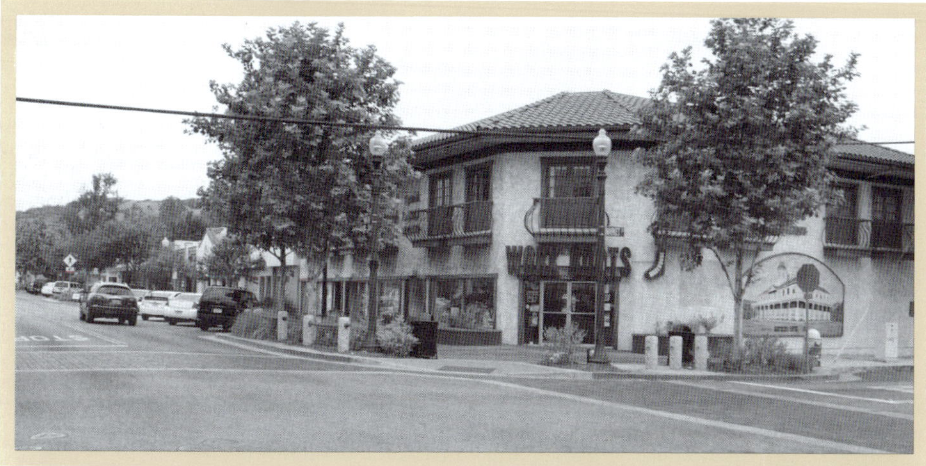

In the 1960s, the Newhall Rexall Drugs occupied this building, located on the southwest corner of San Fernando Road (now Main Street) and Market Street. Albert Swall originally built it in 1914 as the Swall Hotel, and it once housed Newhall's first county library. The present-day stucco structure is a replacement for Swall's original two-story brick building, which was destroyed in the 1971 Sylmar earthquake.

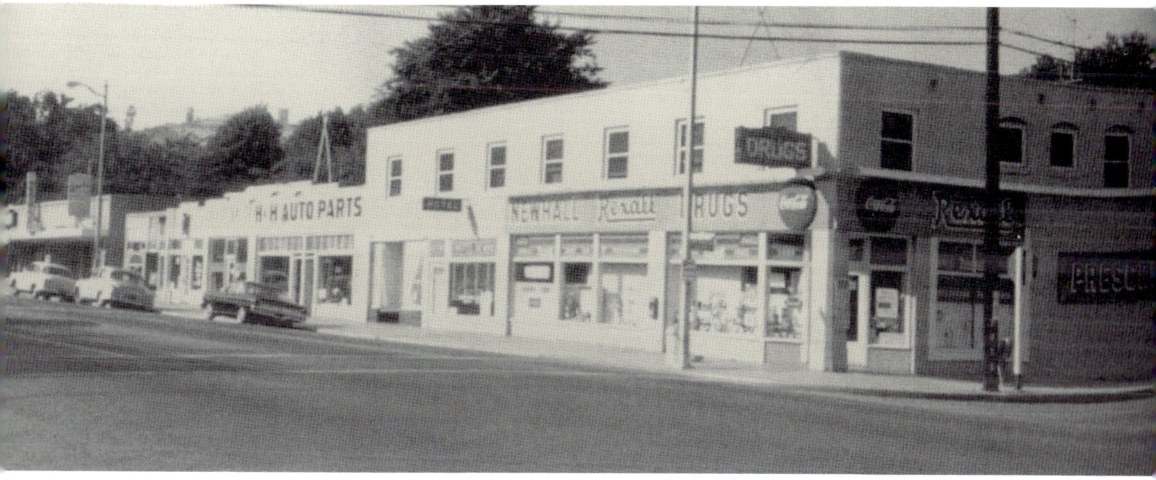

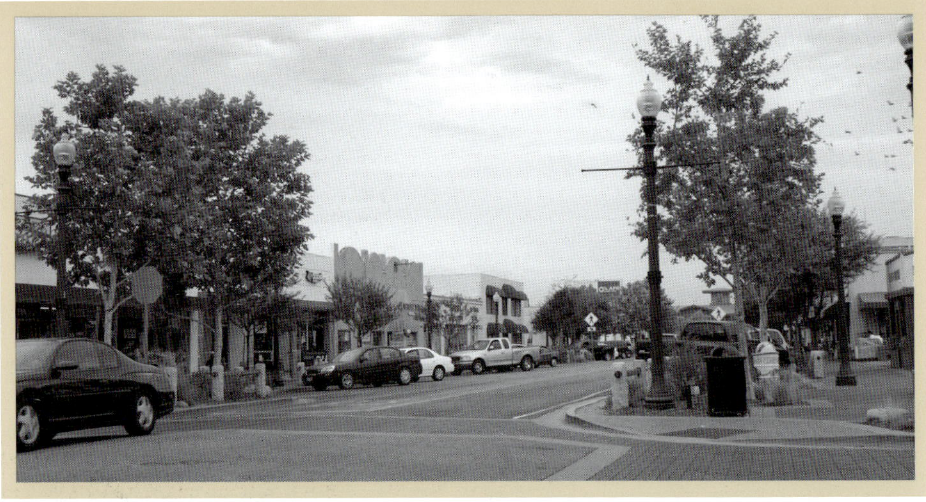

It is holiday time in 1960s Newhall in this photograph of San Fernando Road (now Main Street) and Market Street, looking north. The building with the castle-like roofline on the left was the blacksmith shop, run by Thomas McNaughton Frew II. Frew, a native of Scotland, rode into town in 1900 and purchased the shop from local businessman James Gulley. He was succeeded in the business by his son Tom III and grandson Tom IV. It closed in 1970.

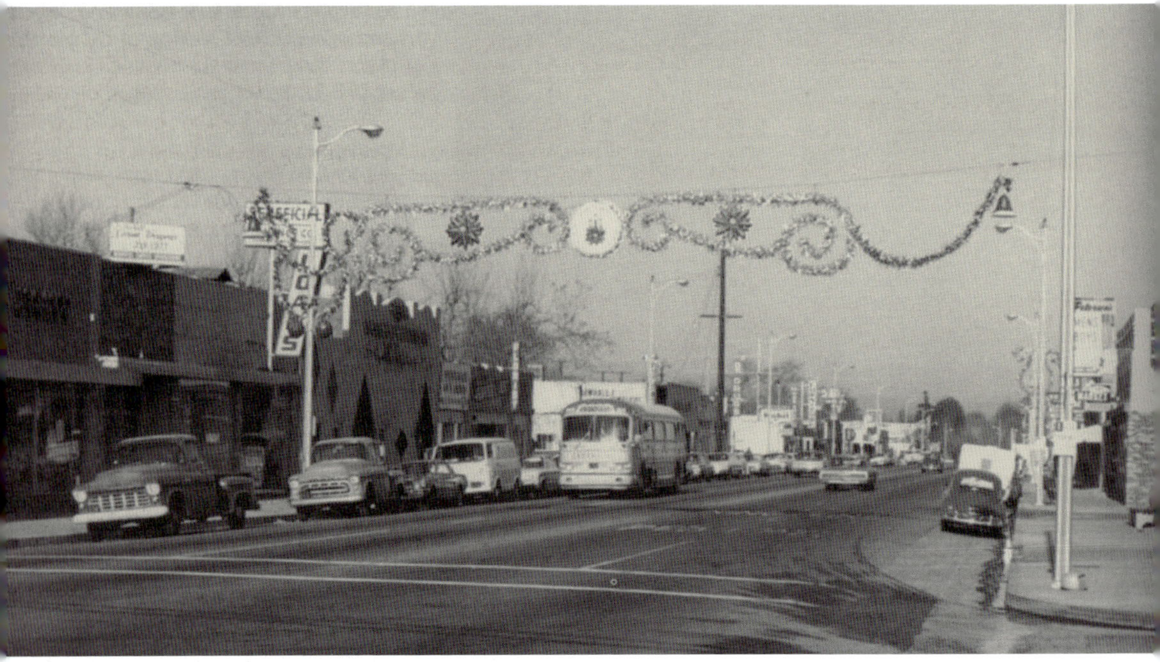

CHAPTER 3

NEWHALLYWOOD

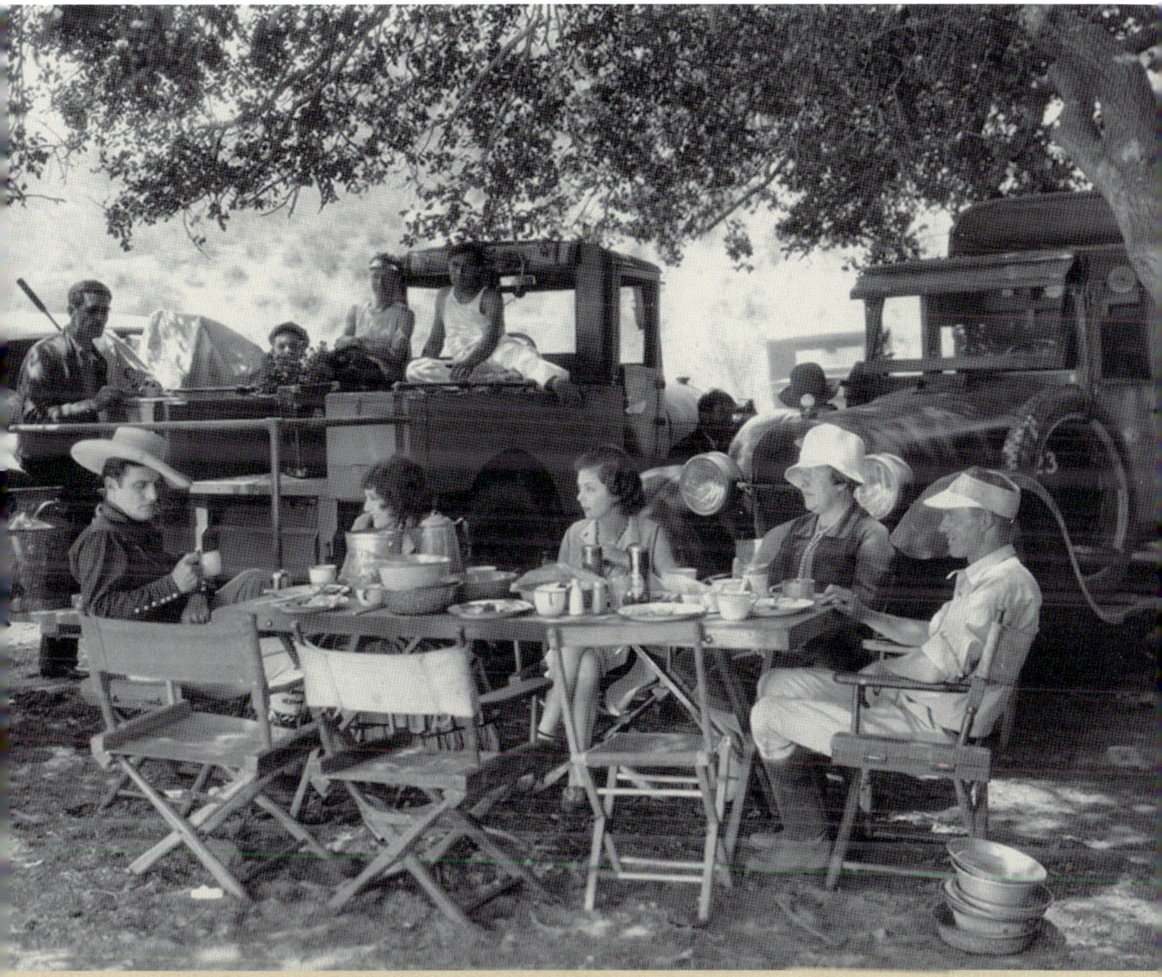

Silent Western film superstar Tom Mix, seated at left in the white hat, pauses in Newhall with some of his cast and crew members during filming of *Tom Mix in Arabia* (1922). Newhall was a frequent filming site for Mix, who earlier had built one of his first "Mixvilles"—outdoor Western sets—in the town.

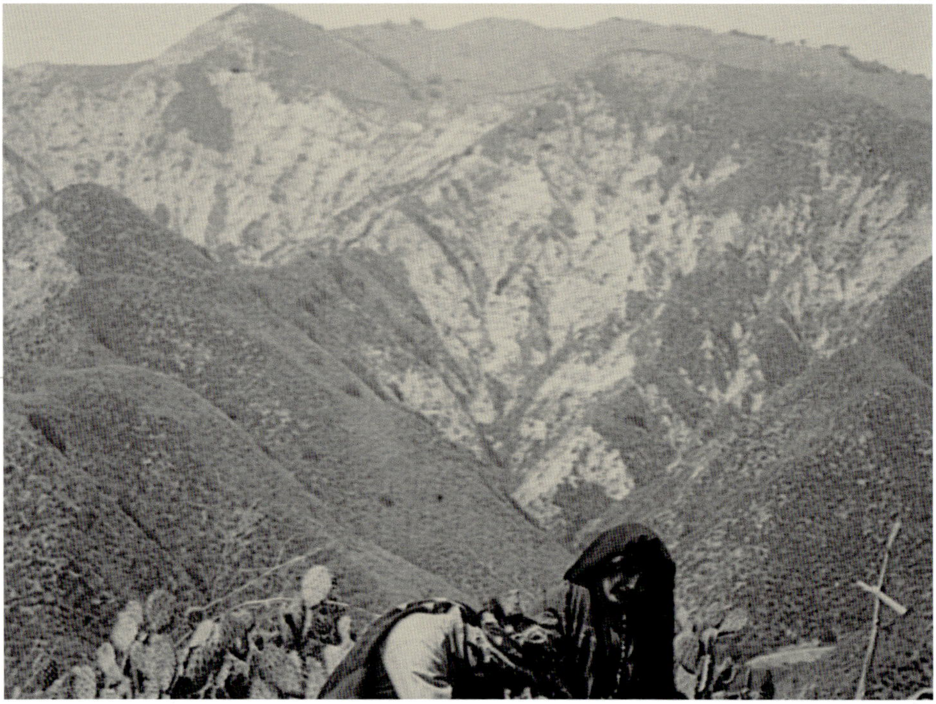

The enormously popular 19th-century novel *Ramona* was first made into a film by D.W. Griffith in 1910. His version starred Mary Pickford and used Rancho Camulos near Piru for its exterior shots. For the final scene, the filmmakers climbed a steep hill near Piru. As is evident from the modern photograph, the landscape has not changed at all over the past century. (Now image by Hugh Munro Neely.)

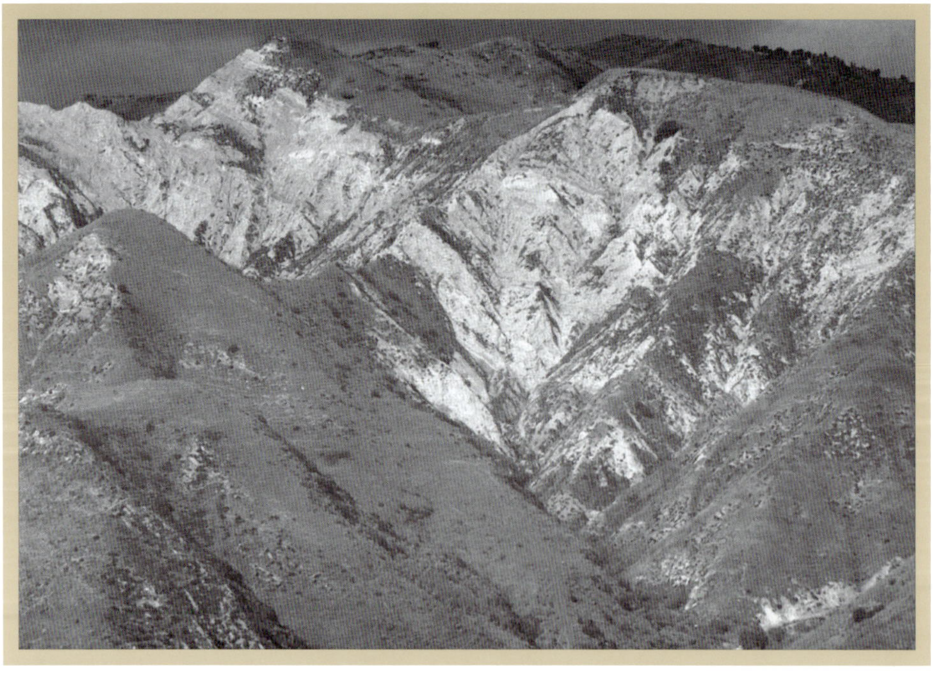

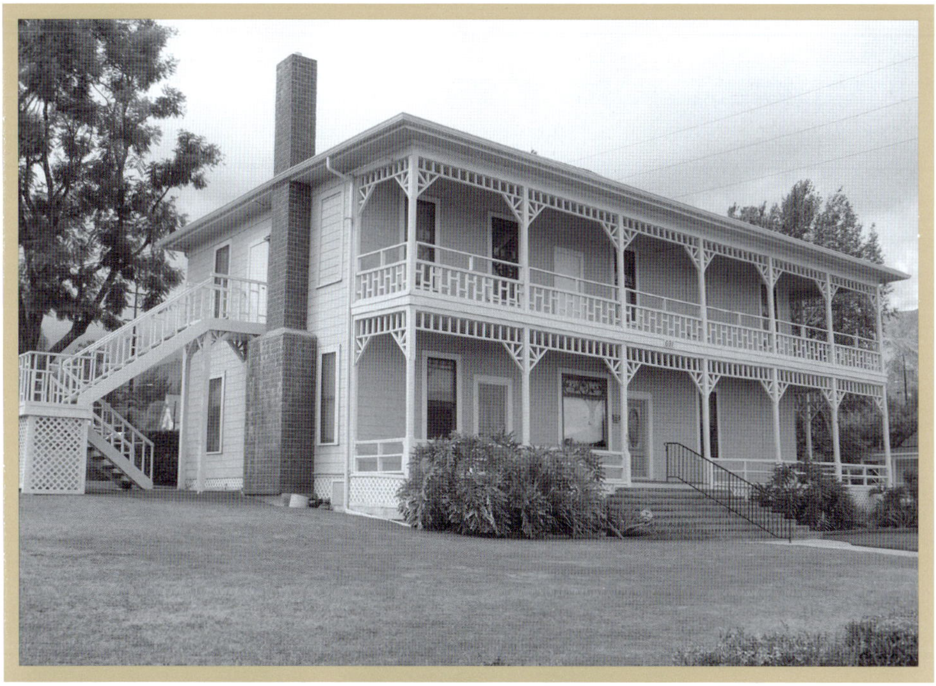

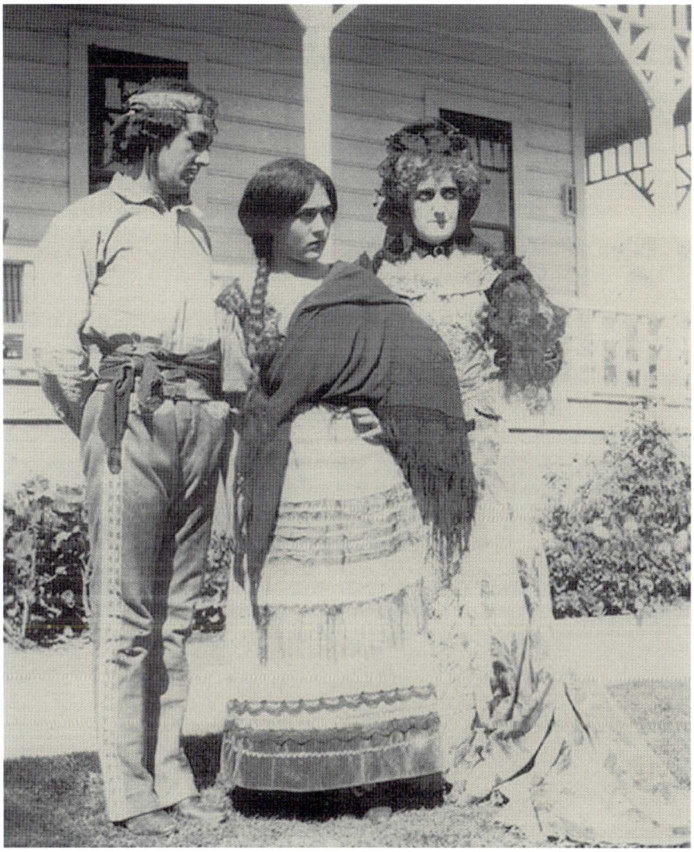

From left to right, Henry B. Walthall, Mary Pickford, and Kate Bruce pose outside of the Piru Hotel in March 1910, during the filming of *Ramona*. This same location was later used in a segment from the ill-fated film *Twilight Zone: The Movie* (1983). The hotel was built in 1887 and was known for a time as the Heritage Valley Inn. It is now a private residence.

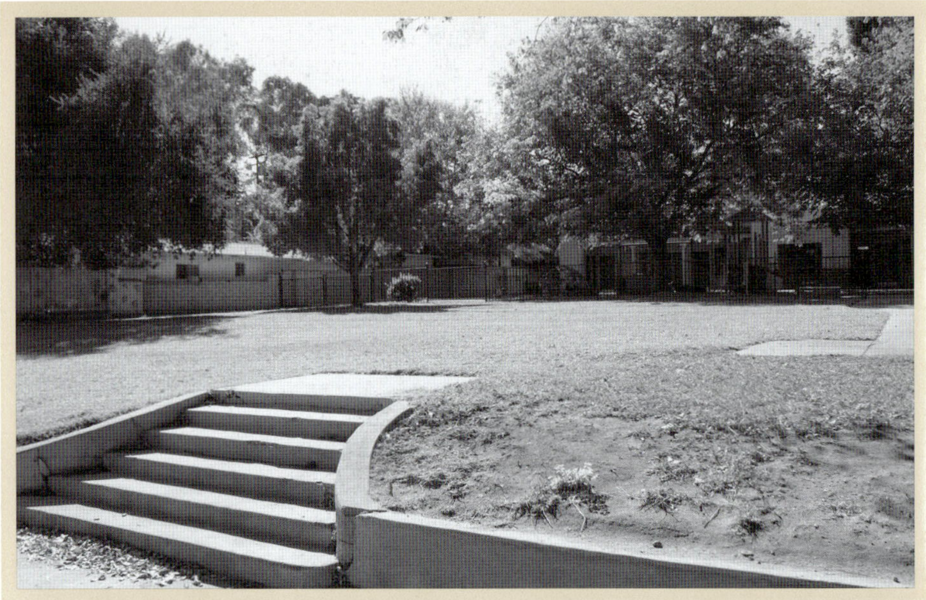

Film crews came early and often to Newhall—so often, in fact, that the town acquired the nickname "Newhallywood." In this photograph, film crews shoot a scene outside the First Presbyterian Church on Newhall Avenue sometime around the late 1910s to early 1920s. The church was constructed in 1891 and was replaced by a brick structure in 1923. This building, which later appeared in the opening credits of 1954's *Suddenly*, was destroyed by the Sylmar earthquake in 1971.

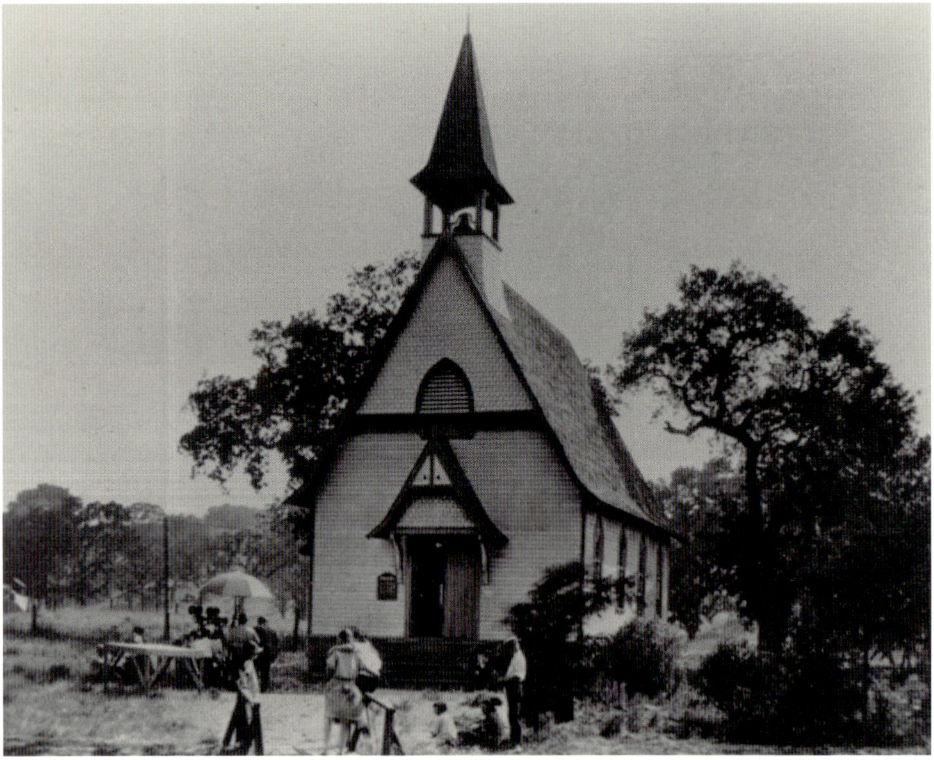

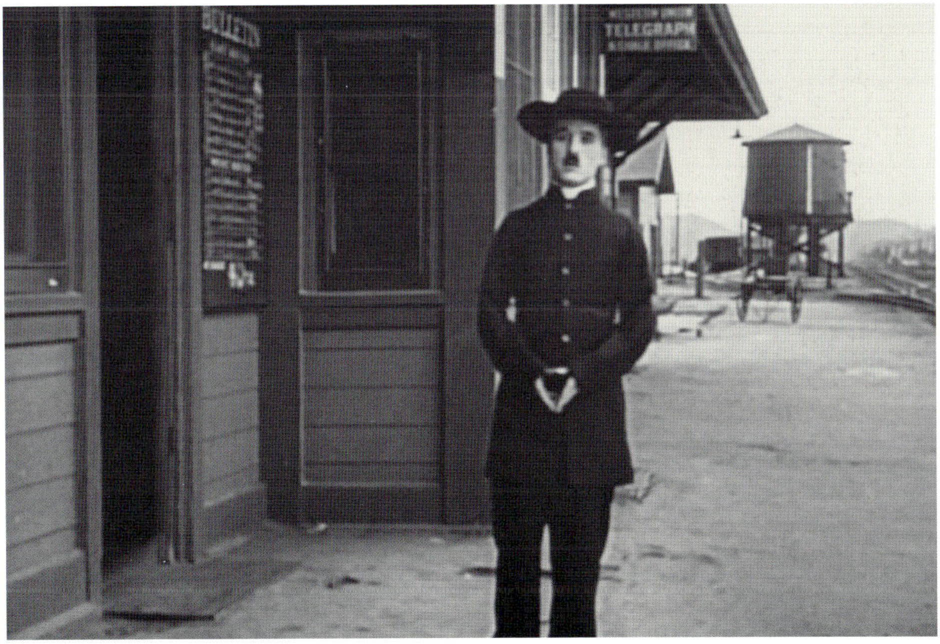

Silent screen comedian Charlie Chaplin came to the Saugus Train Station in 1923 to film this scene from *The Pilgrim*, playing an escaped convict posing as a man of the cloth. At the time of the film, the station was located at the southeast corner of today's Railroad Avenue and Drayton Street in Saugus. In 1980, it was moved to Heritage Junction in Newhall, where it can still be seen today.

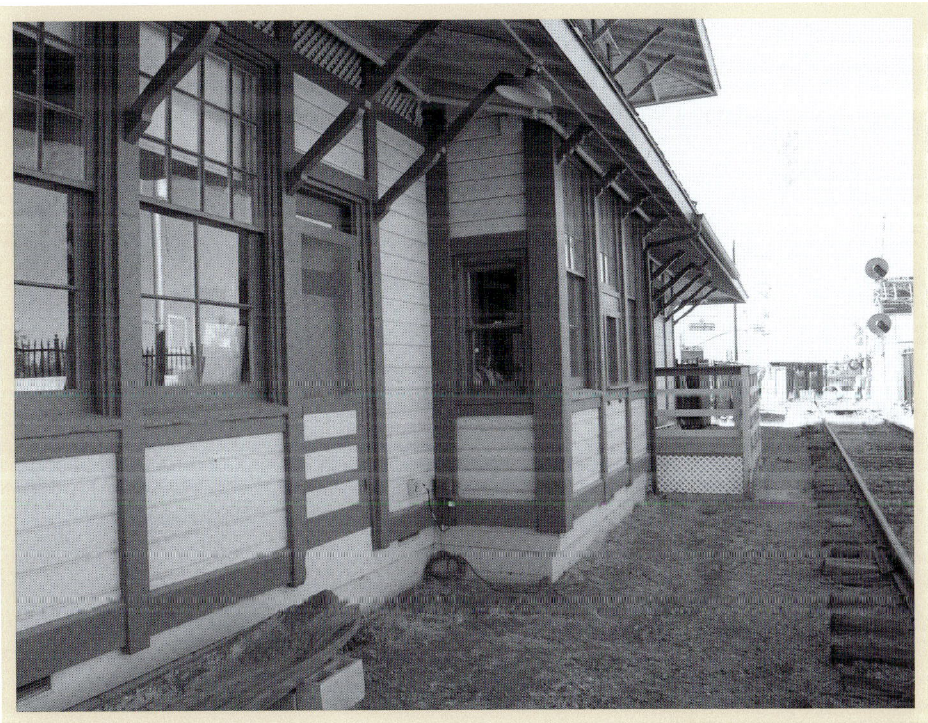

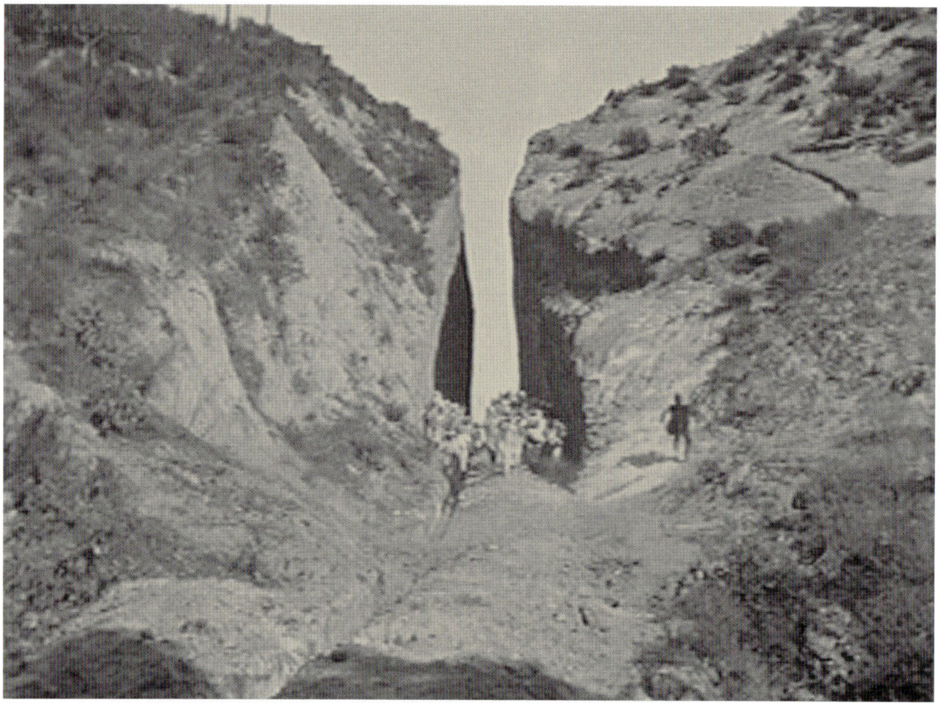

Silent funnyman Buster Keaton came to Beale's Cut in the Newhall Pass to shoot a scene for 1925's *Seven Chances*. This was the second time Keaton filmed at Beale's Cut. He also came here three years earlier while filming *The Paleface*. At right is a modern view inside the cut, with a sliver of the San Fernando Valley visible to the south. (Now image by Bettye Kozlowski.)

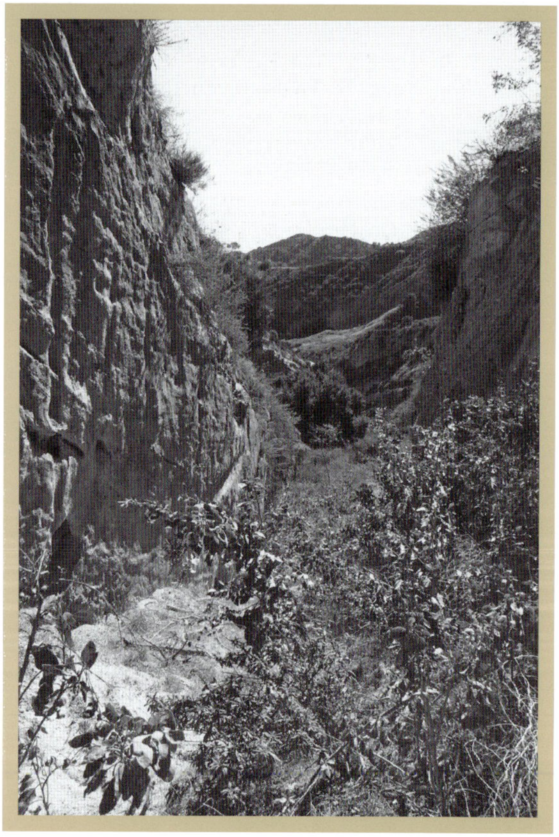

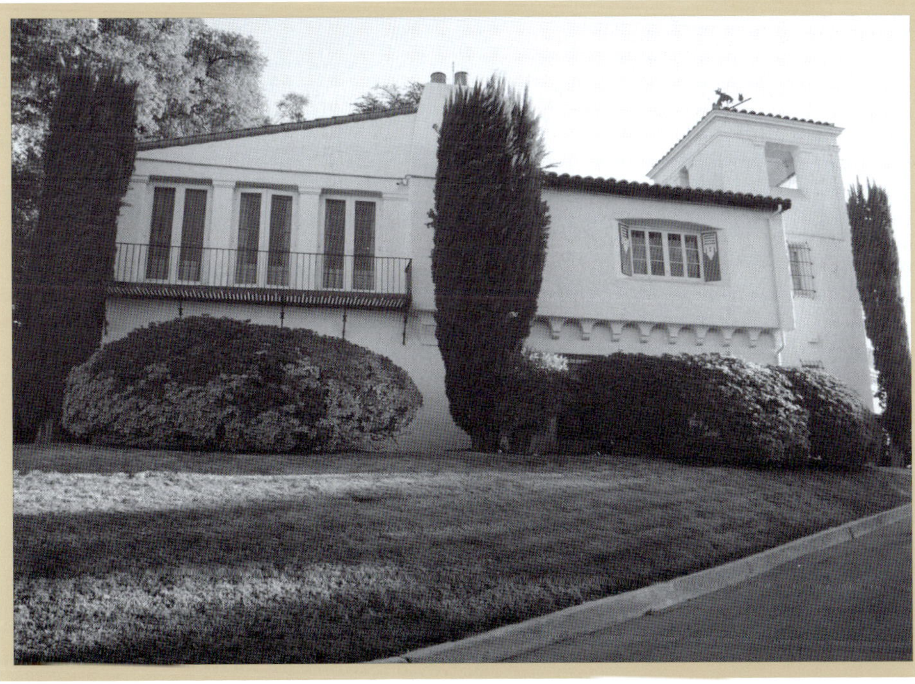

Newhall's favorite son, William S. Hart, was one of the most famous actors in the world when he retired in the late 1920s to La Loma de los Vientos (The Hill of the Winds), overlooking the town. The Spanish Colonial Revival–style 22-room mansion was built between 1924 and 1928 on the 265-acre ranch. Hart lived here with his sister Mary Ellen until his death in 1946. Hart willed the ranch and mansion to the County of Los Angeles to be used as a park.

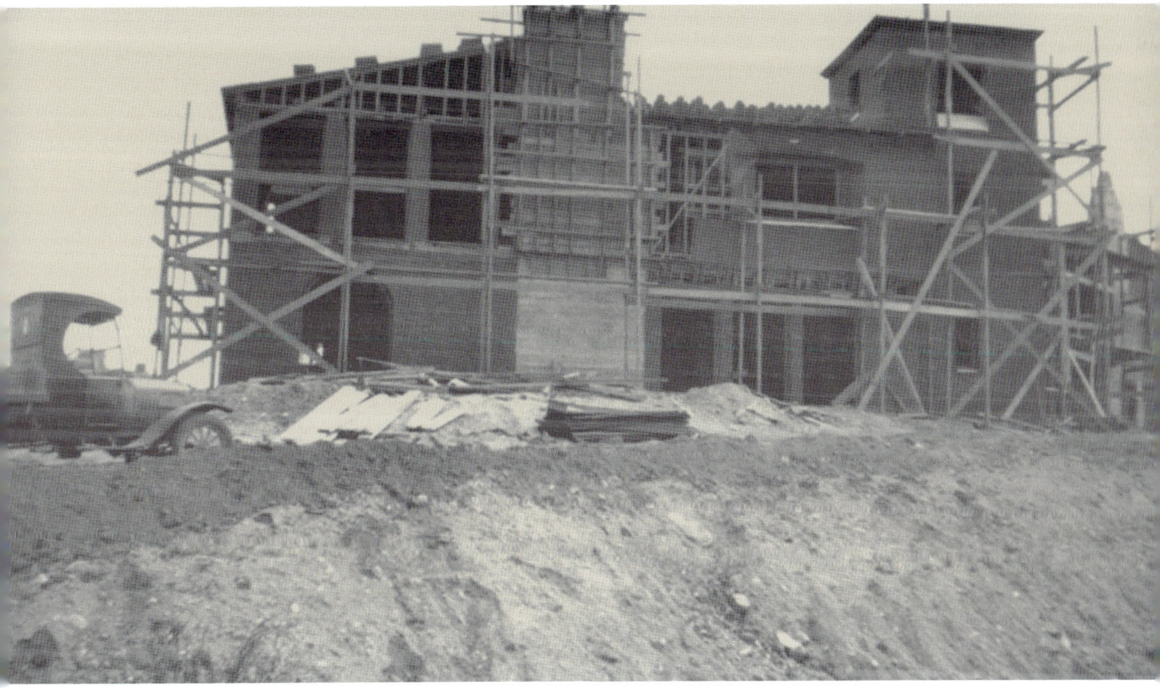

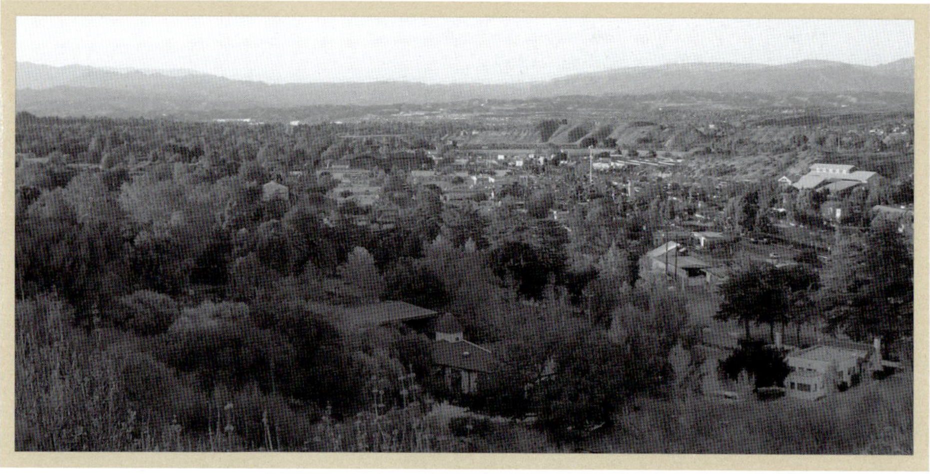

Much has changed in Newhall since cowboy nickelodeon star William S. Hart retired to his Horseshoe Ranch in the late 1920s. As seen from his ranch, Newhall has sprouted from a sleepy hamlet into a bustling district of an even larger city called Santa Clarita. Hart helped this growth by financing the first theater in the valley on Newhall's Spruce Street (see page 57). Horseshoe Ranch is now the William S. Hart Park.

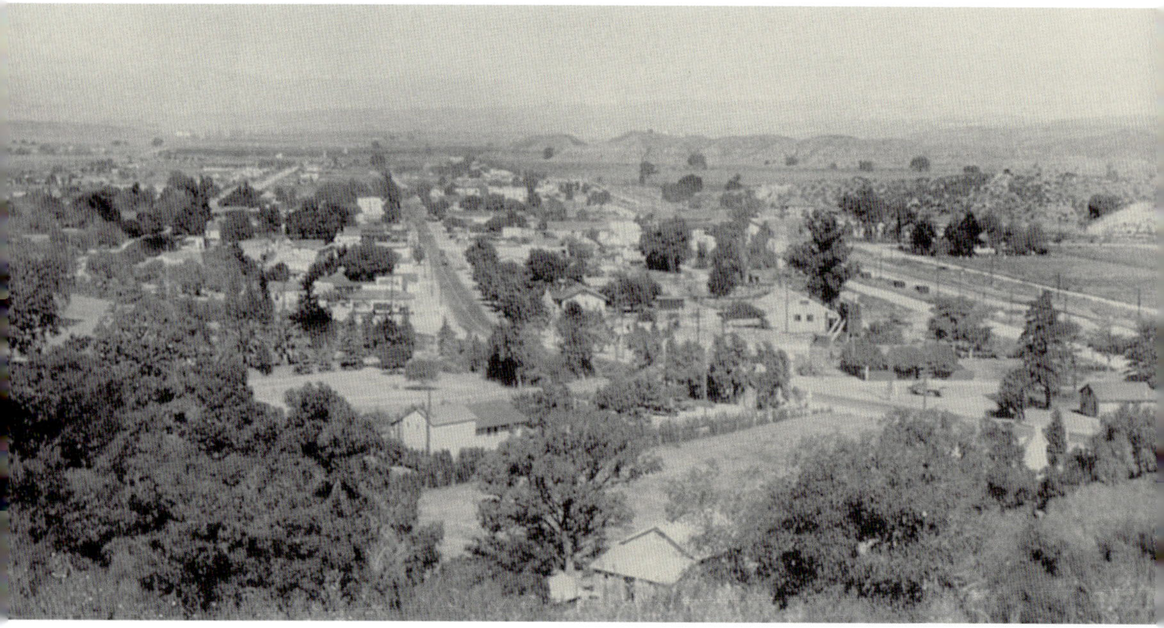

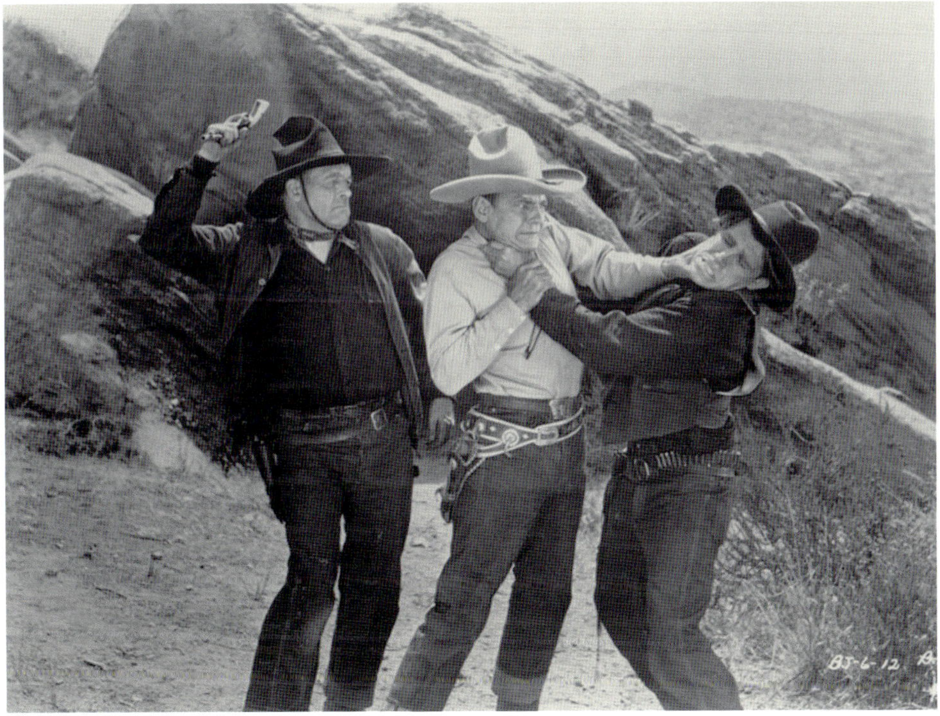

Buck Jones (center) battles bad guys at Vasquez Rocks in a scene from Universal's *Outlawed Guns* (1935). Jones began his career as a $5-a-day stuntman before becoming one of the biggest names in Westerns. His career flatlined briefly in the 1920s before resurging with the arrival of talkies. Jones perished in 1942 in the deadliest nightclub fire in US history at Boston's Cocoanut Grove nightclub. Coauthor Kim Stephens is seen in the modern-day photograph.

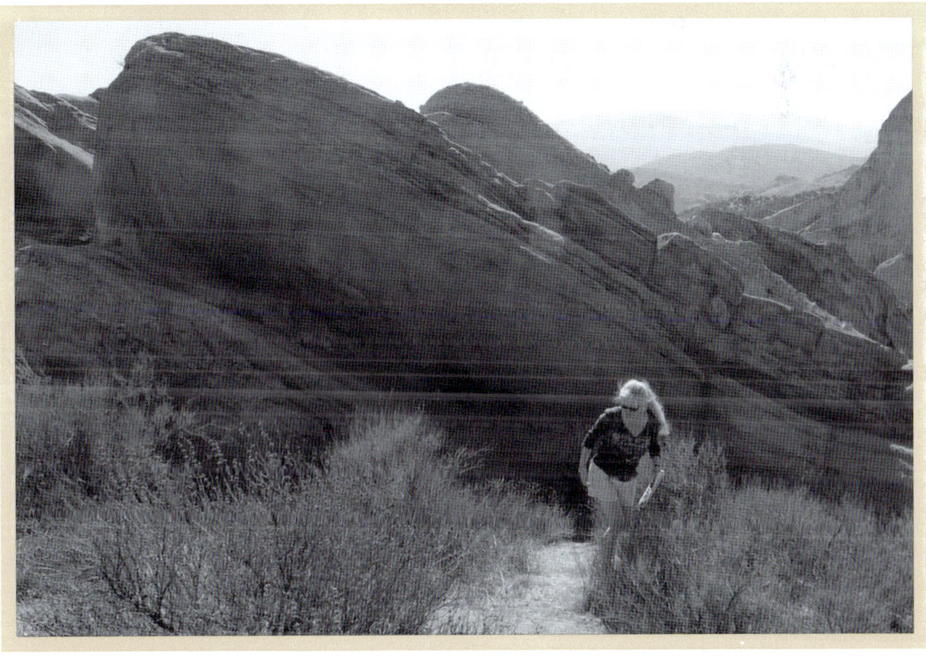

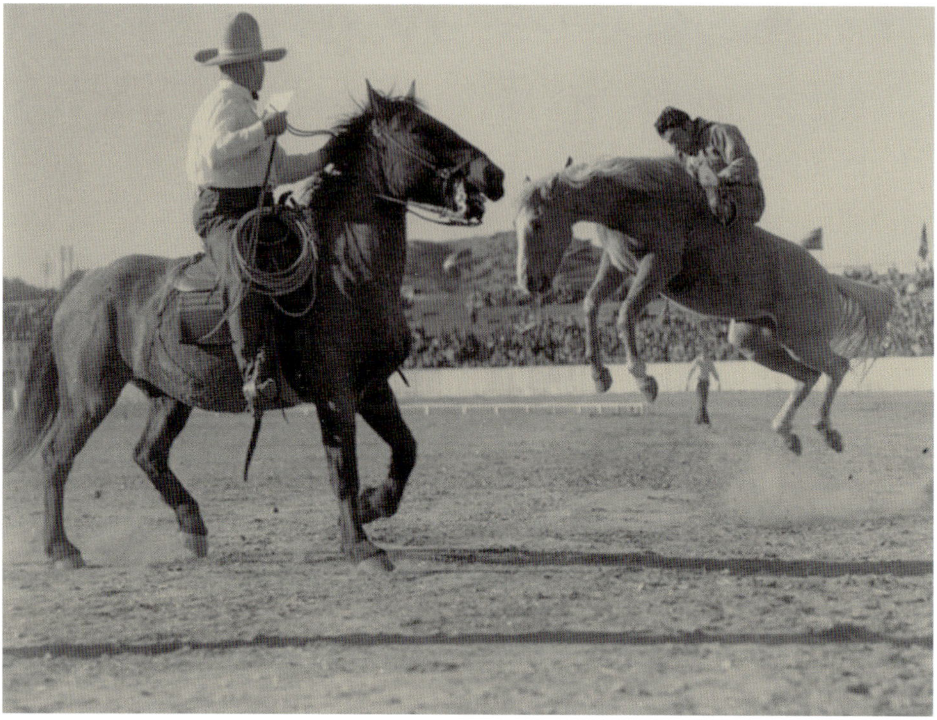

Hoot Gibson was a famous Western movie actor in the 1920s and 1930s. From 1930 to 1934, he owned what would later become the Saugus Speedway, presenting rodeos that drew such luminaries as Tom Mix, John Wayne, and Clark Gable. He is pictured in his signature ten-gallon hat hosting the Hoot Gibson Rodeo Annual Fall Roundup in 1931. Riding the bucking bronco is "Skeeter" Bill Perkins. The Saugus Speedway has been the venue for the Saugus Swap Meet since 1963.

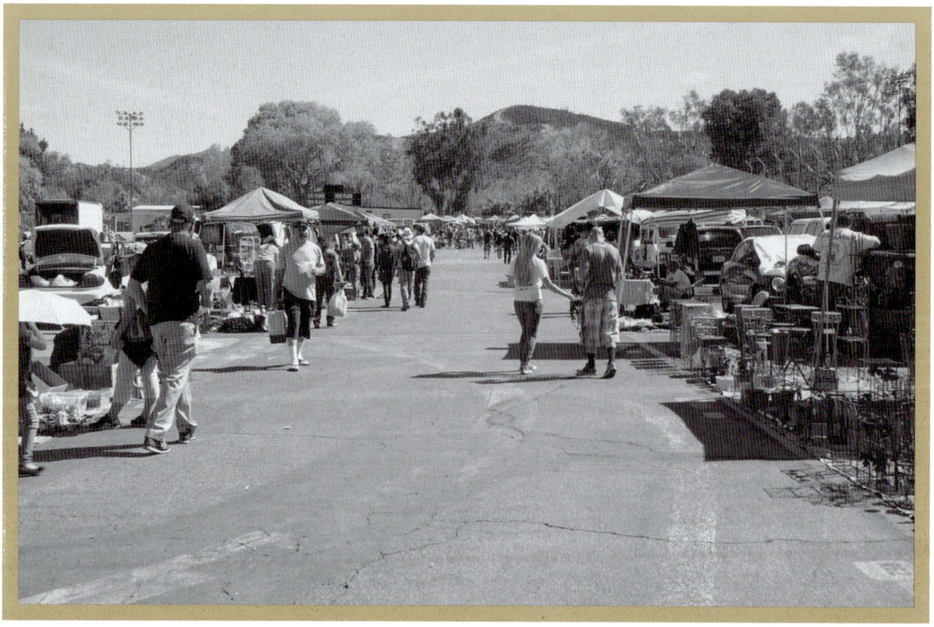

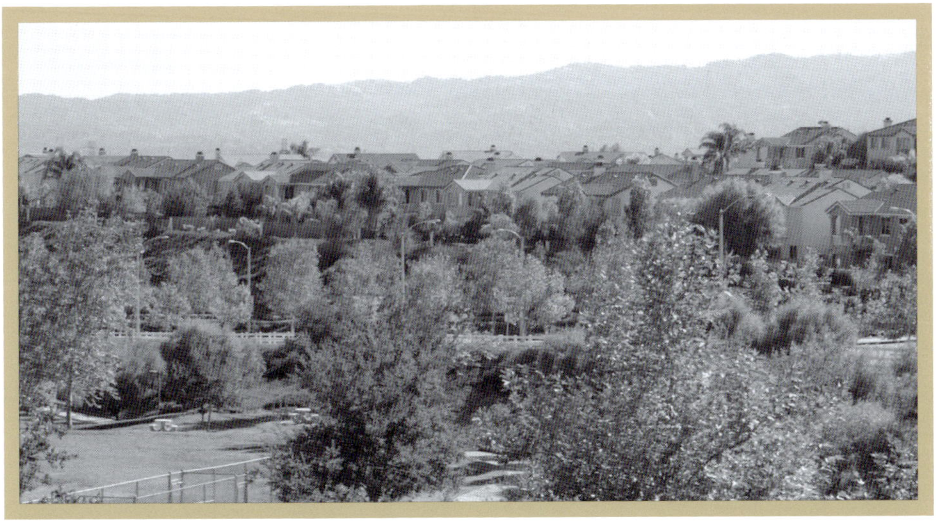

Cowboy film star Harry Carey and his family lived for many years on a 1,200-acre ranch in Saugus. Here, he ran a Navajo trading post as a tourist attraction, complete with 40 authentic Navajo tribe members who made jewelry, raised sheep, and operated the post and a restaurant known as the Navahogan. The trading post was destroyed in 1928 in the St. Francis Dam disaster. Today, Tesoro Adobe Park covers a portion of the former ranch with modern homes filling most of the rest.

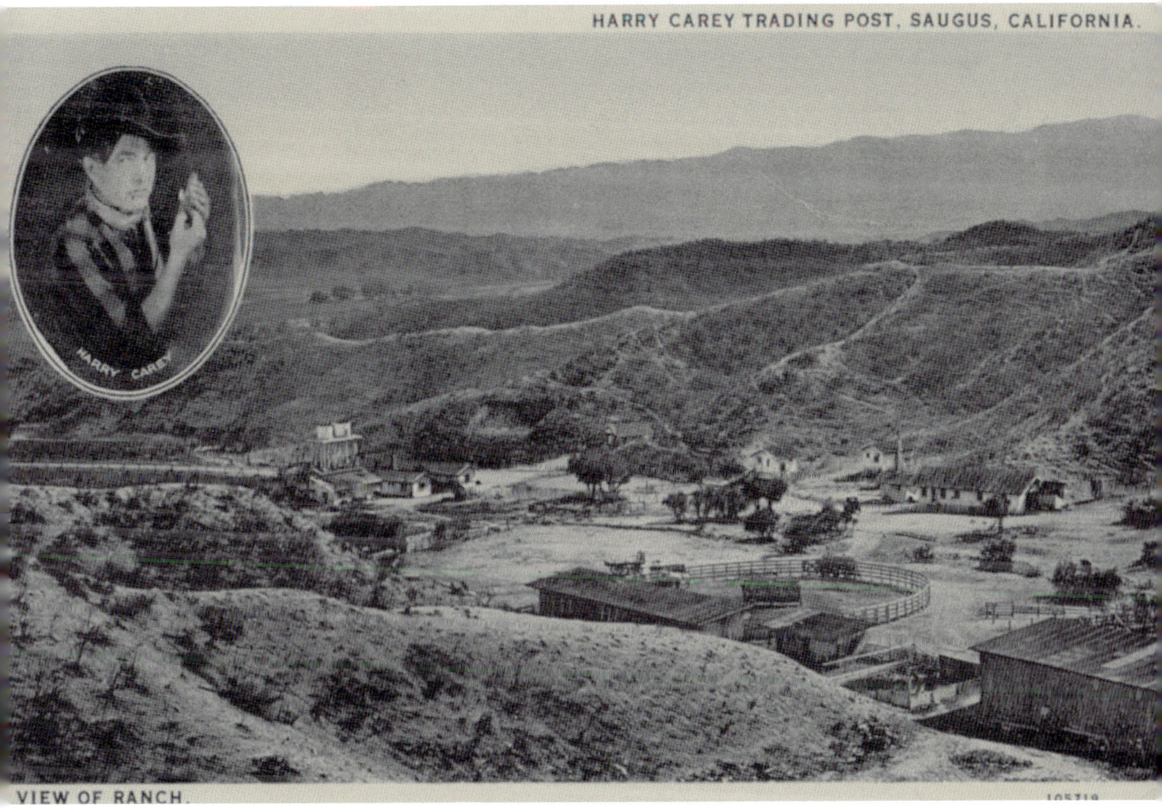

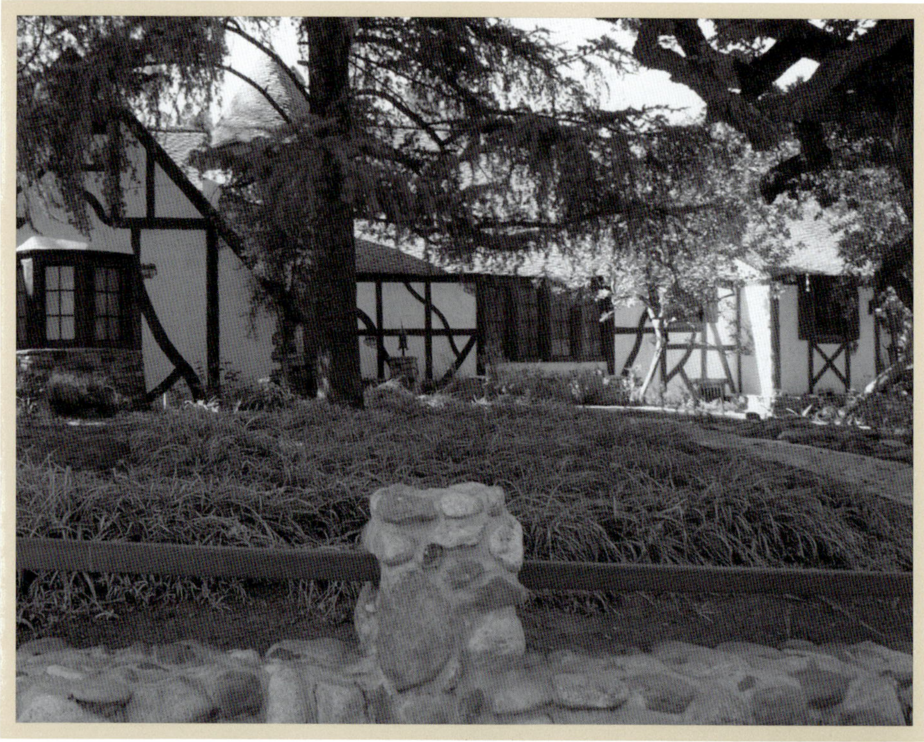

Crowland is a home on Eighth Street in Newhall built by comedian Charles Mack in the early 1930s. Comedian W.C. Fields, seen here, lived in Crowland for a few years after Mack died in a car crash in 1934. The head of Monogram Pictures, Ray Johnston, lived here during the early 1940s. Crowland, named for Mack's blackface comedy act "The Black Crows," was the first of three French Norman–style homes that Mack built on Eighth Street. They are all still in existence today.

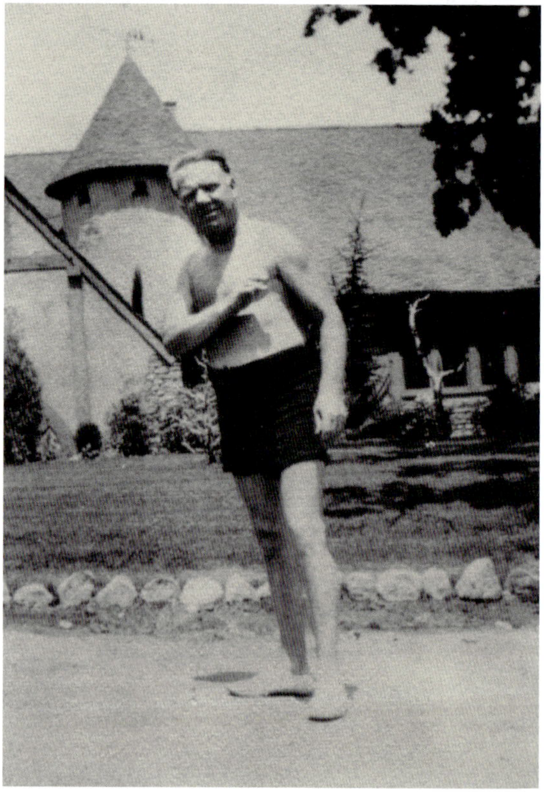

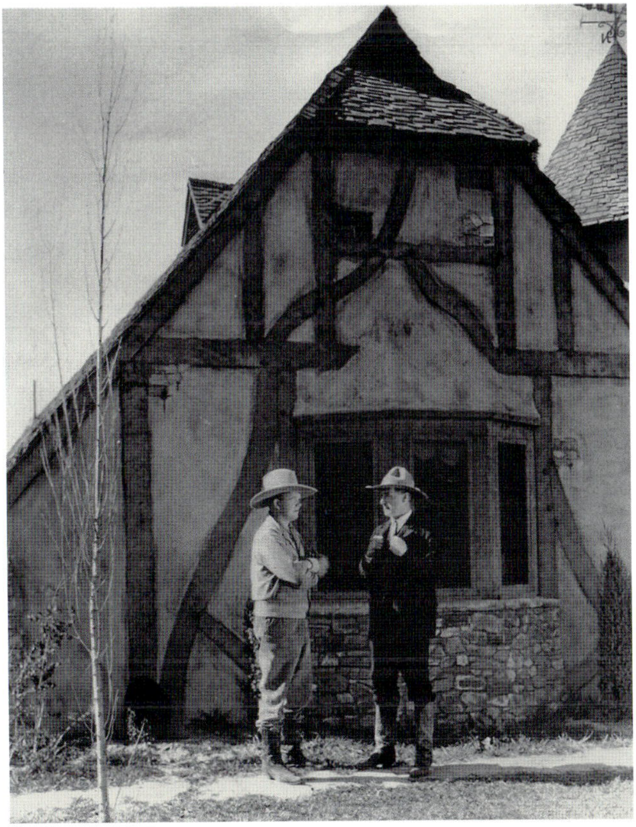

Charles Mack's Crowland was built just down the hill from William S. Hart's Horseshoe Ranch. In this photograph from the early 1930s, Mack (left) and Hart stand outside of the home. After Mack's death in a car crash in January 1934, Hart spoke at his funeral, which took place in Crowland's living room. In attendance that day were many of Hollywood's brightest stars, including Buster Keaton, W.C. Fields, Mack Sennett, and Saugus resident Harry Carey.

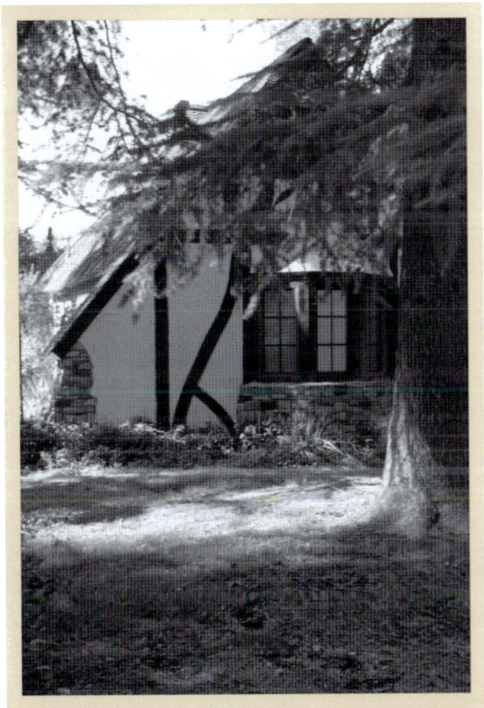

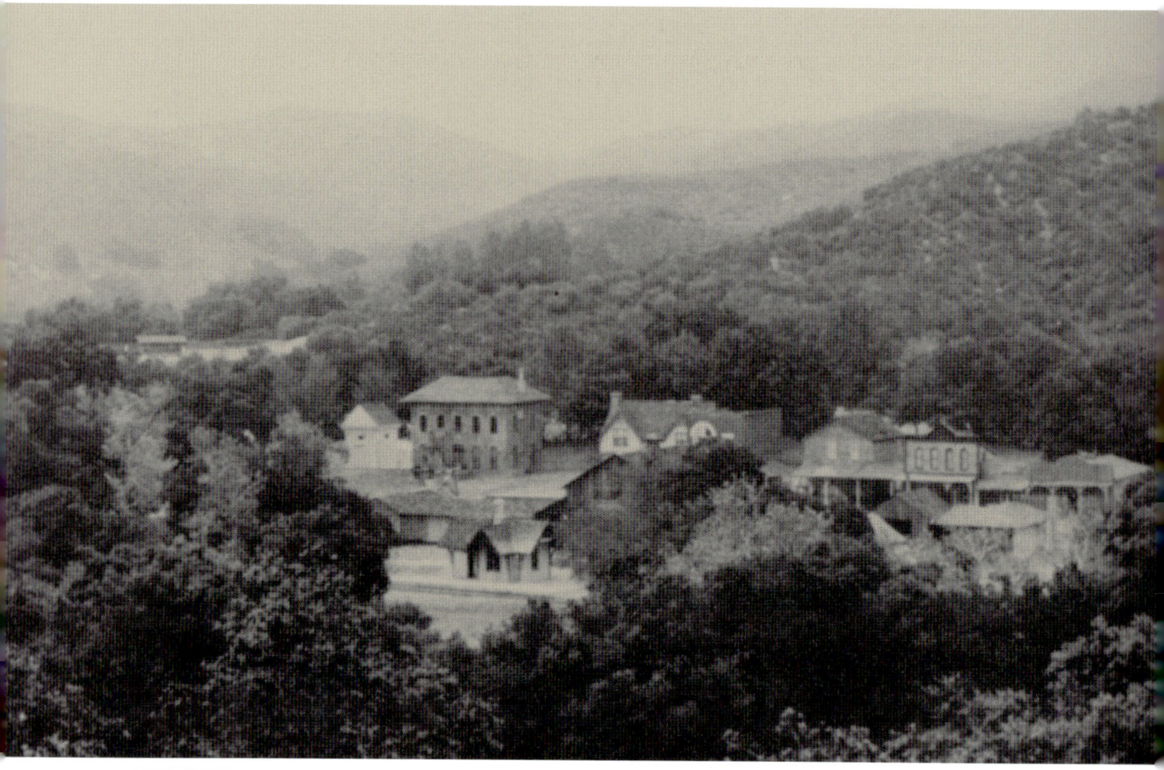

In the early 1930s, set designer Ernie Hickson built an authentic Western town in Placerita Canyon. Dozens of Westerns were made here by companies like Monogram and Republic. In 1936, Hickson moved the sets two miles north, creating what is known today as the Melody Ranch Motion Picture Studio. The original site, now called Golden Oak Ranch, was purchased by Walt Disney in 1959. The Western town was recreated but later replaced by this new modern backlot in 2010.

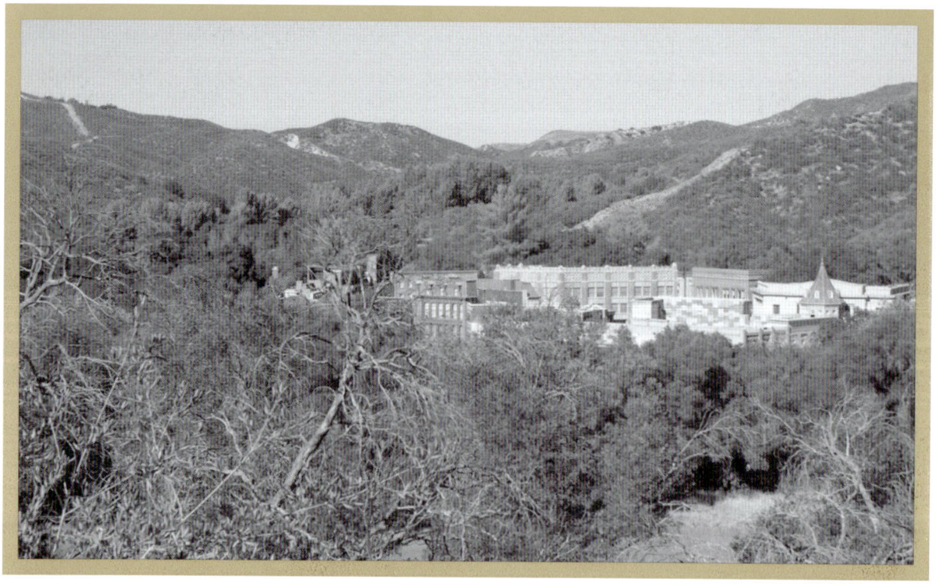

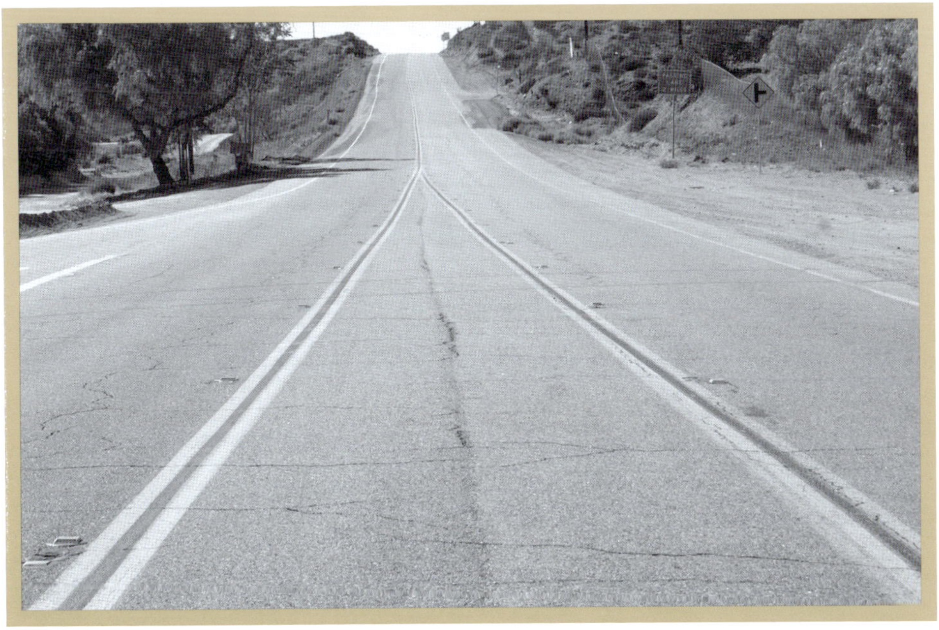

The final two scenes of the silent era were shot on Sierra Highway near Agua Dulce for the conclusion of Charlie Chaplin's epic comedy *Modern Times* (1936). Here, Chaplin (right) and Paulette Goddard stroll down the center of the highway during the film's penultimate scene. The hill in the background looks the same today, and the Los Angeles County Fire Station No. 81, located at 8710 Sierra Highway, is located nearby. The film's final scene was also shot on Sierra Highway, two miles to the north.

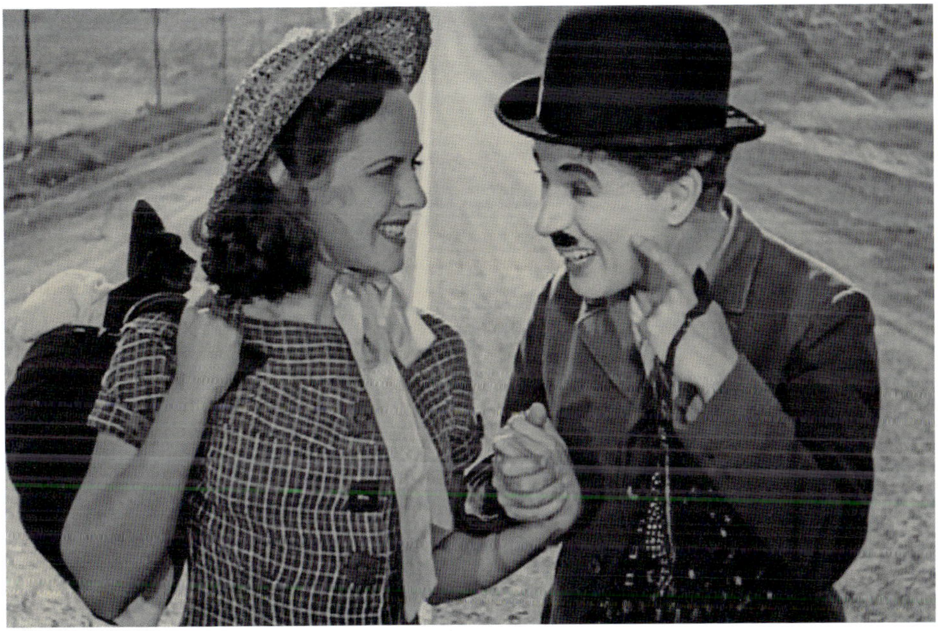

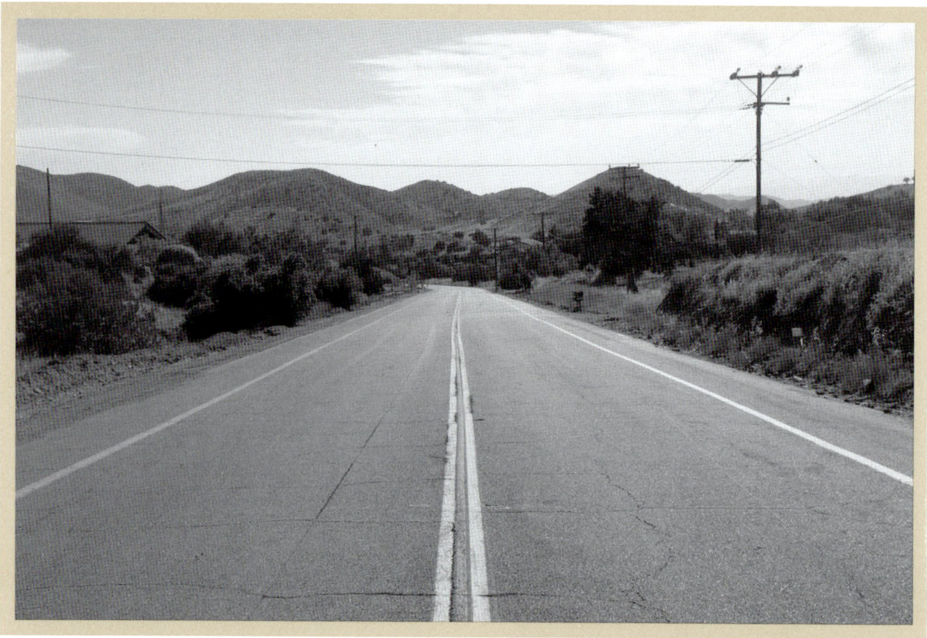

In August 1935, silent screen comic Charlie Chaplin, with Paulette Goddard at his side, walked down this lonely stretch of Sierra Highway at the conclusion of *Modern Times* (1936). The film was shot nearly a decade into the talkie era, but Chaplin avoided giving voice to his iconic character, "The Little Tramp," fearing that language would rob him of his universal appeal. The site on Sierra Highway at Wallace Canyon Road looks nearly identical today.

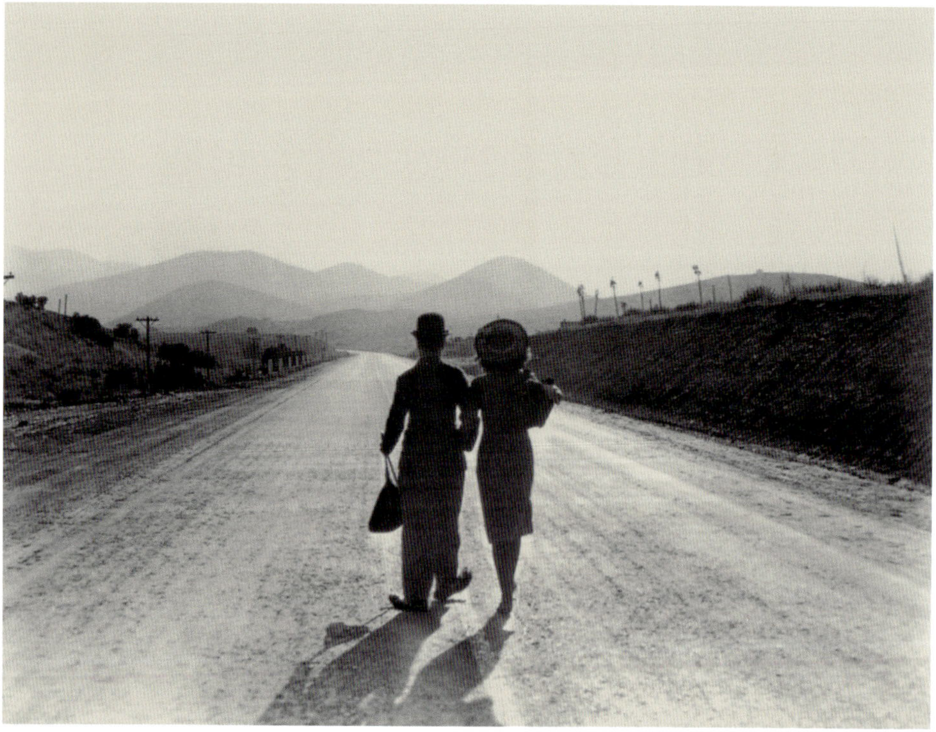

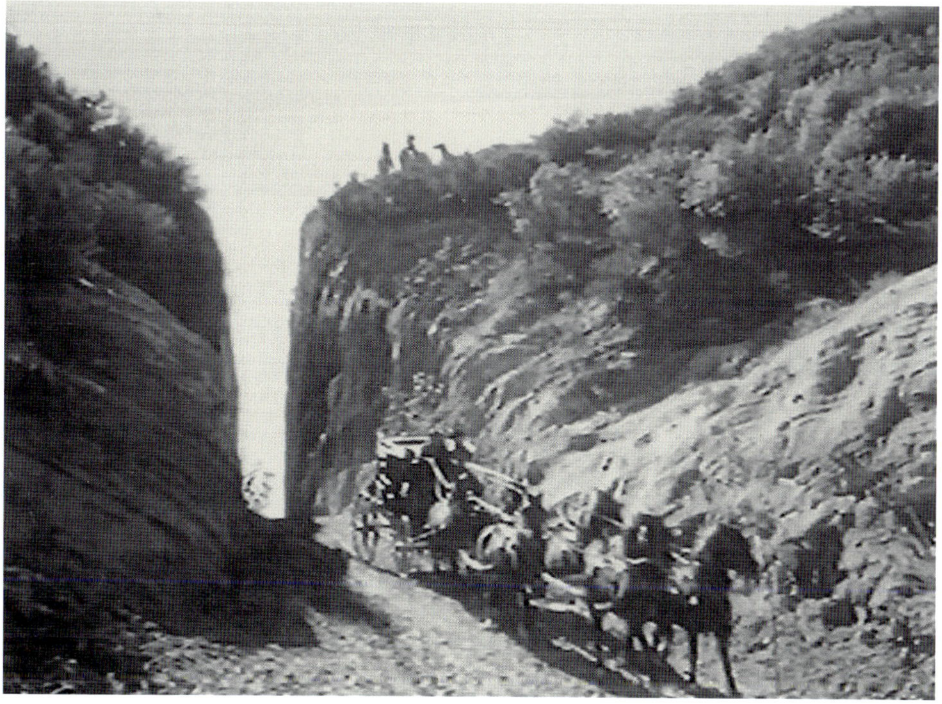

Stagecoach (1939) was the Western that made John Wayne a star. The film, which follows a group of stagecoach travelers who are pursued by hostile Indians, was shot in several locations, including Newhall's Beale's Cut, just south of Sierra Highway. Beale's Cut was a popular filming location for *Stagecoach*'s director John Ford. Ford had employed the spot on screen a few times previously, including in 1923's *Three Jumps Ahead* (see back cover) and the following year in his transcontinental railroad epic, *The Iron Horse.*

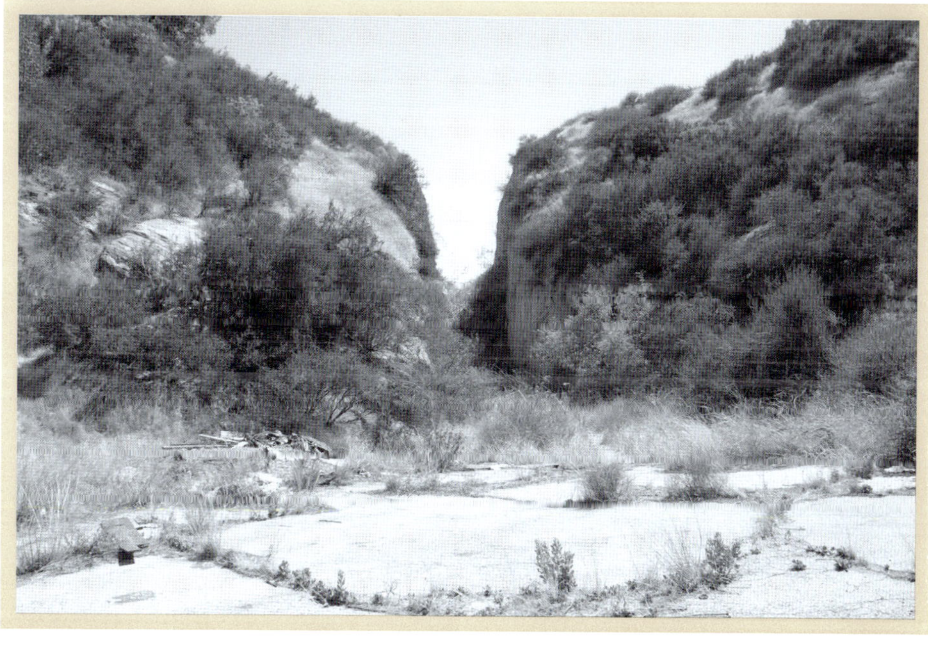

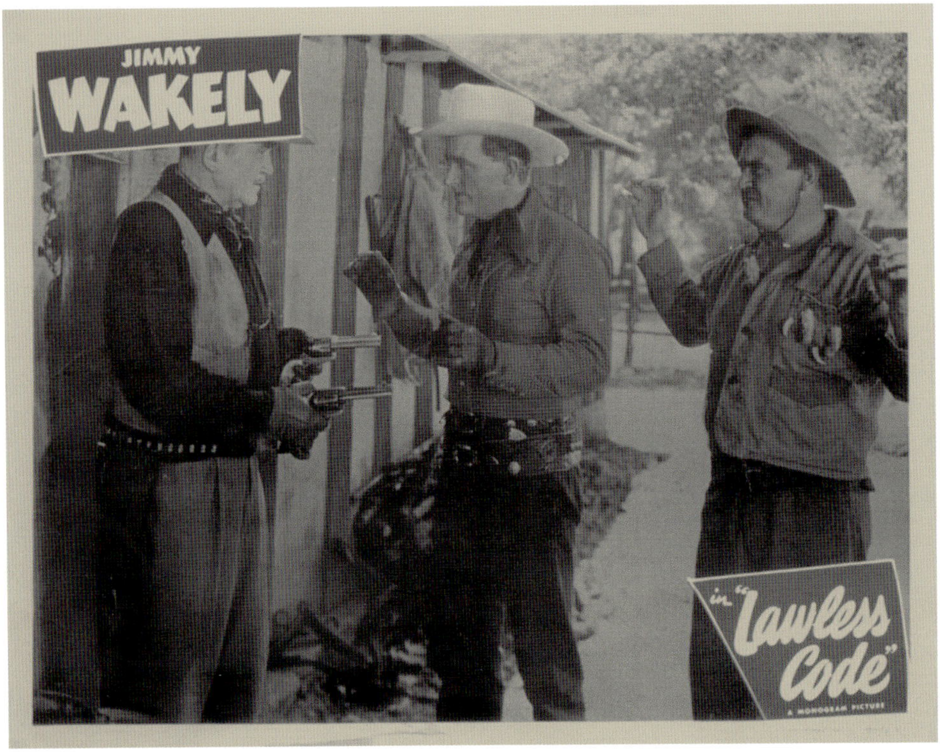

Monogram Pictures' *Lawless Code* (1949) starred singing cowboy Jimmy Wakely. This scene shows a stickup taking place outside of the Walker Ranch cabin, which is today found next to the parking lot for Placerita Canyon State Park. For years, Monogram filmed most of its Westerns a short distance away at Monogram Ranch. Today, the property is known as Golden Oak Ranch, which is owned by the Walt Disney Company.

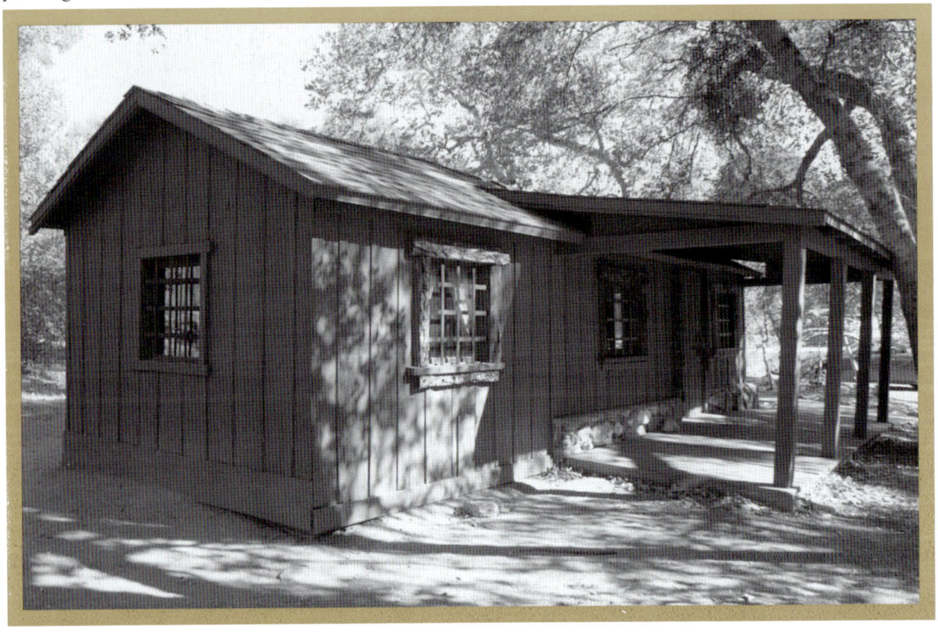

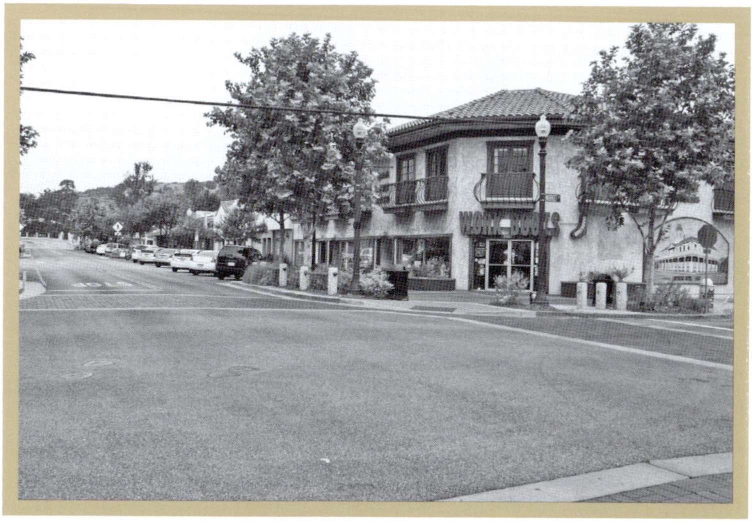

The opening credits of Frank Sinatra's thriller *Suddenly* (1954) shows downtown Newhall from the corner of today's Main and Market Streets looking south. This film follows the attempted assassination of the US president at a train station in the fictional town of Suddenly. Frank Sinatra plays the chief assassin, but the real star of the film is the town of Newhall, which doubled for the town Suddenly.

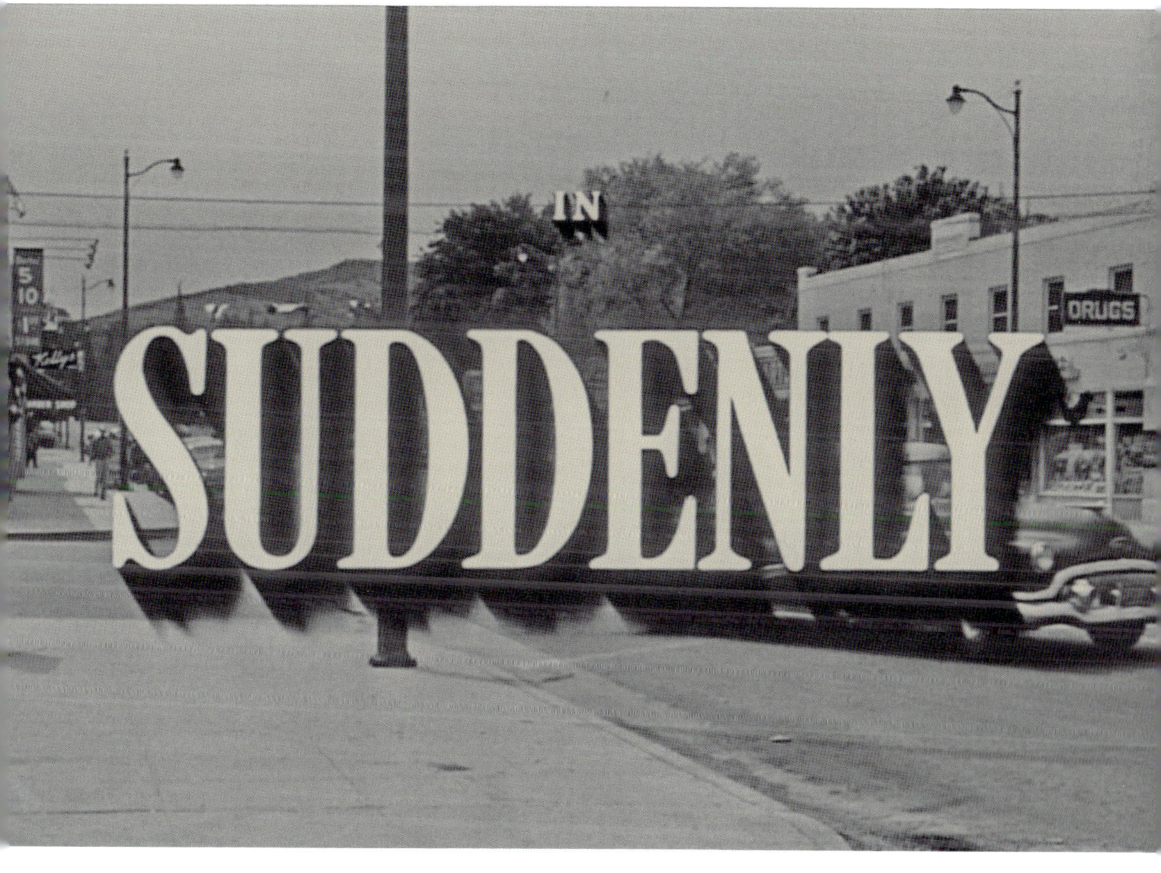

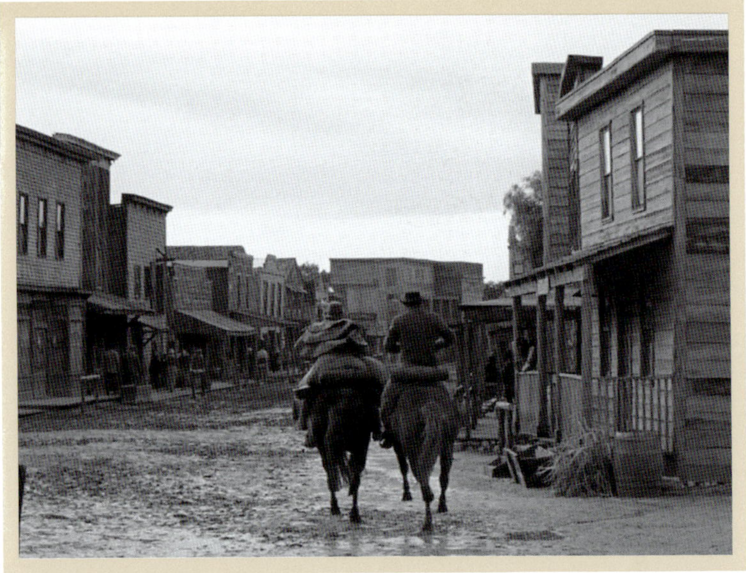

Singing cowboy superstar Gene Autry purchased Melody Ranch in 1952 and used the classic Western town as a background for dozens of Westerns for both the big screen and television. The old photograph shows the empty Main Street of Melody's Western town in the 1950s. In the modern photograph, Christoph Waltz (left) and Jamie Foxx ride through the same town in a scene from 2012's *Django Unchained*.

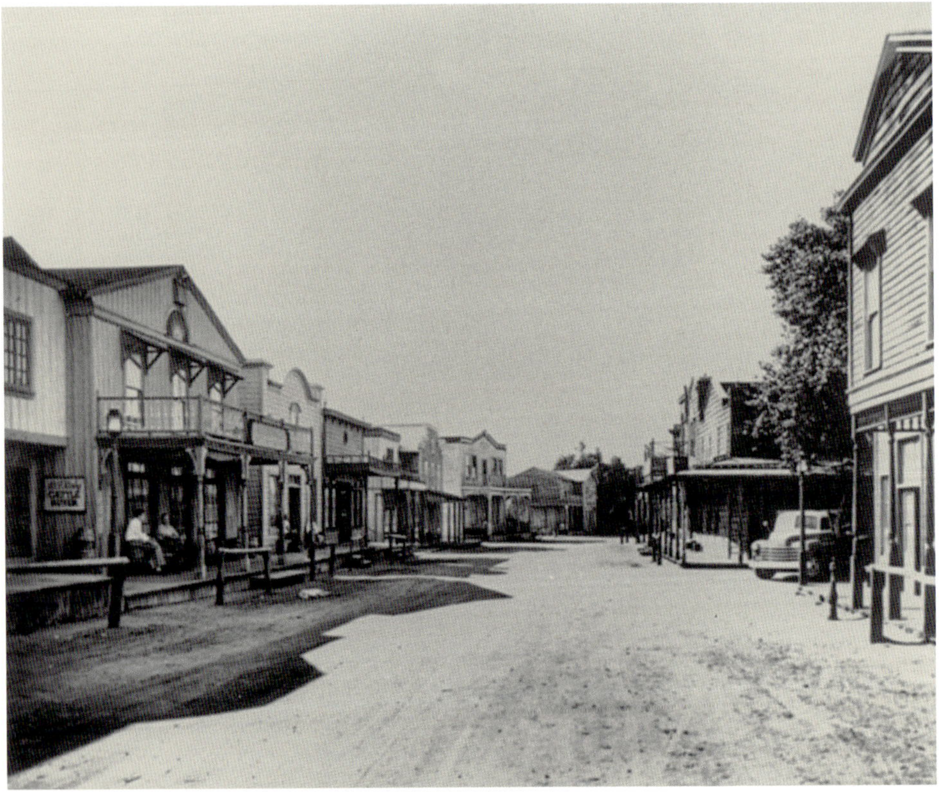

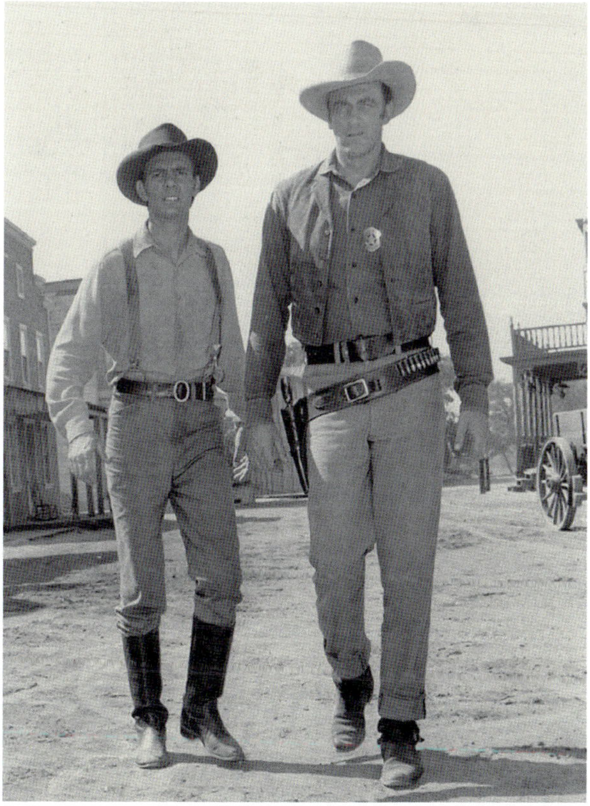

Dennis Weaver (left) and James Arness walk down Newhall's Melody Ranch in 1956, which, for several seasons, doubled for Dodge City in *Gunsmoke*. After the Western town burned down in a 1962 brushfire, the show relocated away from Melody. After the Veluzat family purchased the ranch from Gene Autry in 1990, they painstakingly recreated the town, which is now the site of Santa Clarita's annual Cowboy Festival. The modern photograph shows the Western town in 2013.

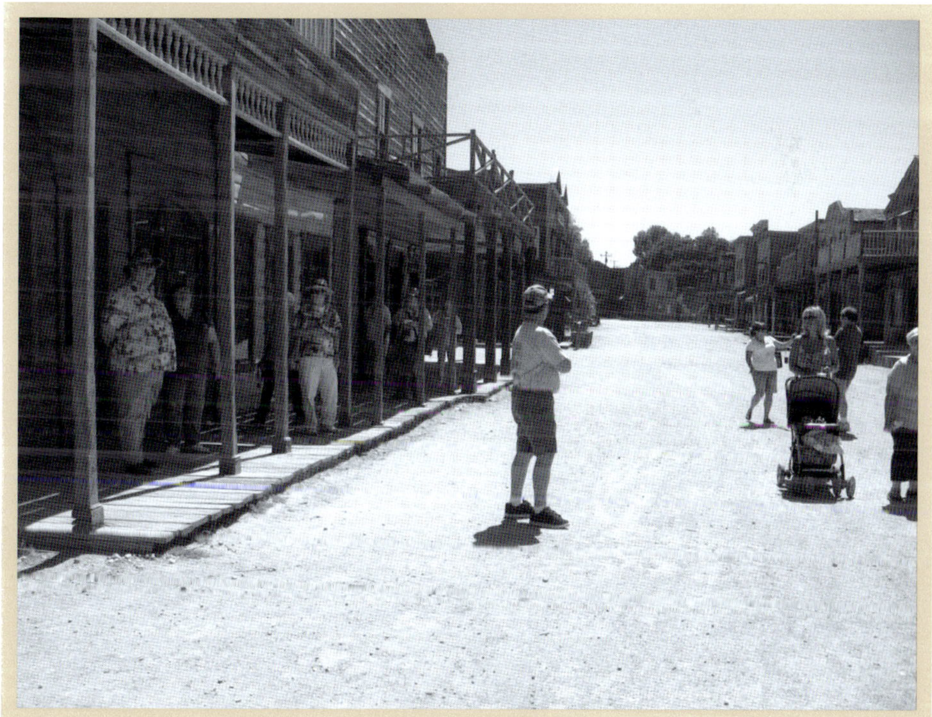

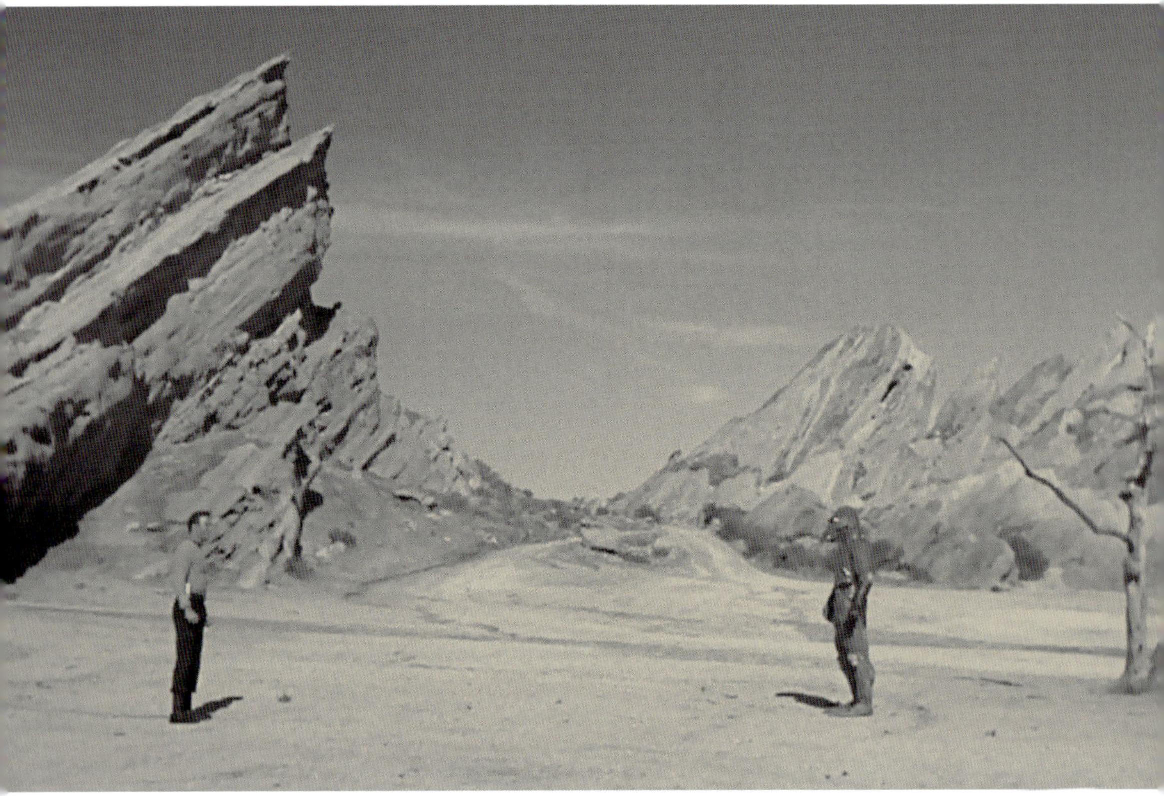

Vasquez Rocks often doubles for outer space. In this scene from the "Arena" episode of the original *Star Trek* television series, Captain Kirk (William Shatner) stares down the lizard-like Gorn creature. Vasquez Rocks has appeared in nearly every version of the *Star Trek* franchise, a fact that has not escaped "trekkers." Fans often show up at the park hoping to see filming whenever a new *Star Trek* production is even rumored to be in the works.

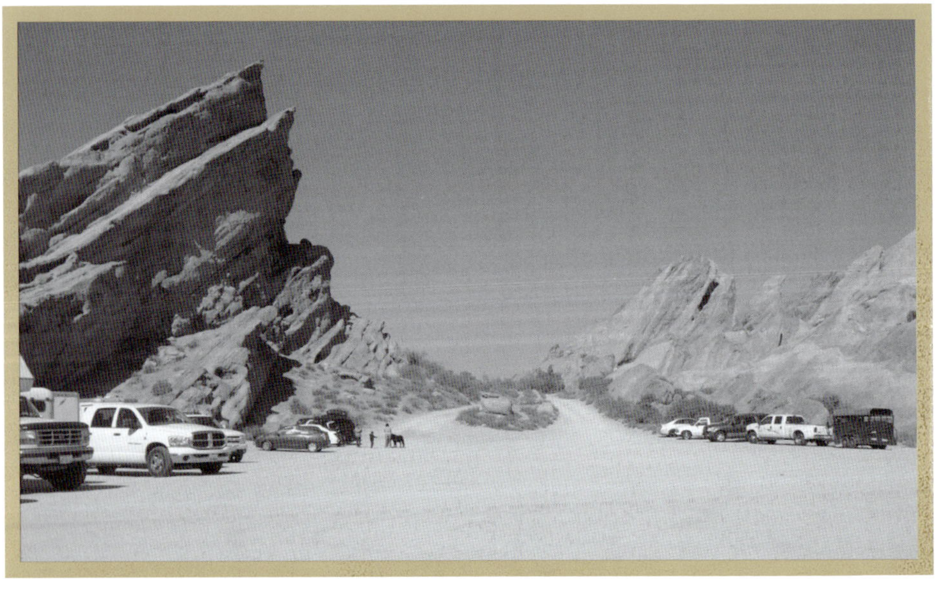

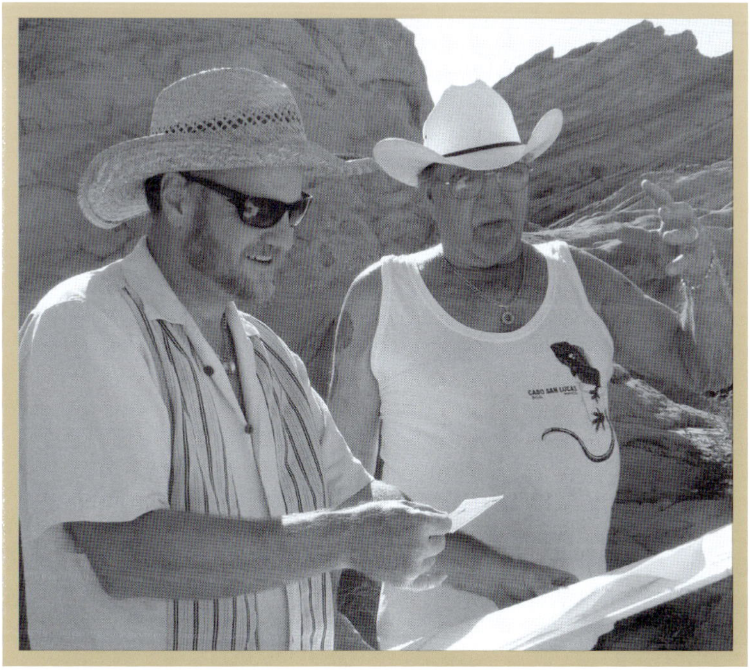

In the photograph from 1966, the Gorn battles Captain Kirk (William Shatner) in the "Arena" episode during *Star Trek*'s first season. In the modern photograph, coauthor E.J. Stephens (left) and Saugus resident Bobby Clark, who played the Gorn on *Star Trek*, meet at Vasquez Rocks. The fight scene from "Arena" was reenacted by Bobby in August 2012 for an episode of *SCV in the Movies*, which E.J. cohosts with Bill West on Santa Clarita's SCVTV television station.

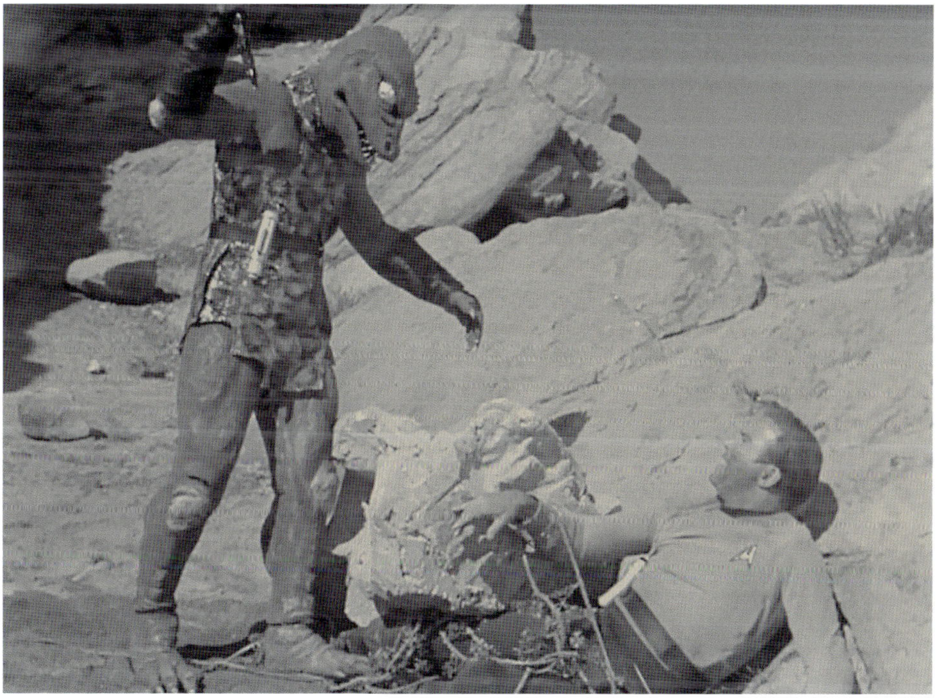

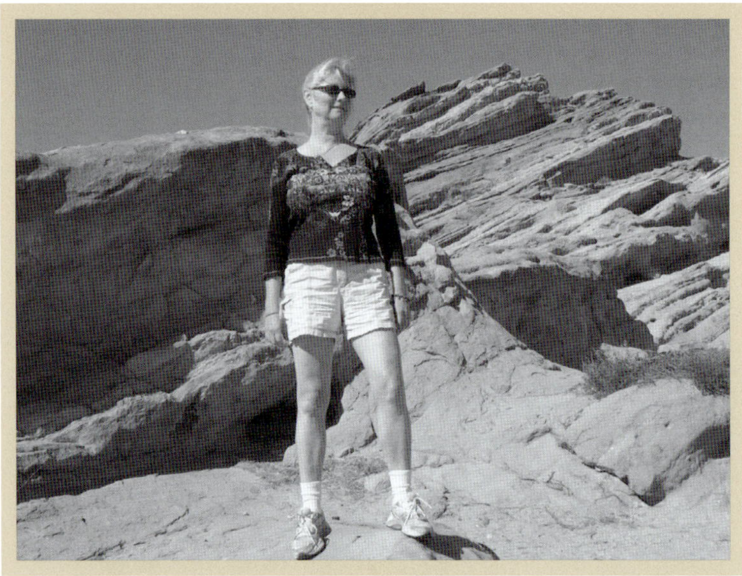

Coauthor Kim Stephens stands at the same spot where Captain Kirk (William Shatner) once battled the Gorn in *Star Trek*. Harvey Korman, playing the conniving Hedley Lamarr, once addressed a gang of ruffians here in a scene from *Blazing Saddles* (1974). It was a fitting location for the classic Western parody, as literally hundreds of legitimate Westerns have been shot at Vasquez Rocks since the dawn of movies. These scenes were shot at the base of Pride Rock in the main parking area.

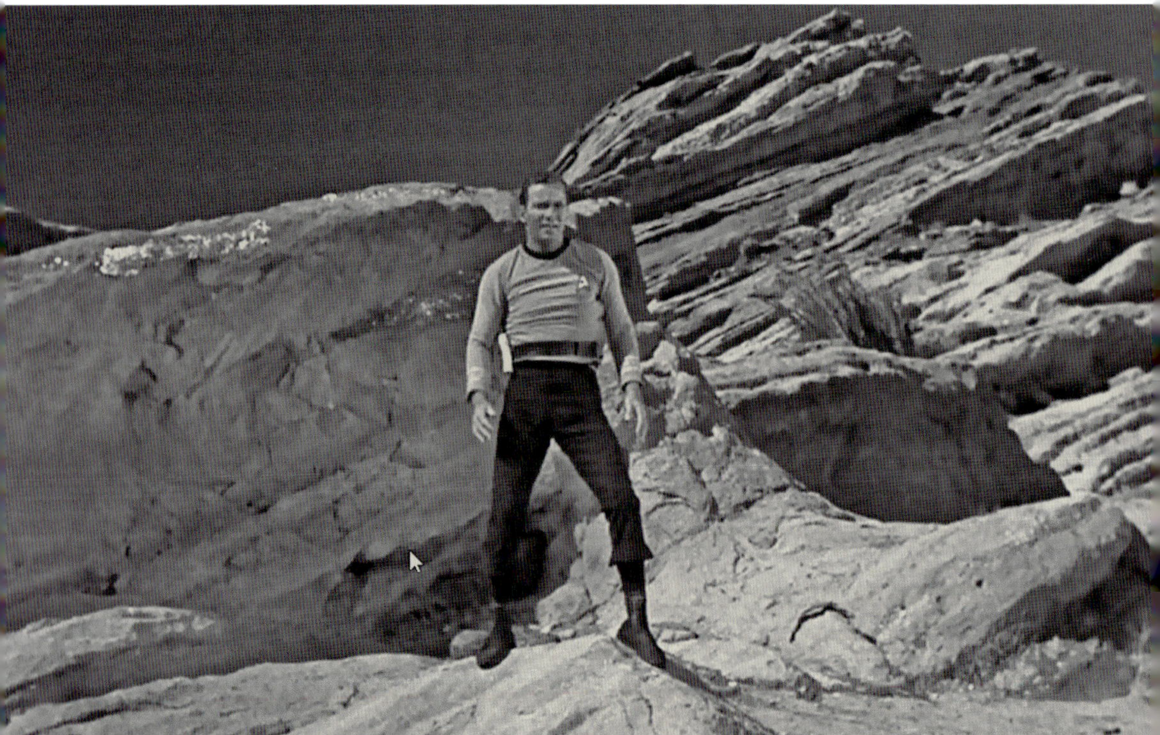

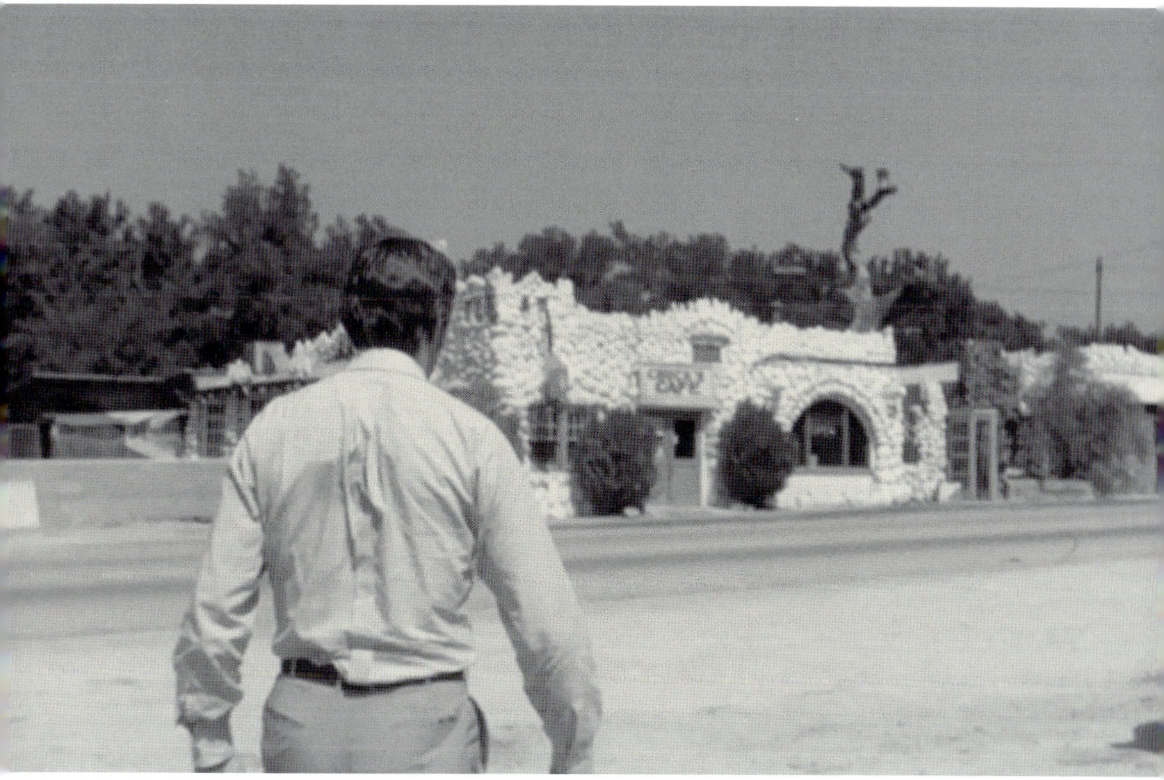

Steven Spielberg's first film, *Duel* (1971), is a psychological thriller about a traveling salesman, played by Dennis Weaver, who is stalked in his red 1971 Dodge Valiant by a huge rusty gasoline tanker truck. One of the locations used was Le Chene, a French restaurant on Sierra Highway north of Canyon Country, known as Chuck's Café in the film. It was here that Weaver's character confronts the man he believes to be the truck's driver.

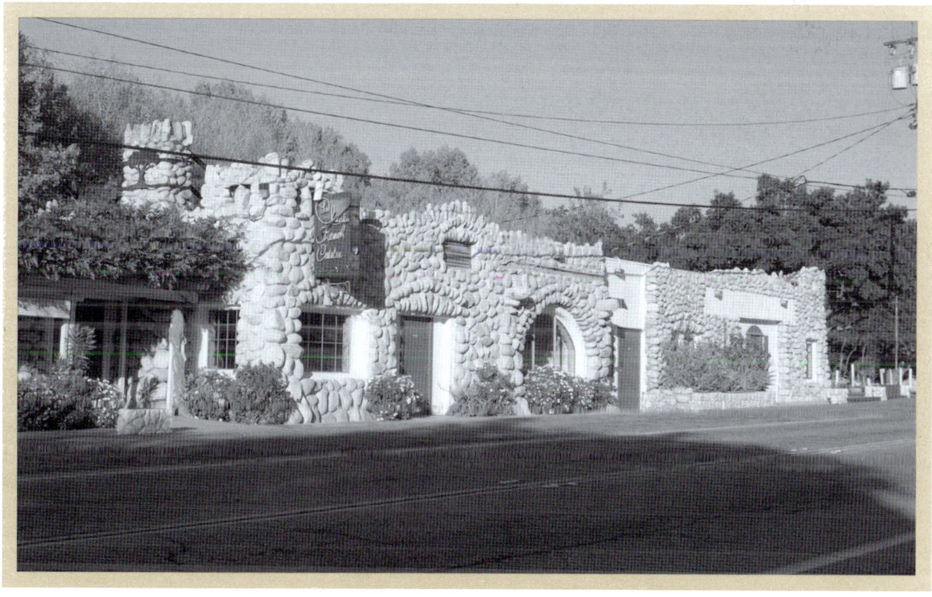

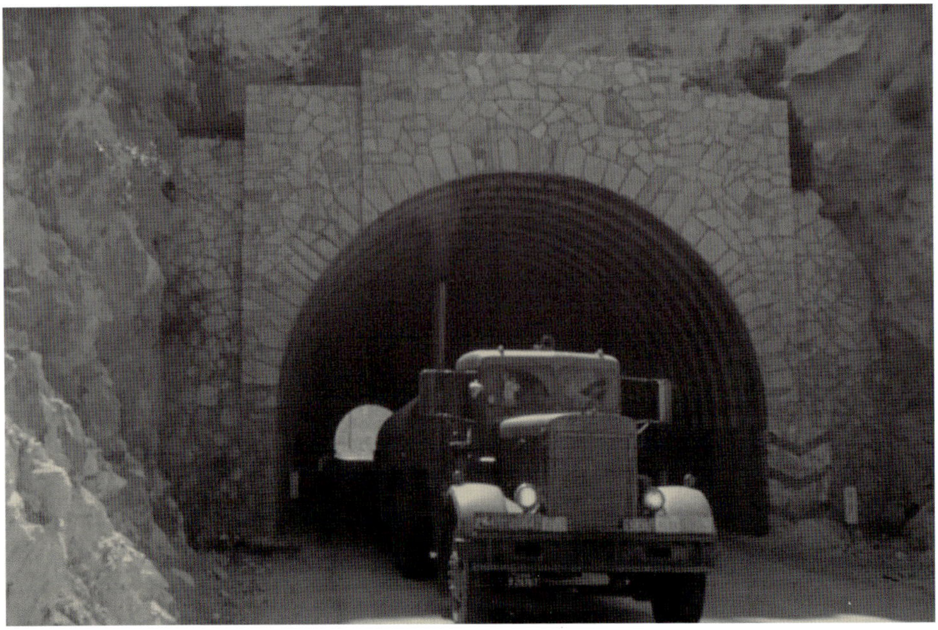

Duel (1971) was shot over 13 days throughout the Santa Clarita Valley, which, at the time, was far from the urban encroachment of Los Angeles. The tunnel used during the school bus scene is located near Acton on Soledad Canyon Road. The film's gasoline truck was a rusty 1955 Peterbilt 281. It was destroyed at the climax of the film, which was originally made for television. Replacements had to be found for additional scenes that were later shot for the theatrical release.

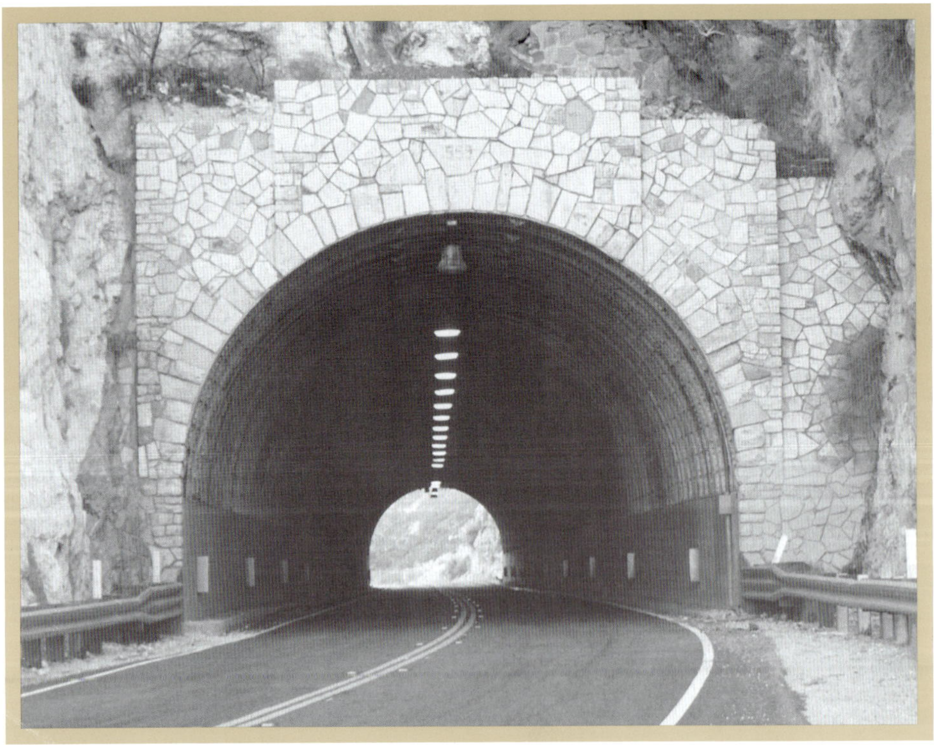

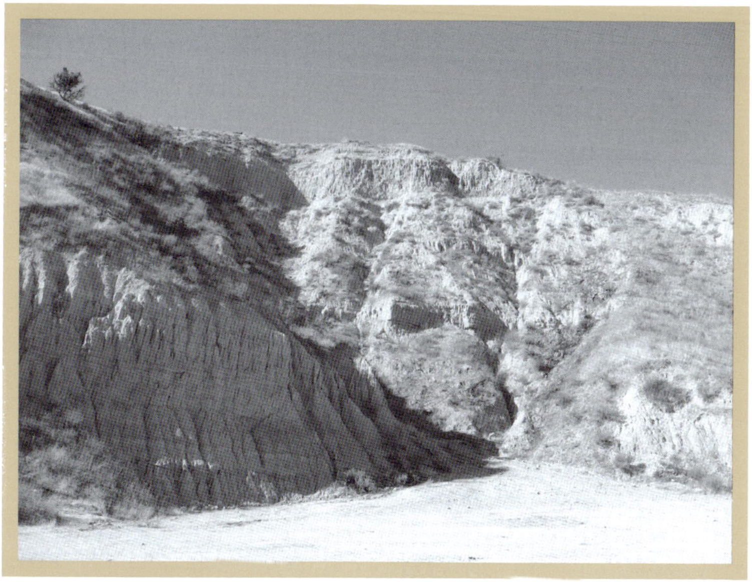

At the conclusion of *Duel*, Dennis Weaver eludes the menacing truck and its unseen driver, which plunges 120-feet from the top of Mystery Mesa to Box Canyon below. Both the mesa and canyon are still frequently used for filming. Steven Spielberg returned here to film a scene for *War of the Worlds* (2005) The canyon is visible from Vasquez Canyon Road, two miles west of Sierra Highway.

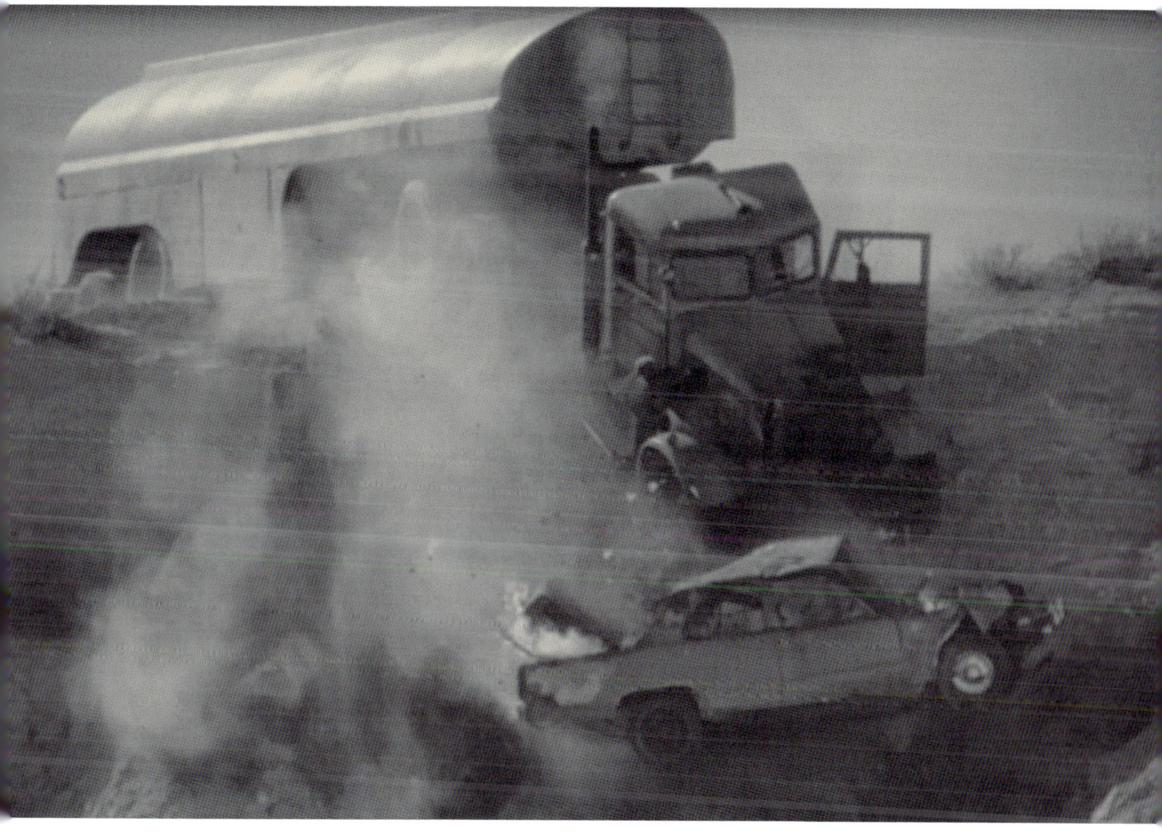

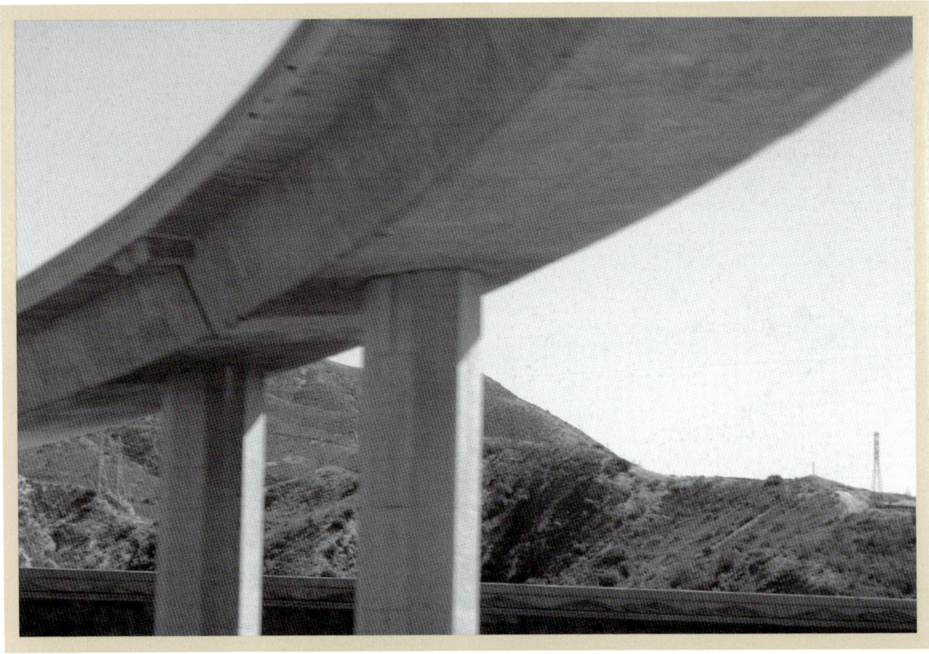

Earthquakes have brought down sections of the Interstate 5/Antelope Valley Freeway Interchange in the Newhall Pass on two occasions in recent memory. The Doobie Brothers took advantage of the first collapse for the cover image of their 1973 album, *The Captain and Me*. This collapse followed the 6.6-magnitude Sylmar earthquake in February 1971, which had its epicenter near Lang station in the Santa Clarita Valley. This same section collapsed again during the 1994 Northridge earthquake.

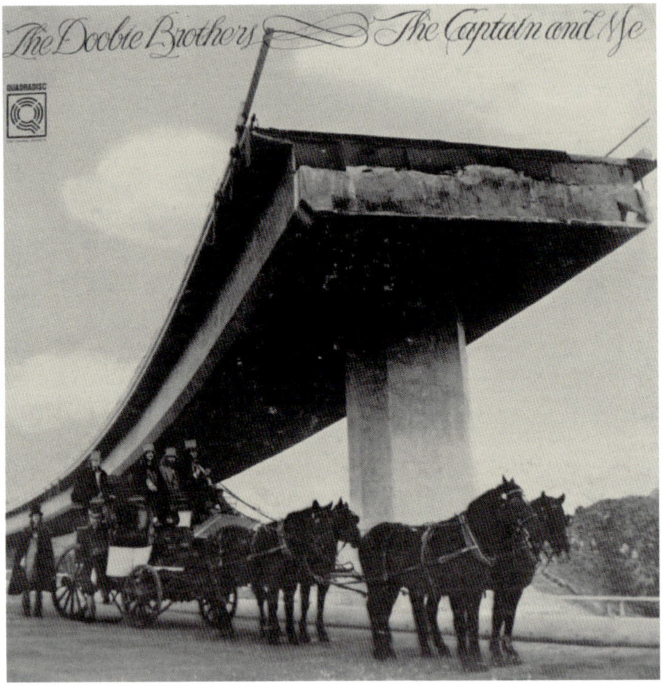

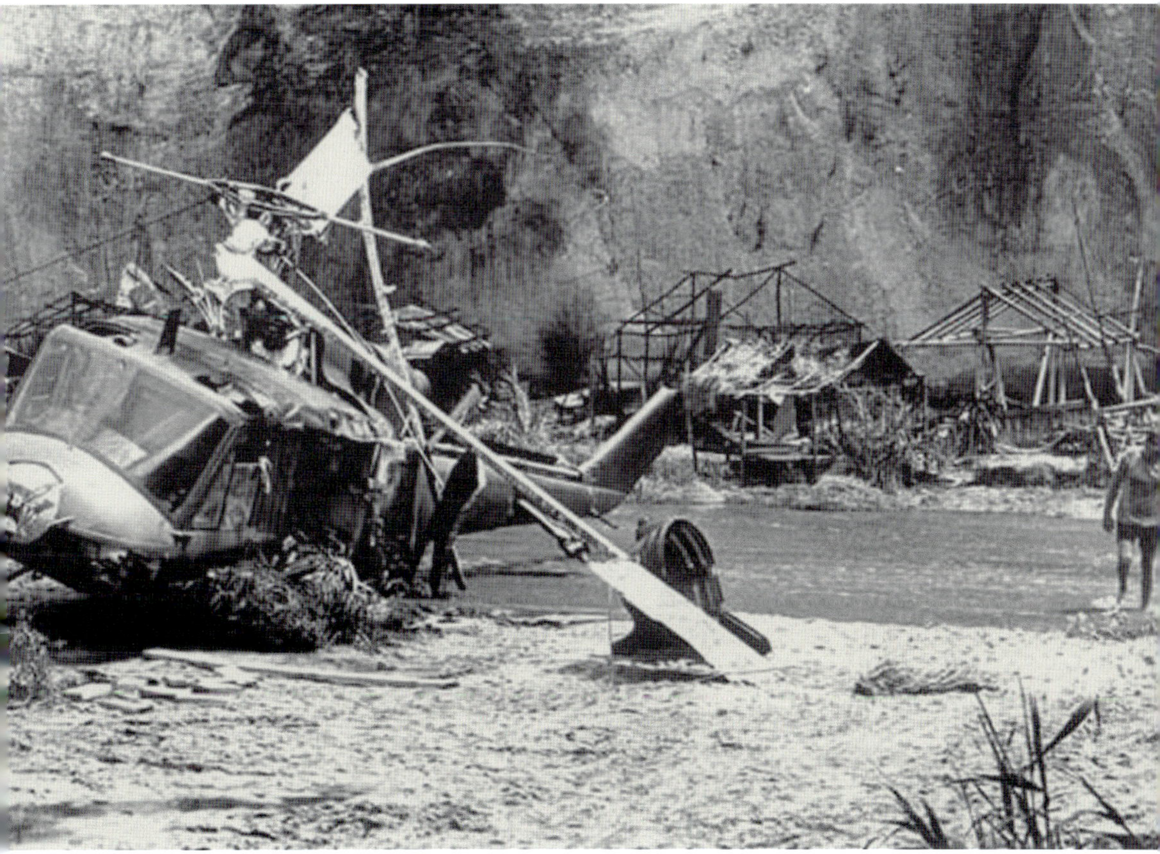

On July 23, 1982, a helicopter crash on the set of *Twilight Zone: The Movie* killed 53-year-old Hollywood veteran Vic Morrow and two child actors. The tragic incident happened at Indian Dunes Park, a 600-acre ranch that was a frequent filming site for movie and television productions. Director John Landis was later charged with three counts of manslaughter but was acquitted in May 1987. This site is near the Six Flags Magic Mountain amusement park in Valencia.

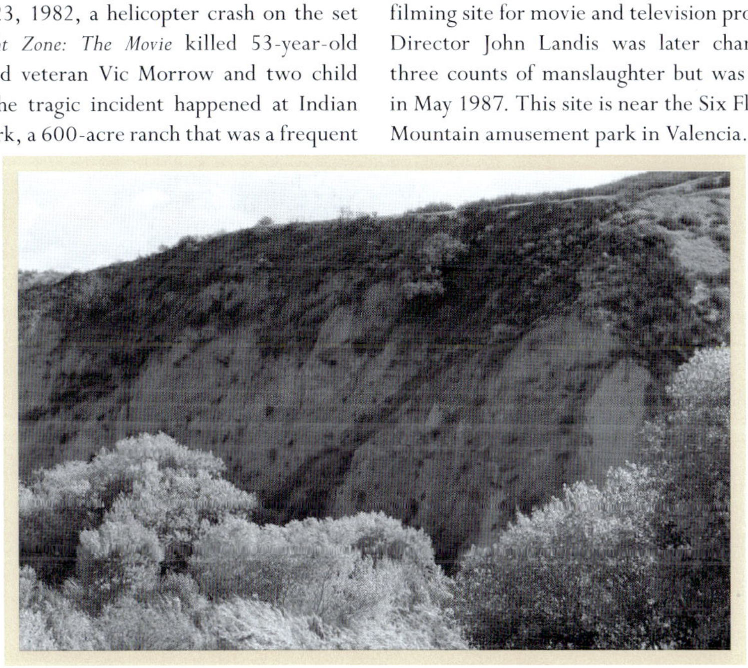

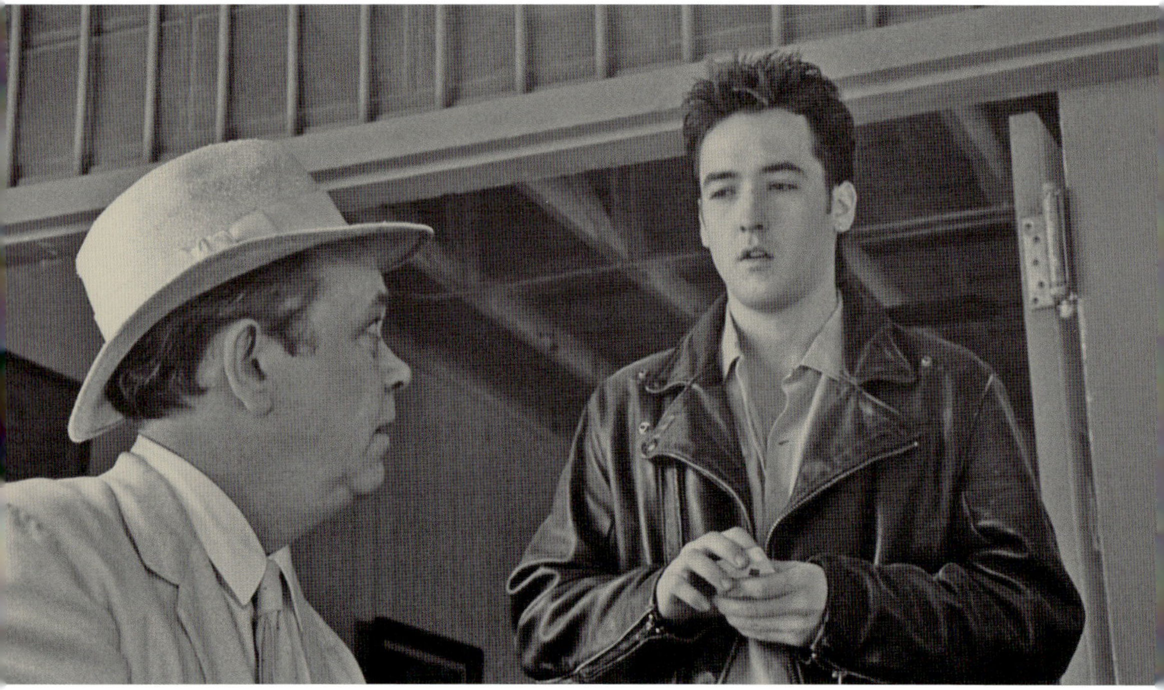

The 1990 neo-noir film *The Grifters* was the first big Hollywood production to employ the Saugus Train Station as a location after it was moved to Heritage Junction. In the film, actor Eddie Jones (seated) teaches young John Cusack how to be a grifter outside of the station's baggage area. The Saugus Train Station, constructed in 1887, is the headquarters of Santa Clarita Valley Historical Society, which is led by coauthor Alan Pollack and is open for tours on weekends.

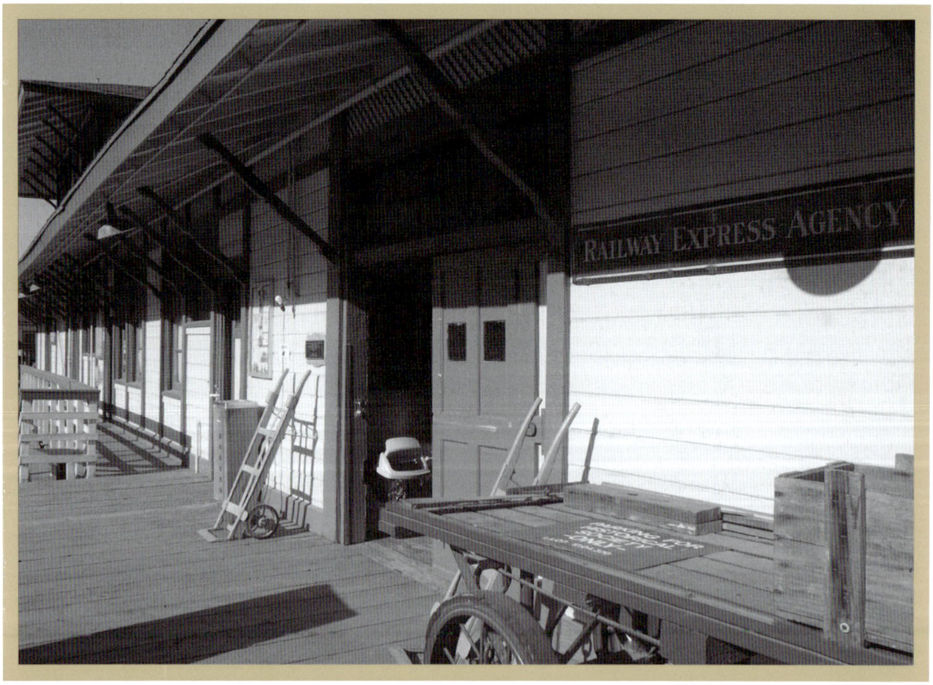

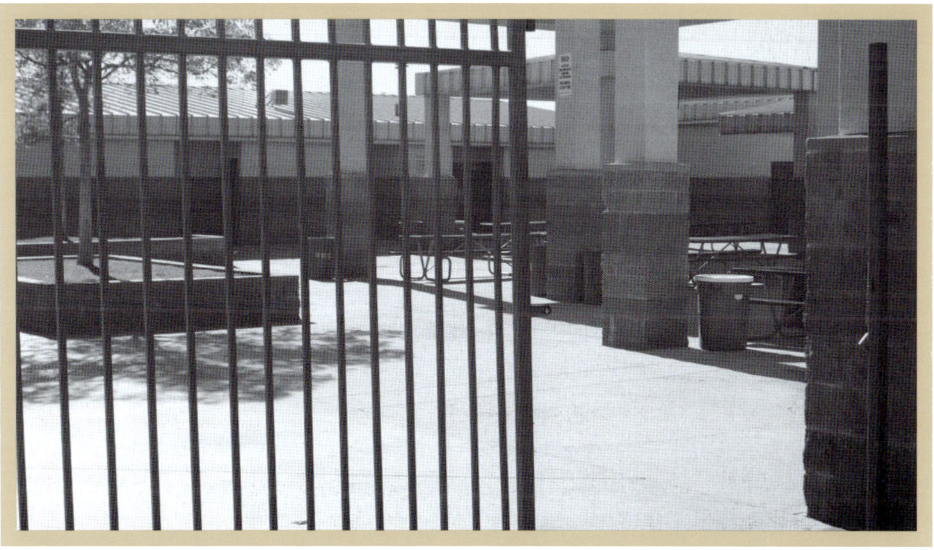

In *Pleasantville* (1998), it never rains, the residents literally see everything in black and white, and the biggest crisis to ever strike is when a cat gets stuck in a tree. This is the world that Jennifer (Reese Witherspoon, seen here) and her twin brother David (Tobey Maguire) are sent to, by way of a magical television remote control. The school that the siblings attend at the beginning of the movie is Santa Clarita's Valencia High.

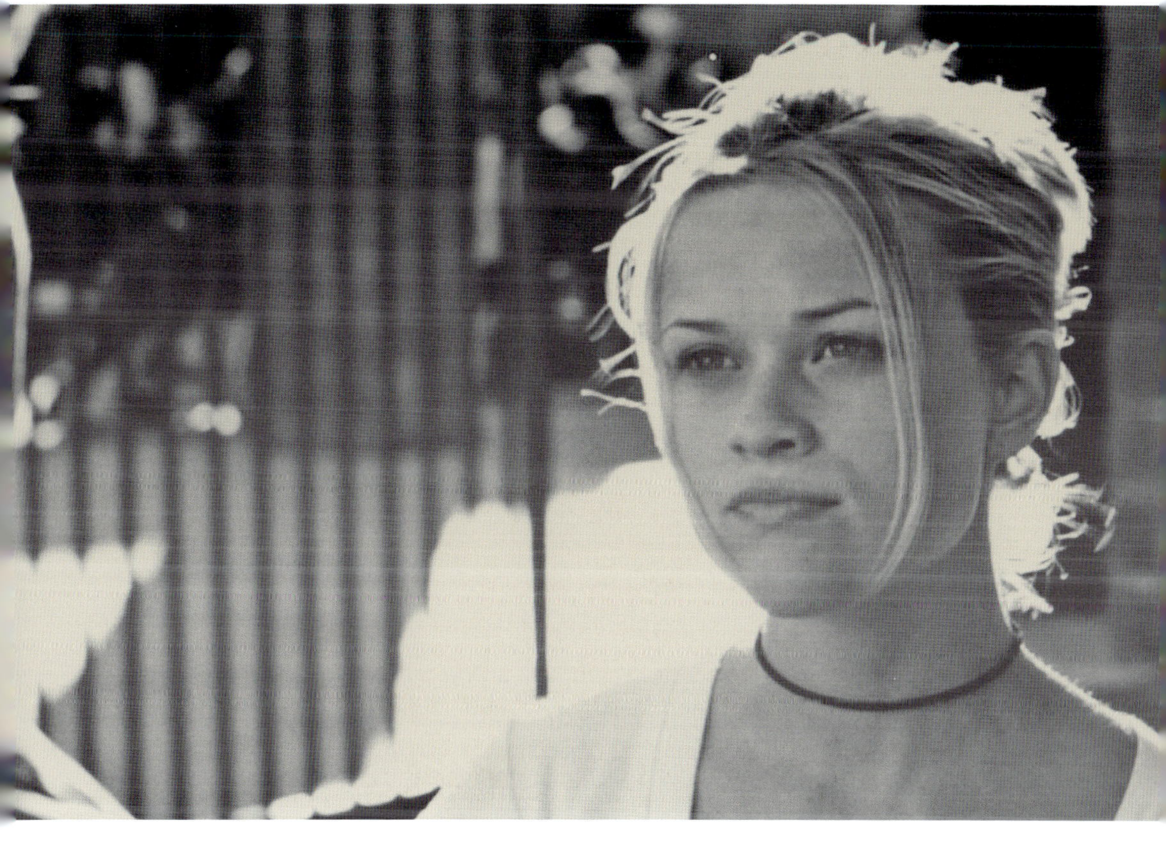